# CONSCIOUSNESS RISING

Women's
Stories
of
Connection
and
Transformation

Edited by CHERYL MALMO
& TONI SUZUKI LAIDLAW

gynergy
books

**Cover illustration by:** Taiya Barss
**Printed and bound in Canada**

*Gynergy books acknowledges the generous support
of the Canada Council for the Arts and
the Department of Canadian Heritage.*

**Published by:**
gynergy books
P.O. Box 2023
Charlottetown, PEI
Canada  C1A 7N7

**Canadian Cataloguing in Publication Data**

Main entry under title:

Consciousness rising

    1st ed.

    Includes bibliographical references.
    ISBN 0-921881-52-5

1. Feminists.  2. Middle aged women.  I. Malmo, Cheryl
Lynne, 1945-  II. Suzuki Laidlaw, Toni, 1939-

HQ1455.A3C65  1999       305.4       C99-950095-3

# Acknowledgements

*Working on a collection such as this is not possible without the significant contribution of many others. First, we want to thank the authors who provided us with ongoing encouragement and support, in addition to their personal reflections. We also appreciate the efforts of those women whose stories we were unable to include for reasons of space and the demands of the publishing world.*

*Barbara Dacks' excitement about the prospect of reading stories of women's connections and transformations was the catalyst for the book's development. Greg Hollingshead's creative thinking was instrumental in our finding the right title. Robin Johnston listened carefully to our concerns when we got stuck and offered helpful suggestions. Sibyl Frei, Managing Editor and Louise Fleming, Publisher of gynergy books, were enthusiastic supporters of our project. They handled difficulties, both large and small, with sensitivity and tact, providing reassurance when we needed it.*

*Finally, we are indebted to our partners, Ray Harper and Eric Hanley. Ray's hands-on support with computer expertise was invaluable as was Eric's willingness to assume responsibility for all domestic chores when the pressure was on. Both, as always, gave us their unwavering emotional support throughout the long process of bringing the book to completion.*

# TABLE OF CONTENTS

# INTRODUCTION

*T*he idea for this book was precipitated by the approaching millennium. Three years ago, while attending a conference in San Francisco, we spent an afternoon reflecting on how significantly the women's movement had influenced our lives and how much we had changed as a result of it. We knew that we were not alone — that this was the experience of our friends and many other women of our generation. A collection of stories that documented these changes would be an interesting and relevant project at this time.

As we thought back to our initial involvement with the women's movement when we were graduate students in the early 1970s, we realized how important our consciousness-raising group was to us. Professors in our graduate classes inundated us with humanistic psychologies, encouraging us to "be here now" and "let it all hang out." What we learned in our consciousness-raising group challenged this individualistic view of the world. The group consisted of a disparate collection of women with varying economic, educational and personal backgrounds. In sharing our experiences, we came to understand that "the personal is political," and, that despite our individual differences, our socialization as females had severely distorted our sense of self, thus limiting our options. We also learned to recognize how our society's organizations, institutions and systems affected us negatively, fostering systemic and personal discrimination of women. With our new awareness we were able to initiate changes in ourselves and in our relationships. We also applied our growing knowledge to our academic work and got involved in grassroots political action. Our raised consciousness was the primary catalyst for the many changes we initiated.

While we knew that documenting changes in women's lives would be an important theme of the book, we also wanted our collection to focus on women's deep connections to themselves and others. By this, we mean those powerful beliefs that strongly affect our outlook on life, our feelings about ourselves, our motivations, decisions and behaviours. We know that in a culture that devalues, restricts and discriminates against us, we cannot help but internalize negative messages. When these messages are transformed into core beliefs about the self, they become internal barriers to a fulfilling life, damaging the spirit and crippling the capacity to thrive. If these negative messages and beliefs remain unconscious, they have a hypnotic effect, resulting in the repetition and persistence of unhealthy behaviours. Even though we may want to change and make attempts to do so, we stay "stuck" in old patterns, the unconscious negative messages providing a blueprint for our lives.

As feminist psychotherapists who work with women to help them recover from the destructive effects of living in this culture, we have long understood that personal change must go hand in hand with social and political change. While women's status can greatly improve through important advancements in the public arena, including policies and laws, this is not enough. Women benefit from making those difficult and often painful personal changes that ultimately give them the strength and determination to take control of their lives in ways that are meaningful to them. To do so in a healthy and constructive way, women must first become aware of internalized negative beliefs, and replace them with positive ones. In psychotherapy, this work is called reframing; in the women's movement, consciousness raising. Whatever the label, this process is basic to the internal change necessary for women to transform themselves and their lives. The transformation that occurs when women move from negative to positive connections is the central theme of *Consciousness Rising*.

As we reflected on our own changes over the past thirty years, the obstacles overcome and the positive connections made to ourselves and to others, we knew it was this kind of change that we wanted to portray in the book. From the vantage point of mid-life, we could look back on the many barriers that we and other women have faced — internalized negative beliefs as well as external barriers to equality that are part of women's experience under patriarchy. With the help of the contemporary women's movement, our struggles to overcome these obstacles and make significant changes in our lives has been possible. We wanted our contributors to share their struggle and their connections to themselves, to others, to community — connections that enabled their particular transformation. What were the obstacles they had overcome? What were the positive connections that helped them develop conscious, healthy and life-affirming beliefs about themselves? Who or what supported them in their process of change? We looked for contributors with considerable life experience who would be willing to tell their own stories of personal growth and transformation. Not surprisingly, they too, are in mid-life.

Because such transformations are deeply personal, we asked our authors to write from a personal perspective. For those of us, including the editors, who are trained in an academic style that intentionally distances the writer from what is being written, this was very difficult. Even more difficult was the feeling of vulnerability we experienced by exposing our personal lives and risking judgement and dismissal from others. Whether academically trained or not, many of us worried that what we had to say would be seen as little more than egotistic self-indulgence. But if we were to talk about our own connections and transformations and use our personal experiences as examples of the transformation process, we had to take that risk. What gave us the courage to continue was the reassurance that others in the project shared our fears. We were not alone.

As the book developed, it took on a life of its own that we had not anticipated. We were confident that women's personal stories would be interesting and valuable, but were amazed at how, as a collection, they illuminate the issues central to an understanding of women's psychology today. Each personal story of psychological connection and transformation engages the reader in a very direct and moving way, thus making academic discourse both visible and accessible. The psychological particulars of each lived experience, in collection with the other narratives, portray the psychology of women far more powerfully than any textbook is able to do.

Many of the contributors talk of negative messages, expectations and experiences that damaged their sense of self-worth and self-esteem. Through their stories we come face to face with the pain of sexual, racial and religious discrimination. We hear tales of discouragement and despair, limited and limiting expectations and institutional as well as personal sexism. A number of the authors write about difficult childhoods involving abuse, neglect and abandonment. Some write of failed marriages and abusive relationships in adulthood. Most "got stuck" at different times in their lives as they struggled to cope with the after-effects of these destructive experiences. They experienced first-hand the damaging repercussions of powerful negative connections that remained unconscious and hypnotic for some time.

The stories also make apparent the tremendous energy it takes for women to overcome barriers, instigate changes and thus transform their lives. All had to tap into some inner resource and find the courage to initiate changes on their own. Many also acknowledge the support of particular individuals who made significant positive contributions to their lives. Some speak of how they were mothered by women other than their birth mothers when they were children. Others talk of the importance of special friends, teachers, partners, therapists or groups who supported them at crucial times, providing a necessary sanctuary from the harsh realities of their worlds. For many, the women's movement also played a central role in supporting change.

Most of the contributors make direct reference to powerful personal transformations. While the focus of the transformation may vary, the results do not. All of the authors in this collection are spirited, competent and energetic middle-aged women, living fulfilling and diverse lives.

As we look forward to the new millennium and back on the one that is passing, we realize that none of these transformations would have been possible without the contributions of the generations of women who came before us. It is our hope that our stories will resonate with women who are our contemporaries, as they too look back on the significant transformations in their own lives. For those still struggling to find the connections within and without that will act as catalysts for change, we hope that these narratives will support their quest. And for the young women who read our book, we offer these stories as a legacy from an older to a younger generation as they create, in the next millennium, the narratives of their own lives.

*Cheryl Malmo*          *Toni Suzuki Laidlaw*
*Edmonton, AB*              *Halifax, NS*

*April 1999*

# EVA PANDO RADFORD

## CIRCLES

### SPEAKING OUR TRUTHS

*You will be teachers for each other. You will come together in circles and speak your truth to each other. The time has come for women to accept their spiritual responsibility for our planet.*[1]

— *Sherry Ruth Anderson and Patricia Hopkins*

There is an intriguing drawing in my *Gage Canadian Dictionary* that illustrates the words *nadir* and *zenith*: a tiny figure straddles a minuscule globe and peers through a telescope. A circle surrounds this tiny being and the globe she stands on. Directly midpoint on the circle below the figure is the nadir; directly opposite, above the figure, is the zenith. The nadir, we learn, is the opposite of the zenith. The figure, however, is looking not at the zenith, but just below. The figure, or the "observer on Earth," as the drawing identifies her, illustrates my relationship to the circles I belong to: I stand, a good Taurus, firmly on the round earth, in the centre of a larger circle, and try to keep my vision aimed at, if not the zenith, then some perhaps more attainable point just below it. The circles centre me; the inner one is my terra firma, the surrounding circle represents all that gives my life meaning. My circles help direct my vision up to where the good possibilities of life lie, and away from the downside, the nadir, that easily-slid-into place many of us know.

I live in Edmonton, Alberta, the northernmost large city in North America, a long way from where I came. I was born in Santa Fe, New Mexico, a venerated, ancient city in the piñon-dotted foothills of the Sangre de Cristo Mountains. I've been in Edmonton for nearly thirty years and discovered a long time ago that, because I live this far from "home," relationships with the people around me are crucial to the quality of my life.

My little dictionary icon has only one circle surrounding her. I'm luckier. I have many circles around me: my family, good friends, peers and community. Circles are the reality of my life. Most of us have circles, based on interactions and relationships. They form and dissolve like the organic creatures they are. But in addition to the circles that I am part of due to the circumstances of my life, I have also belonged to circles that arose from consciousness: a reading circle, a solstice circle and a yoga class. They have different purposes, but each one nourishes me as a spiritual, social and intellectual being.

## READING CIRCLE

In this, my oldest circle, women from varied backgrounds, with differing careers, tastes, opinions, gather to share a love of books and another common ground — women's spirituality and personal growth. Our circle is not a "religious" group, but we are spiritual women with feminist beliefs and values. We don't always read books on women's spirituality, but our sensibilities and perspective determine our choice of books. As well, our reactions to the books we read, and the discussions we have about them, reflect who we are and where we come from.

Our reading circle was formed many years ago, by two good friends and book lovers who each invited another woman. Some of us had degrees in English literature or library science; we were all working with books or authors in some way or other, whether as librarians, writers, editors or book publicists. Our circle began to meet once a month, and we took turns hosting, creating a celebratory mood with candles or flowers, serving fruit or cheese, sometimes dessert, with wine and coffee or tea.

Over the years, there have been a few changes. Some members moved away; new members joined; we decided to expand the circle to six. Initially we chose the books we would read in a casual discussion, agreeing on a list for the months ahead; now the host for the next meeting chooses the book for discussion in her home. This assures that everyone has a say in the reading list.

Our discussions about books are always stimulating and fun. We don't often agree, and this can lead to the most interesting debates. When we read Doris Lessing's *Love, Again*, I didn't "get" the book; I thought it was boring, repetitive and pointless. But after the evening's lively exchange, I realized that it was much more complex and rich than I had thought. The group helped me appreciate the profound nature of the novel and I decided to reread it. Another time, one of the members refused to read Diana Gabaldon's *Outlander*, saying it was "junk." We agreed that the book was not up to our usual literary standards, but it was a hell of a read and we needed a great escape. Entertainment aside, my views have been broadened by our books: Leslie Feinberg's *Stone Butch Blues*, the autobiography of a butch lesbian, was an insight into the difficult, vulnerable and risky lives of women who live outside the norm. *The Feminine Face of God*, by Sherry Ruth Anderson and Patricia Hopkins, knocked me off my feet with its insights into the nature of women's spirituality and intimacy.

We all bring our own experiences to the circle — we "speak our truths." All of us are married, have children and hold day jobs. We range in age from late thirties to late fifties, enjoy cultural heritages that range from Hispanic to Icelandic to Norwegian to Greek to English/Scottish, were born and lived in other places in the world before coming to roost in Edmonton. We lead completely different lives, with full-time jobs, part-time jobs, young children at home, empty nests, blended families, adored grandchildren, ex-partners or partners in different cities.

One of our members, Lillian Macpherson, beautifully described a circle:

> *A circle is a unique space for women to celebrate their lives, the passages in their lives, their unique bodies, their loved/hated bodies. It is a time to honour that which is woman/female/feminine without reference to or comparison with that which has defined us. It is a space where we can speak our truth, our uncertainty, our pain, our power, our strength, our love.*

Our reading circle honours this definition. We are a support group when support is needed, say for the illness of a loved one, or the trials of work-related stress. We celebrate the arrival of children and grandchildren, new jobs, trips to exotic cities; we commiserate over truculent teenagers or surly co-workers, and sometimes cry together when one of us decides to move to a new city. The circle has become a special place outside of "real life," brought together and held together by our common intention — to read and to talk about what we have read. Commitment is an essential ingredient in our success: we make a real effort to read the book and to make it to the circle. I'm surprised by the cavalier attitude of other reading groups whose members can't find time to read one book a month, and who treat the group as little more than an excuse to share a bottle of wine and gossip. Our circle has become so important to me that I would not dream of missing a meeting, unless I was ill, and I am sure the other members feel the same way.

## Solstice Circle

Three women form the core of another of my circles, although we began as four and occasionally invite guests. This circle arose from a get-together at one woman's home, in 1989, to view the National Film Board's stunning *Goddess Remembered*, directed by Donna Read. When the film ended, we sat with tears in our eyes around Sylvia's oak table. Like Germaine Greer's *The Female Eunuch*, the film gave us powerful insight into what was wrong with mainstream religion. Many of us had been brought up in a Christian environment but had left the church over the years. Our spiritual natures had been subsumed by child-rearing and the grit of daily life. The church had little to offer. The film awakened us to what we were missing, and showed us the way to begin to realize our deeper natures. It was an epiphany, and soon we were on the road to rediscovery of our spirituality.

We decided to meet at the winter and summer solstices, to reflect on our lives and mark the cycle of the earth in a meaningful way. Our first time together was in my backyard, because I had a firepit. (We use fire as part of our ritual.) Now we often gather at Cheryl's home, in front of her fireplace. One of the women traditionally brings champagne; there is always wonderful food — the ceremony turns into a party.

Our evenings begin around a table beautifully decorated with a special cloth on which are set goddess images, candles and flowers. The goddess images are part of Cheryl's collection from all around the world, and the evening's ritual includes choosing our favourite goddess images for the night. I always bring to the table the little, fierce-eyed Minoan Goddess, in her amazing flounced skirt and bared-to-the-waist bodice, with a tiny cat perched calmly on her elegant coiffure. She is feminine, yet a force to be reckoned with. I like to wonder about the cat, and how it relates to the snakes clenched in her upraised fists. Was she the goddess of nature, in control of the storms and earthquakes that charged over the Cretan mountains? Was the cat her familiar, or her earthly representative, worshipped like Bast, the Egyptian cat-god? Do the snakes represent wisdom? Another goddess who inevitably joins the celebration is the palm-sized Goddess of Willendorf, whose rounded shape suggests that she was a fertility symbol.

We have evolved a few other rituals over the years. We burn sweetgrass and bathe ourselves in the sacred smoke. In a fireplace or firepit we burn representations, in words or poetry or art, of the negativity that has accumulated in our spirits since the last time we met. The contents of these missives are private but are sometimes shared. While the others watch quietly, we take turns placing our packages or letters on the fire. Some are largish, elaborate, well-sealed affairs that take a lot of time to burn, or meaningfully full envelopes that are surprisingly quick to catch flame; others are folded slips of paper, hurriedly prepared. No matter the size or shape, they all burn brightly. We watch in fascination how one expands and changes shape as the fire breathes into it, how unearthly and beautiful it looks just before it implodes. As all this bad karma becomes a delicate structure of ash and finally collapses, we heave a communal sigh of relief.

Our ritual burning of negativity reminds me of Zozobra, or Old Man Gloom, who is burned at Fort Marcy Park, a few blocks from the Santa Fe plaza. Zozobra is burned on the first night of the Fiesta, a fall celebration to commemorate the reconquest of Santa Fe from the Pueblo Indians in 1692, but I suspect that the event has been layered over a much older festival of harvest. Zozobra is a huge, crepe-paper figure stuffed with fireworks. He has large, black, staring eyes and a thatch of fiery red hair. His mouth is wide and red. He is rigged so that his jaw moves up and down, so that he can be seen to moan and groan while loudspeakers emit his tape-recorded pain. He wears a long white garment with a rather natty black belt and three large black buttons. He looks, standing there against the indigo sky, as if a first-grader drew him. A fire dance at his base, performed by a local ballet troupe, culminates in setting him aflame. As the fire rises high into the night sky, his cries grow louder and louder, competing with the crackle and snap of the flames. The burning of Zozobra ends with the fireworks in his head bursting over the cheering crowd.

The burning of this effigy is a strangely moving event. When I was a child, I used to get terribly upset for poor Zozobra. How he moaned! How his arms moved helplessly up and down! But how happy everyone was when it was over, and the gathered hundreds paraded in their fiesta finery to the city plaza to enjoy the mariachis and flamenco dancers on the bandstand. *"Que viva la fiesta!"* we called out. It is an ancient, pagan event, this burning of our "gloom" before the party can begin. One shivers to think that the burning of heretics and "witches" held the same sense of relief. But with Zozobra, the overriding sense is that the old, burdensome troubles have disappeared like so much crepe paper. A cleansing by fire is cathartic, be it in the plaza in Santa Fe or — one winter — in Barb's barbecue grille.

The solstice ceremonies mark a time of reflection, not only on what has passed, but also on what is to come. After the burning ritual, we read the tarot or runes for each other. I remember one special reading on December 21, 1997. We had spent most of the evening discussing our mothers and ourselves. We had talked of the way our mothers had lived, comparing their lives to ours and understanding that we were indebted to them for our own degrees of success and for our feminism. Our mothers valued and encouraged our education; we went to university and joined the feminist movement. And now, because of our work, the next generation of women, our daughters, can take courses in Women's Studies at university. One of us noted ruefully that witches had in all likelihood been burned for the kind of evening we were enjoying! I added that my husband's family was descended from a Salem judge who sent women to their death during the hysteria of the burning times. Not surprisingly, this information was received with a shudder. I hope the spirits of those unfortunate women, burned at the stake for their special knowledge, are resting easy, knowing that they have finally been recognized as victims of ignorance and fear.

The first rune of that night, representing us then, was Teiwaz, "warrior energy, the Rune of the Spiritual Warrior," who tells us to "remain mindful that all you can really do is stay out of your own way and let the Will of Heaven flow through you."[2] The second one, representing our challenge, was Dagaz, the rune of transformation in attitude, of seizing "radical trust" and leaping into the void. Finally, our best-outcome rune was Algiz, the rune of mindfulness, of "staying with the pain" and controlling the emotions during a time of self-change. It reminded us to "learn from whatever happens." Good advice. Six days later, my father died. I am still learning from that painful event. The issues concerning me that evening have remained, but I have tried to stay back, keep an open mind and let things unfold, trusting that the future will be all right.

The gathering of a solstice ritual always ends reluctantly and late. The ceremony continues to grow and change; recently I have been including with my burnt offering a thank you to the Spirit that infuses all life, for the blessings my loved ones and I have enjoyed. If negativity can rise to the sky in smoke, why not send positive messages as well?

There seems to be a new circle forming in my neighbourhood: a "women's-pause" weekend. I've just returned from our second annual get-together, this time of a dozen women, in the country-side for an entire weekend. This group evolved from the fact that many of us are entering menopause and want information on the issue. We thought the most enjoyable way to learn was to get together, away from our responsibilities, and talk and listen to each other. That was the first year. This spring we hardly mentioned menopause, which caused one woman in the group to comment, "So what? Maybe enjoying life is where we are in our menopause, so why talk about it?"

I know from my sister-in-law, who lives in Maine, that women's circles there meet on a monthly basis and have for years. These groups are everywhere, I believe. It is a wonderful thought that, every full moon, women come together to celebrate the feminine face of God.


## Yoga Class

I first took a hatha yoga class shortly after moving to Edmonton, in the early seventies. At that time I saw it simply as physical exercise, a way to keep limber. My twenty-five-year-old body responded to the asanas (postures) easily and I felt energized by them. Then I quit yoga for twenty years — years of marriage break-up, remarriage, children, career — years when I didn't think I had time for it. I realize now what a mistake that was. Not only would I have kept in touch with that youthful body, had I continued, but yoga would have helped alleviate the stresses those years accumulated. Still, remnants of yoga remained with me; I kept up with a few stretching postures and practised meditation whenever I could. In time, a combination of stresses from my job as manager of a small publishing house and health problems caused me to realize that I had to centre my life, to get on a path to wellness. The path led to a teacher who believes that yoga is not just a series of asanas but is rooted in a profound spiritual practice.

My women-only Friday morning class became one of my circles, a place for body and soul. My teacher is a beautiful woman with a deep spiritual sense, a gift for teaching and enormous tact. The class was a place where I unkinked the week's physical and psychic knots, where I celebrated my middle-aged body's ability to flex, to align, to bend, to breathe. We began with an exercise to help us focus our awareness on pranayama, or breathing, to help us concentrate on our yoga practice and to strengthen our ability to centre ourselves later on, and draw on conscious breathing when we were challenged by the stresses of life — the traffic jam on the way to work, the endless lineup at the grocery store. The class ended two hours later, in a circle where we chanted a few "oms" and closed with hands on heart in prayer position, gentle bows, and the blessing and thank-you word, *namaste*. This class fed my body and mind and spirit for several years. Now, with a different job, I have had to switch to a Monday night group. The new class is different, but being without my group of friends has made me dig deeper to bring a conscious effort to my practice. This class is more inward-focused for me, and I expect that this has not been sent to me without a reason.

## PAST CONNECTIONS

During the late fifties and early sixties, when I was a teenager, we girls were pretty much on our own emotionally and psychologically, subject to the influences of television and film. At least I was, in spite of regular church attendance. My teen role models were the perky blonde actress Sandra Dee and the perfect Betty Anderson, eldest daughter on "Father Knows Best." Growing up in Santa Fe, where the dominant social group was Anglo, had its own challenges for me, a high achiever with low self-esteem, a Hispanic kid from a working-class neighbourhood. My membership in the honour society and marching band did little to qualify me for a satisfactory social life in high school. I learned that what mattered was how you looked, where you lived, what your dad did for a living, what you wore and whom you dated. A circle would have helped get me through those confusing and emotional years, but my groups outside of school were limited to the crowd I hung out with, my church young people's association and, for a very short time, the Rainbow Girls, the female youth group of the Masons. My participation in all of these was due to the necessities of time and place, and parental expectations.

In my mother's day, I think, similar circles existed, but they were disguised as "stitch and bitch," bridge games or women's church groups. I remember my mother's regular attendance at church groups, including the choir and the women's fellowship. Later she was invited to join groups outside the church — a sorority group and Eastern Star — groups that gave her a chance to dress up and move outside her work and household roles, to connect with other women on her own behalf.

During my college years in St. Paul, Minnesota, from 1963 to 1967, young women all over North America began to realize how important our relationships with each other were, but this knowledge did not develop into consciously organized support of each other in today's sense. Many of us were trying to understand and cope with revolutionary social changes at the same time as we were learning to live away from the shelter of home. We drew together in dorm lounges, after a day of classes and a night of study, and gained comfort from girl-talk. But while these gatherings let us support each other, we had little awareness of our deeper needs, and no goals beyond our immediate ones.

During the sixties such circles evolved from small groups with similar interests into a broad political movement on university campuses. The atmosphere of those years is difficult to convey to young people today. Those of us who were in our late teens or early twenties then were very lucky to live in a time of social change. The Vietnam War was raging. Student protest movements gathered momentum across North America and made us realize that adults did not have the answers, that we had a political voice and that even the president of the United States could be dead wrong. I was dating a philosophy graduate student in Ann Arbor, Michigan, a university town that teemed with vitality. The streets buzzed with life and colour, from psychedelic head shops to open-air groups of students arguing over philosophical and political issues, or listening to the dynamic words of a Black Panther or a member of the SDS (Students for a Democratic Society). The languid, hypnotic acid rock of The Doors wafted from open windows, and more than incense filled the air. I took my first baby steps in learning to think for myself during that time, and began to turn away from the social and cultural mores of my upbringing. I also got my first job, my first car and my first bank loan.

After the student antiwar protest and Black Is Beautiful movements, it was a natural step for the next disenfranchised group — women — to seek its rightful political power. The political is always personal. We quit wearing makeup and bras, to symbolize the fact that we did not want to be sex objects, but wanted to free ourselves from the clutches of male control. The birth-control pill gave us more freedom to be sexual beings, if we chose to. Women began to aim higher in the workforce, in academia, in industry; we broke limits everywhere. Our voices grew stronger and we opened more and more doors. We began to meet, with our own agendas.

## CONSCIOUSNESS-RAISING GROUPS

In 1969 the philosopher and I got married and moved to Edmonton, where he had been hired to teach at the university. I found that my teaching degree was useless in Canada, and drifted from clerical job to clerical job. I took up silversmithing, began to study printmaking and revived my interest in becoming an artist. By 1973 my marriage was on the rocks and I needed support from outside our social group. I became close friends with a female student, and she introduced me to an entirely different social circle, particularly when she began dating a local filmmaker/musician. She invited me to join a fledgling consciousness-raising group, and I leapt at the chance.

The group was made up of women connected with the developing film community in Edmonton. I was an exception, being married to an academic and working part-time in an ear-nose-and-throat surgeon's office. Our agenda was to read and discuss the works being published by women writers who were part of the new "women's liberation movement." We read Gloria Steinem and Betty Friedan, and discovered the works of earlier women writers such as Simone de Beauvoir and Virginia Woolf, but I think we began with *The Female Eunuch*.

*The Female Eunuch* educated me on the realities of the lives of girls and women. Until then, I had not questioned the way things were between men and women or, more to the point, between men and me. I had been was brought up in a patriarchal household and, although my mother worked to supplement our income, she deferred to my father on major decisions. I may have thought I was liberated, but I was still living in the old paradigm: the man's career came foremost; the woman was responsible for keeping up the home and directing the social life. Greer's book was an awakener. Indeed, many of us were profoundly affected by the discussions in our circle, and so were many of the men in our lives. I went back to school to earn a post-graduate degree so that I could find a better job and be financially independent.

In the consciousness-raising group, our discussions were lively and fun. I no longer felt isolated in my new city. I had connected with other women who wanted to explore the issues that concerned us: independence, self-awareness, relationships, our biological selves, our sexual selves. Together we arrived at the exciting notion that we had emotional needs and that they deserved to be met. Thinking back on the difference between this group and the group of women I had shared a house with during my college years, I see clearly that the consciousness-raising groups of the seventies had a political agenda we college coeds of the sixties had not even dreamed of.

I was not at all the same person in 1975 that I had been in 1967. Few of us were. I had (consciously and unconsciously) gone as far as possible mentally, culturally, physically, from my people and place of my birth. I had left the organized religion of my parents, earned a couple of degrees, begun to support myself, married, moved to a new country, made new friends, divorced, remarried, had two children, made more friends, joined some circles. During the process, I had reinvented myself. I found myself proud to be who I am, proud of my father's Spanish-Indian roots in the northern New Mexico mountains, proud of my mother's Mexican origins in the apple-growing valleys of Chihuahua. I had learned that my ancestors gave strength, perspective and richness to my life. My centre was within me.

RETURNING TO THE CIRCLE

When I left the landscape and culture of the Southwest to attend college in the Midwest, I did not realize that it would take me years to find my centre again. Belonging to my circles has given me a place to do this, friends to do it with and an awareness of the importance of the celebration of our lives. In my circles I have learned that it is essential to connect to the centre of my being, my spirit, and my circles nurture this spiritual aspect of me. Now, as I move through my fifties, my circles are showing me that the future looks interesting and stimulating, and are supporting me as I face the daunting prospect of an empty nest in the coming years.

Sometimes I wonder if I'm the "observer on Earth," in my dictionary sketch, or the circle around her. Perhaps I am both. Belonging to a circle makes me a participant, a provider as well as a recipient of its energy — a giver and a taker. My yoga teacher tells us that as we breathe we are breathed. We are circles in the endless stream, moving and touching, expanding and blending, growing and dissolving, affecting those around us and being forever affected by others. I am thankful for the circles I have been given, as well as those I have chosen for myself, for it is in these circles that I have discovered an essential part of myself.

## ENDNOTES

1. Sherry Ruth Anderson and Particia Hopkins, *The Feminine Face of God: The Unfolding of the Sacred in Women* (New York: Bantam, 1991), p. 4.

2. This and the following quotations about runes are from: Ralph Blum, *The Book of Runes: A Handbook for the Use of an Ancient Oracle, The Viking Runes* (New York: St. Martin's, 1987).

# ROSA SPRICER

## *BODY IMAGE*

### A LIFE PROCESS

*I* am more accustomed to listening to life stories than to telling my own. As a therapist I work with many women, and occasionally men, whose connection to their bodies is conflicted and painful. I am thankful that I no longer suffer as they do.

Body image is a complicated concept, one that is often poorly understood. The term refers to our experience of our bodies, which takes place on several levels: the visual level — how we see our bodies; the kinesthetic level — our felt sense of being in our bodies; and the auditory level — how we think about and talk to ourselves about our bodies. Body image starts forming at birth, is continually affected by life experiences and keeps changing until we die. It is a developmental process and therefore my story needs to start at the beginning.

I have many bodily memories, which manifest as spontaneous physiological and emotional reactions, but few conscious memories of my early years. My parents were Holocaust survivors. They were in their thirties when I was born and had already suffered innumerable traumas. The Holocaust was a darkness that followed my family everywhere, permeating everything. My mother has told me that she could not hold or nurse me as an infant. She would begin to shake, terrified that I would die as her first baby daughter had, in her arms. For me, my mother hired a nurse. I have no idea whether the nurse was loving, gentle and attentive. I can only guess at what I began to believe about my body, myself and the world at that time. As a psychologist I know that infants learn about their worth and about trust in relationships through their senses, according to how their bodies are treated. I do know that trust does not come easily for me and that even as a young child I was uncomfortable with physical affection or closeness.

I spent the first year and a half of my life in a displaced persons' camp in Germany. My mother has often recounted how she would barter and fight for oranges for me. I wonder if I was malnourished then and, if so, whether that is one point of origin for my lifelong sense of deprivation.

I remember vividly being a sickly child with recurring colds, infections, fevers, numerous allergies and asthma. For many years there were weekly hospital visits for injections, visits that for the most part I made alone. Although my mother was caring and nurturing at such times, I hated being sick. Perhaps I had already decided I never wanted to be like my parents, who suffered on-going medical complaints and what seemed to me to be regular medical emergencies. Later, I came to understand their ailments as echoes of the relentless pain of the Holocaust. By age five I already preferred to be at school — in fact, to be anywhere but at home. To me, home was a dingy, ugly, sad and stressful place. When there, I escaped into daydreams, drawing and books. School too was an escape. Illness meant staying home and this I would not do. I believe that my reaction against sickness, my refusal to succumb to it, was a crucial part of my salvation as a child and a significant motivator for me as an adult.

Illness, however, was only one of many early influences on my perceptions of my body. Each influence was significant but, in fact, all were interwoven into the fabric of my life. My elementary school years were the most difficult of my life, shadowed by my being an immigrant, by poverty, and by my parents' pain and fear and stress.

My parents' fears were wide-ranging. Perhaps because they had already lost so many people, or because they saw the world as unpredictable and dangerous, they could not bear for me and my sister and brother to take physical risks. When we did, they reacted with terror. For as long as they could, they prevented us from climbing and jumping from high places, doing balancing acts or even riding bicycles. I learned to mistrust my body and to fear loss of control. I eventually became determined to do things in spite of my anxiety, but the anxiety is almost always there, just below the surface. To some extent, I have passed this fear onto my son.

My parents' fears for their children extended also to food and eating. Their traumatic wartime experiences of starvation and death, including my older sister's death from either malnutrition or starvation, made food another primary focus in their circumscribed lives. Food healed, food soothed, food kept you alive, food was how you showed love. We were cajoled, bribed, manipulated and forced to eat, not one helping but at least two. The fridge and cupboards were always packed with food. My mother, who worked fulltime, would cook and bake on the weekends. My father, who by the time I was nine stayed home because medical and emotional difficulties made work impossible, would rouse himself from his miseries to feed us. To refuse to eat was unthinkable. It would put our lives at risk; it would negate my parents' lives. My sister, brother and I quickly learned to ignore our bodily cues and to eat on demand. By the time I was nine, eating had become for me a complicated emotional activity that had little to do with hunger. Instead, it was a way of bonding with my family, connecting with my Jewish culture and comforting and nurturing myself.

To further complicate my relationship with food and with my body were other conflicting messages. Junk food was forbidden in our home. My father seemed to view it as a symbol of the corrupted, inferior culture of North America, and he refused to spend money on it. This made it all the more desirable, and consuming junk food became one of the many things the rest of the family would do in secret. In addition, my father was concerned about our appearance and weight. He commented on both continually, looking us over, appraising our clothing and judging whether we had gained or lost weight. Looking back, my guess is that he was as concerned as I was about our status and our place in the world and that our acceptability represented his. Luckily, my mother did not seem concerned about weight or appearance — hers, or ours — and gave the impression that things like work and responsibility mattered much more. In this respect, thankfully, she modelled self-acceptance and a healthy sense of priorities.

Still, my preoccupation with image was by no means solely attributable to my father. For me, the immigrant experience, as well as the experience of poverty, was pervaded by feelings of profound humiliation. I remember my feelings of shame and anger at my parents' treatment by shopkeepers and social workers, as well as by acculturated relatives. Our impoverishment seemed extreme even within the context of our immigrant slum neighbourhood. My clothes were homemade and badly sewn, my frizzy hair was cut short by a barber and when the weather was cool I wore a babushka, not a hat. My parents spoke Yiddish at home, and they rarely socialized. My verbal abilities and my understanding of social rules and etiquette were limited. My home was empty of anything ornamental or playful. I was mocked and called names by schoolmates. It was obvious to me that I was being judged by how I looked and behaved and I began to concentrate on my appearance. By age twelve I was plucking, shaving, tweezing, and straightening my hair, and by age fourteen I was working so that I could buy my own clothes. I now understand that my appearance was one of the few things I felt I could change and control. I was desperate to escape my world and in order to do so I believed that I needed to look acceptable. Outsiders often survive by becoming very watchful and attentive and I became a sharp observer of class, race, status, power and social groupings, and of the images that convey them. I believed I needed to learn to read the signs quickly and accurately to avoid humiliation and to push myself in the direction I hoped to go.

Furthermore, Montreal, the city in which I grew up, was sophisticated and fashion-conscious. We lived close to downtown and the women I saw and wanted to emulate were elegant and stylish and knew how to express themselves through their clothes. By the time I was ten or eleven I hungered for the girls' and women's magazines that would tell me what to do. I read them wherever I could find them, even though they were forbidden in our home. The more I read them, the more I realized the extent to which my body did not measure up to their standards, and my dissatisfaction with my body grew.

By age ten I had sizeable breasts and around my eleventh birthday I began to menstruate. I hated my body for both these developments. My periods devastated me, bringing excruciating cramps and migraine headaches which invariably meant bed rest for one day each month. My large breasts added to my sense of being different and brought me more unwelcome attention. I learned to try to hide them. I had no one to speak to about these matters and I suffered alone.

I spent my elementary school years in an ethnically mixed, poor inner-city neighbourhood, where life was lived on the street. Sexual harassment and molestation were normal. Men seemed to lurk everywhere, in alleys, by the corner store, in the parks, on crowded buses, their hands always ready to grope, their bodies insinuating themselves, closing in on mine. Several times, coming home after dark, I was followed. My parents took in boarders to help subsidize their rent and when I was nine years old one of them molested me as I sat at the kitchen table doing my home-work. I told my mother and, to her credit, he was gone that same day. She rescued me again, this time from an employer, when I was fourteen.

In adolescence, I used to equate my experiences of sexual harassment with poverty. While poverty certainly had a part to play, I see now that the pervasiveness of these incidents was largely due to the extent to which I was unprotected and out in the world alone. My parents were overwhelmed and I had to learn to fend for myself. I am forever grateful that my mother believed me and protected me when she could.

The effect on my body image of these sexual incidents was subtle, I think. I became street-smart at a young age. My body learned to be hypervigilant, alert at all times to signs of danger. I could feel it becoming stiff and contained in order to be less accessible to men. I learned how to shield myself and how to move quickly. I was growing even more wary and aloof.

I learned that it was not safe out in the world, but even more significantly, I had already learned that it was not safe at home. After my father had stopped working, and as his emotional state deteriorated, his unpredictability, his rage and his violence had increased. My mother was afraid for us but she worked long hours and could do little to protect us. Because my father's behaviour was so extreme and because he gave us so little, it became easy for me to hate him. (In fact, I remember telling him so for the first time when I was only five years old.) I became angry; I defied him. Even so, my father's verbal and physical abuse had a profound effect on my sense of self, and therefore on my body image. In his eyes I felt worthless. My body and my needs were obviously completely irrelevant to him.

Luckily, my mother's covert empathy for me and the closeness I had with my sister and brother — who shared the same reality — enabled me to trust my anger. My anger fuelled my will to survive, allowing me to fight for myself as well as for my mother and siblings. However, in order to do this as a child, I unconsciously had to lock away my own childhood needs, my terror and my physical and emotional pain. These came to be stored deep inside my body, only to emerge, as they always do, as uncontrollable overreactions to people and events or as confusing physical symptoms. My emotions and unmet needs found their outlet in eating and my seemingly inadequate body became the ultimate proof of my unlovableness.

At a conscious level, I made significant life decisions. I resolved that I would never again be a victim, never again be abused. I would never allow myself to be dependent or vulnerable or needy. I would learn to be strong and self-sufficient. And if I were powerless to prevent my body from being subjected to scrutiny in public — where it could be commented on, leered at, touched or hit — I decided that my thoughts, at least, could always be mine, to share only when and with whom I pleased, and only when I felt safe. I became closed, protective. I erected innumerable barriers, especially against boys and men. I could not have articulated my beliefs about men and heterosexual relationships at that time, but I did believe that prostitution — demanding payment for the use of one's body — made sense. Otherwise men just seemed to take what they wanted.

I had already made these life decisions by age twelve. At age thirteen I entered high school. Unlike many adolescents, I loved it. I discovered sports and found to my amazement that I had athletic ability. For the first time in my life I felt physically strong and capable, even powerful, and I have treasured this feeling ever since. I was finally able to connect and work with my body in a positive way.

Sports also gave me a legitimate reason to avoid going home, one I used as much as I could. And sports gave me my first sense of belonging to a group, of being with people who made few emotional demands on me. I experienced my first taste of empowerment and liberation. Soon I was enjoying many other extracurricular activities and I began to have female friendships. I was very busy and successful. In addition, I developed a relationship with a guidance counsellor who became a lifelong mentor to me. He asked nothing of me; he was genuinely interested in me as a person and he consistently believed in and encouraged me. At a very crucial time in my life, he modelled behaviours that were completely different from what I had learned to expect and opened up a world of possibilities. I was eating compulsively

during those years; my family life was fraught with conflict and
tension; I had daily crises about my appearance; but I was also
growing, and I had hopes and dreams for the future.

After high school, against my parents' wishes, I entered university and the larger world. Although I behaved as if I were worldly
and in complete control, now that I was alone, with no support, my
latent but deeply rooted sense of inadequacy emerged. I felt stupid,
ugly, inarticulate and socially and intellectually inferior. I rarely
spoke, lest I give myself away and most of my energy went into
obsessing about how I appeared to others. Body-image issues began
to consume my life. I dieted and binged continually. I experimented
with diet pills, diuretics, laxatives and fasts. Luckily, I hated feeling
weak or unwell; my concern for health was consistently stronger
than my desire for thinness and the pills and regimens were only
experiments. I did straighten my hair daily and worked long hours
to afford the right clothes. I was desperate to create an image that
would make me acceptable, desirable, that would camouflage and
compensate for my failings, that would do for me what I felt
incapable of accomplishing in any other way.

I think of those undergraduate years with sadness. I now
understand that I was terrified to go out into the world alone and
that I was doing my best to survive. For four or five years much of
my "real" self went into hiding, and I consistently chose safety
instead of growth. I simply did not have the inner resources that
would have allowed me to take risks. I gave up physical activities;
I took classes that did not challenge me; I developed relationships
with people who would not threaten me (and who often bored
me); and eventually I even married someone "safe" in order to be
able to leave home. His background was similar to mine. He spoke
little and expected even less. He was indecisive and confused and
in his presence I could feel strong and smart. When he and I left
for our first trip to Europe I managed my terror at having left my
family and at contending with the unknown by weighing myself
anywhere and everywhere I could. The weigh scales of Europe
provided me with an anchor, something concrete and familiar that
would tell me whether I was okay or not.

My obsession with food and weight stayed with me for many more years, but after I graduated with a BA, a series of almost imperceptible internal shifts began to occur. I had my first jolt of insight on my wedding day, as I was walking down the aisle. I was twenty-one years old, and I heard my internal voice telling me that I was making a huge mistake. My wedding did not feel real; it was in no way a reflection of my true self, of my hopes or dreams. Suddenly I could see how much I had been permitting my life to be directed by fear and I felt deeply disappointed in and ashamed of myself. Instead of vowing to commit myself to this marriage, I was promising myself to find a way out of it and back to me. Although the circumstances were far from ideal, for the first time I was able to think about changing the direction of my life rather than the shape of my body.

Shortly thereafter (in 1969) I saw an advertisement for a consciousness-raising group for women. I went by myself. I cannot remember the women in the group, the specifics of our conversations or how many times I attended, but I do know the profound and lasting effect it had on me. My discovery of feminism felt like a miracle, like corrective surgery after lifelong partial blindness. Finally, I had the words and concepts with which to articulate what I had always sensed and dimly known: there was something wrong, something unjust, in the lives of girls and women and in the relationships between males and females. At last my perceptions, as well as my needs and desires, had some legitimacy. Whereas before I could dismiss them as subjective, neurotic, now they were validated by many other women. I no longer felt so completely alone. For the first time since high school I felt empowered, and the long, slow process of learning to trust myself could begin. Taking baby steps, I started to turn away from dreams of being rescued and from the all-consuming need for acceptance, both of which hinged on having the perfect body, and began to ask what I might want for myself.

My husband and I moved to Toronto to attend teachers' college. At that time, Toronto was smaller, less sophisticated and less fashionable. Although feminism had provided me with an

intellectual understanding of the oppressive nature of the quest
for beauty, it was only in this more casual environment, away
from family and old friends, that I could begin to free myself from
the constant tyranny of clothes and makeup. I met a young
woman from New York, a feminist like myself, who was very
informed about health and healing. She introduced me to the
notion of healthful eating and living. For her this meant choosing
organic, unprocessed, whole foods, because she believed the body
needed to be well nourished and well cared for in order to be
strong. She felt, also, that the body needed rest and calmness as
well as activity, and she made me aware of the practice of
meditation. I learned a great deal from her and, although I was
still dieting and binging and suffering, each move I was able to
make towards health seemed significant to me.

Over the next few years food and weight remained obsessive
concerns, but I began to take a few risks. I worked and travelled,
and eventually found the courage to leave my husband. I felt
exuberant, liberated and full of hope. For a period of time, I made
myself slim and attractive and I experienced the power that
comes with being single, youthful and seductive. It frightened
me. I allowed myself to fall in love for the first time, and this too
was scary. At about the same time, I entered graduate school.
More fear. I began to gain weight again.

My new relationship proved to be loving but very painful. We
were both emotionally immature, terrified of being hurt and of
committing to each other. When this relationship ended I found
myself deeply depressed. I could see that I had no idea how to be
in a relationship and that intimacy scared me, made me feel too
vulnerable, defenceless. Unnerved by the depth of my hopeless-
ness and despair — qualities I had abhorred in my father — I
found a therapist and began the arduous process of self-explora-
tion with the intent to change.

Slowly, imperceptibly, I began to change. Feminism had
provided me with a political analysis, and now therapy allowed
me to make sense of my own way of being in the world. I looked
at my life experiences, my family, my relationships. I began to

understand the reasons for my self-hatred, my sense of unworthiness and my debilitating fears, and as I did so their power over me diminished.

My therapist, a man, had no understanding of body image or food/weight issues. However, I was determined: I hated feeling disempowered. With his emotional support, but without his knowledge, I spent considerable time reading, thinking, watching and trying to understand the role these issues played in my life.

I was now in my mid-twenties and overweight, but I decided to throw away my scales; I was tired of their tyranny, the way they controlled my day. And I stopped dieting. I no longer wanted to live with the anxiety and tension that diets impose. Somehow I knew that dieting was not the answer, although I did not quite know what the answer was. Unconsciously, I think I had realized that periods of being slim had solved nothing, had not protected me from pain or brought me happiness, and that I used excess weight to shield me from men and from intimacy. As I gave up deprivation and allowed myself to eat what I wanted, my frantic and crazed binges gradually diminished in number and intensity. I was still overeating but I felt better because I no longer seemed so completely out of control. And very gradually, as my tension concerning food subsided, I was better able to hear my body's messages about what it liked or did not like, or whether it was hungry or not. I was not always acting upon what I heard, but the process of reconnection was beginning. I was turning away from fighting with my body and toward listening to it. With therapy, I was also becoming aware of my inner voice, which was harsh, unforgiving, completely critical and abusive. I started to redirect my mental energy away from self-hatred whenever I overate or examined my body. Instead I cultivated curiosity, a desire to understand why I needed these behaviours and feelings. I learned merely to notice my emotions, my reactions, my judgements. Over many years, I came to know the many and complicated reasons for my compulsions and more important, over time and with my therapist as a model, I started to internalize a questioning and compassionate attitude towards myself.

Gradually, my harsh, punitive inner voice, while still there, became less powerful and pervasive.

At the same time other aspects of my life were changing. I began to take more risks, to expand my world. I reclaimed my love for physical activity, which I had abandoned since high school, and pursued yoga, aikido, t'ai chi, running and cross-county skiing with a passion. I remember telling myself, and others, that if I couldn't be thin (without the stress of deprivation), I could still be strong and active. I chose jobs that might be challenging or enjoyable rather than merely safe. I started to travel by myself, wherever I wanted to go, and allowed myself to meet a variety of people. With weight as my unconscious protection, and in spite of fear, I allowed myself to get to know men as friends and, occasionally, as lovers. Slowly, my focus began to shift from other people's approval or disapproval of me to my own. This made it possible to think about what I wanted for myself and to go after it. I spent less time hating myself and more time living fully.

By the age of thirty, I gained enough courage to pursue a Ph.D. It is probably more accurate to say that the part of me that believed I was intelligent and capable grew stronger, because I certainly still had a part that was insecure and doubtful. That first year, in yet another city miles from home and from anyone I knew, was hard but satisfying. I still ate more than was comfortable, but my assessment of my body, and therefore of myself, no longer held me back from doing anything.

During this period, I decided to share an apartment with another graduate student. She was the first close female friend I had ever had who seemed to have a healthy relationship to food and to her body. Unlike many slim women I had known, who prided themselves on being uninterested in food, being able to ignore their hunger or eating very little, she ate when she was hungry and she ate with gusto and without guilt. She also stopped when she was full and I never saw her eat when she wasn't hungry. She cared about her health and her appearance, but in a relaxed sort of way. By watching her, I learned what I needed to do. As I practised, these behaviours came to feel right and my body responded. It took another year or two, but by my mid-thirties I had made peace with food, and I was comfortable with my body, which was neither thin nor overweight. I also met a man who became my partner, and he too had the same easy relationship with food and with his — and my — body.

Of course, I have had, and will continue to have, many more challenges. Life is never static and we do remain the product of our experiences. My obsessive thoughts about food and my painful, hateful feelings towards my body are gone. I have learned to listen to my body, to respect it and to work with it, as opposed to against it. Had I not done this, I would not have been able to help my son do the same after he was diagnosed with diabetes at twenty-two months.

Traces of my old behaviours remain. If I feel like having a "treat" and I'm not particularly hungry, I now know to look a little deeper; usually I am tired or overworked or have not taken enough time for myself. This is my body's way of telling me that something important is missing in my life, that I need to make a change. Physical complaints such as headaches often have a similar message for me.

I am not completely free of body-image concerns. I don't expect to be; I live in a world that makes such freedom impossible. There is a part of me that automatically notices every imperfection and every new sign of aging. I am as aware as ever of my failings. The difference lies in my responses to my awareness. Most of the time, I can notice and let it go. Like the voice of an advertisement or of a politician I know is suspect, I am able to hear it and give it minimal credence. It is there, but usually has little power over me.

My story is hardly unique. Our culture systematically teaches girls and women to be dissatisfied with their bodies, to view them as objects to be inspected, controlled and improved. And emotional, physical and sexual abuse, as well as neglect, is rampant. When this is the cultural norm, the backdrop to our daily experiences, it is not surprising that we try to fix our bodies when life becomes difficult. Our bodies become the focus for everything that is wrong in our lives, a focus that is tangible, concrete and completely socially acceptable, something that bonds us to other women. Body-image issues are really metaphors for our unhappiness and for our desire to change.

I believe there are three fundamental areas that need to be addressed if we are to come to terms with our bodies. They are all of equal importance. First, we need to explore and grapple with the real-life problems that lie behind our dissatisfactions with our bodies. These are different for every woman, but they usually include painful childhood experiences (blows to our sense of security or confidence) and unsatisfying relationships. One common element is the level of perfection we are encouraged to attain: this must be questioned if we are to free ourselves. Examination of our real issues inevitably entails some risk; however, without this, change cannot happen. For some women the risk may be too great, and we must respect this fact.

Secondly, it is crucial that we learn to reconnect with and work with our bodies. To ignore, disown or reject our bodies is to be cut off from ourselves, and so from reality. Our bodies house our truths; they hold our emotional responses to people, events and things. These emotional responses are not good or bad, right or wrong, but merely the fundamental raw material with which we must work, by which we must be guided. Without this vital information, which body hatred suppresses, we are limited in our ability to know ourselves, and therefore in our ability to care for ourselves, to act on our own behalf. We are disempowered. Empowerment entails being able to know what is right for us and what is wrong for us and to act accordingly. To be empowered, we must reconnect with, learn to listen to and honour our bodies in all ways. Our bodies are fully capable of telling us when we are hungry or satiated, what or whom we like or don't like, when we are tired or energetic, whether we feel sad or afraid or angry or lonely. Only by listening can we figure out what to do — that is, how to live. One of the most satisfying gifts therapy can provide is the ability to work with the powerful information stored in our bodies.

Thirdly, we cannot reconnect with or improve our relationships with our bodies if our self-talk is consistently harsh, critical, judgmental and abusive. This voice, which so many of us have internalized, creates anxiety and prohibits growth. Human beings, young and old, learn and thrive best in an atmosphere of acceptance and compassion. While our bodies will invariably change and age, it is the empathic and accepting inner voice that will heal.

Support is very important for women with body issues. Our support may come from reading material, friends, groups or a therapist. I do not think I could have learned what I needed to know on my own. In an atmosphere where it is normal to dissect and criticize our bodies, to deprive ourselves, to go to extremes to try to fix our bodies, it is an act of courage to begin to question the game, to declare that we have needs and appetites and that there is something wrong, not with our bodies, but with the bigger picture. But I do know that significant and lasting change is possible.

Over the course of my own journey, I developed greater patience and compassion toward myself, because the path was long and circuitous and connected to every area of my life. My work as a therapist — like other therapists — is always informed by my life experiences, by my beliefs and values. I take body-image concerns on the part of my clients seriously because I remember how these concerns took over my thoughts, directed my life and drained my energies. I try to bring the same patience and compassion that I offer myself to my clients.

When I first went into therapy, I believed there would be an "end," a point at which everything in my life would work perfectly. I thought I could figure everything out and fix whatever needed to be fixed, and all would be neat and tidy. But I have learned that, just as there is no perfect body, there is no perfect state of mind and no end to life tasks. What I have attained is greater self-knowledge and self-acceptance. When we are willing to know ourselves, we become our own best authority; we know whether something fits us or not, and we feel grounded. When we can accept ourselves, we experience a comfortable way of being in the world. The sense of being grounded in our lives provides us with the very feeling of empowerment that we seek but cannot attain when we focus on body image.

# SHEREE FITCH

# DANCING WITH DRAGONS

## EMBRACING THE FIRES OF CREATIVITY

*I am in a school surrounded by a group of children. They look like a bowlful of jellybeans jiggling in front of me. Happy faces. I have just spent forty-five minutes "doing" poetry with them, reading from my books. Now it's question time. How manychildrendoyouhavewhat-isyourfavouritecolourhowdidyoubecomeawriter?*

*I am in a small community centre surrounded by women. We are intense. Fragile. We have been writing and reading together. I read from my "adult " book. Then questions. How can I say what I have to say? Is it worth saying? Why did you become a writer?*

How and why. Good questions.
   I want to say that it's a long story. There is much I must leave out, much that remains mysterious.

Some days, still, I think maybe I dreamed all of this. I will wake up. I will end up back in my other life. The one before. The quicksand life. The cave.

Pinch, pinch. I am awake. Here. Now. I am a w-w-w-writer. Say it. Claim it.

Writing for me is not a job, it is a way of life, and not always a joy-filled one. I feel in the midst of a never-ending dance of becoming. In this dance there has been a lot more to contend with than sore feet and bruised toes. At times it has been a foxtrot that changed into a tangled tango, a waltz that became a jitterbug. If only I could use this dance metaphor to describe how it all flowed like a ballet. *Ah yes, with the beauty and skill of a Karen Kain I have pirouetted my way to the present.* But her apparent effortlessness is the result of years of discipline and sore toes and sweat. That is the truth for anyone who commits to a path of creating. Or maybe a truth of being human.

Most of the time I embrace the solitude my dance requires, but often I feel lonely. Yet I am rarely truly alone in the dance. How could I ever imagine that my dance partners would be dragons? Some real, some of my own making. Even more surprising, each of these dragon partners has more than one face. Those faces can stop me, paralyze me, even attack me. Then somehow they transform, show me the flip side of that face. They can push me, provoke me, make me dig in my heels. They can make me a better dancer than I ever dreamt of becoming. They can help me defend the dance I choose to make my own.

Dragons? Let me defend dragons.

Like most women, I grew up with the archetype of the evil dragon — the one that wanted to abduct me, carry me away and — what? Rape me or swallow me or just hold me hostage? Of course, as the story went, it would take a prince or a knight to slay the dragon and rescue me from its fire. I don't believe in those fairy tales any more, and my understanding of dragons has changed. They do not need to be killed; they just need to be transformed. And the one who must come to the rescue is the fearless warrior/witch/alchemist within myself. I have learned to transform evil dragons into benevolent guides. I have learned to be the intrepid dancer in the midst of the fires of creativity. At least, some days. On those days, the good days, I acknowledge that the fires are needed, and I am so very grateful the dance continues.

Whatever else it means to embrace the creative life, it means a commitment to ourselves to live our lives in authenticity — as hard, as painful but as ultimately rewarding as that can be.

## PREHERSTORIC SNAPSHOTS

My mother and I together in the kitchen with the sun shining through the window — a square of melted butter on the tile floor.

*Mares eat oats and does eat oats*
*And little lambs eat ivy,*
*A kid'll eat ivy too,*
*Wouldn't you-ooo?*

My mother sings and sings and sings. I try these delicious, tongue-tangly, lip-slippery syllables and discover it is fun to make mistakes. Tongue twisters are more fun, the more your tongue gets twisted. I don't know what the words mean. It is a secret language, this language of nonsense.

*No sense.*
*Ridiculous.*
*Rididculikulickyoulous.*

Why does something so silly feel so good?

It is time to peel potatoes now, time to go to work. But somehow the word "potatoes" seems odd. Potatoes. Pot a toes. Pot of toes. What fun to take a word and play with it, stretch it, slide it, bounce it off my tongue and into the air. Will I have my pot of toes baked or mashed?

✧  ✧  ✧

The teacher is printing on the board. "Write this in your notebook," she tells us. So I copy down words about fog, about fog coming in on little cat feet.

I stare at these words and something strange begins to happen. The page begins to glow. The words wriggle across. I see underneath the page. I see fog. Yes — yes, it's just like that, isn't it? That's just the way fog moves. But I never would have thought of it that way.

This, says the teacher, is a poem. Right here and now, I know what I want. I want to write and have someone say, *Yes, oh yes, it's just like that, isn't it, only I never would have thought of it that way.* I want to let people see words wriggle on a page until they see underneath the page to what it means.

✧  ✧  ✧

I am in front of the class, reading a poem. At the end of the poem, in print, is my name. I wake up. I tell my parents in the morning that I had a dream that a poem I wrote was in a book. Maybe you will do that someday, they say. Maybe I will. But I look around the neighbourhood I live in. There are no real, living, breathing people I know who are writers. It is a dream, just a dream.

Still, I practise writing my name over and over. My mother finds pieces of paper, napkins, magazines with my name written hundreds of times. She wants to know why I am practising so hard. *So when I am a published writer and people ask me for my autograph, I will have a nice signature.* Signature — I like that word. She smiles and kisses me. I know it is a dream, just a dream, but if I believe it hard enough and practise long enough, could it come true?

✧  ✧  ✧

Today, class, we will write a poem. We groan. We don't know what to write about. Nonsense, you can write about anything. The sun, a shoe, your name, whatever. But write! I cross out words and erase many times. My first poem, at age seven:

*I'm an itchy fitch*
*I live in a ditch*
*I'm not very rich*
*I look like a witch*
*Sometimes I itch.*

This, says the teacher, is a poem. A nonsense poem. She writes it on the board and everyone laughs. But it's okay to write funny poems that make people laugh. For weeks I am called itchy fitch, until the teacher puts my poem up in the school fair. There it is, thumbtacked on our class display. Poem by me. My parents put it on the fridge. Poem by me. Dream coming true.

✧ ✧ ✧

The oak tree in front of my grandmother's house is ancient. Its limbs are many; they reach out and call to me. The leaves whisper secrets. This is the first tree I ever climbed. Inside the first branch is a tiny hollow, a perfect seat where my bottom fits as if it were made for me. Here is the place I learn, finally, to tie my sneakers. Here is the tree where I read my first book alone in silence. I can look up from the pages and out from the tree to the ocean, which shines like crinkled foil in the sunlight. I can hear the bleating of sheep and see them, tiny flecks of sand that freckle the green hill on the other side of the basin. Their baahhs blend into the caws of the gulls. The ocean laps lazily against the rocks. The leaves rustle with the breeze, heavy sighs above my head. Everywhere there is music. Everywhere there is a poem waiting to happen. I return to my book and I am far away from here, around the world and back in time. Magic. Magic.

✧ ✧ ✧

The rain taps a tin tune on the roof above my head. I am writing in my journal. I cross out lines and erase many times.

*How can it rain on a Sun-day?*
*Why isn't Monday called Moon-day?*
*Will I ever be a writer some day?*
*Sun-day, Moon-day, some day dreams.*

I never saw the sun in Sunday until now. Words. Words. Wonderful words. Dreams, dreams, wondering dreams. There's a poem in the drip drop tip tap tap drip drop tap tin tune of rain.

✧   ✧   ✧

Four o'clock Monday afternoon. I sneak past my friends in the cafeteria, hoping and praying no one will ask me where I'm going. They don't notice and I make it all the way to the classroom on the third floor. Six students have joined the Creative Writing Club, but no one I know. No one else in Grade Ten, either. I don't want any of my jock friends to know about this side of me. They think I am a runner, a field hockey player, a basketball guard. They do not know I dream about writing poetry and stories. We learn about the short story each week for a month. We do short paragraphs and character sketches. We talk about plot. After a month, I write a story about a woman who becomes a pediatric nurse. One of her patients dies and the nurse, full of sorrow, kills herself.

"Why this ending?" the teacher asks.

"The pain is too great," I say.

"Is that a good solution for ending pain? To give up?"

"Well, I think it might not be the best way, but it's her way."

"You didn't convince me," says the teacher. "A writer must make a reader believe."

She wants me to rewrite it with a different ending. That is her story, I think. Mine ends with death. I rewrite the story with a different ending in mind and it becomes a different story altogether, about why the girl wanted to be a nurse in the first place. We all agree it is a much better story than the first try.

But I stop going to class. Partly because I am in training for a big track meet. Partly because a boy in Grade Twelve in the club asked me out and tried to kiss me good-night, and he had dog breath and it was gross and I don't want to face him again.

✧　✧　✧

Years pass. I study to become a nurse, I get married, I have a baby. I no longer dream of writing.

My two-year-old son has eyes like brown Smarties. They are wide and shining as he watches the bathwater swirl down the drain.

"Look at that little man down there," he says.

"What?" I laugh.

"That little man down there!" He points again at the whirlpool of water.

"Honey, there's no little man down …" Suddenly I remember. When I was little and stared at the drain, I used to think there was a whole universe that lived down there. I used to be afraid that if my toe got stuck, I could be sucked down there too.

"Oh, yeah, I know what you mean. That little man down there." He nods in excitement. "So what's his name, do you think?"

"That's easy," he says. "He lives in the plug so his name is Mr. Blug."

"Mr. Blug! Of course."

My son goes down for his nap. I get out a notepad and pencil and begin to write. I cross out lines and erase many times. Finally, after about two hours, I am finished.

> *At the end of my bath*
> *When I pull out the plug*
> *There's a monster down there*
> *We call The BLUG!*
> *There's a blug in the plug in the tub*
> *It gurgles and swirls and rumbles*
> *It gobbles up toys*
> *With thunderous noise*
> *And burps and swirls and grumbles*

*Blug in the plug blug in the plug blug in the plug*
   *in the tub.*
*Glug! Glug! Glug! Glug!*

My son claps and laughs. We blug together every day. Sometimes I wonder what kind of person does forty rewrites to produce nonsense. We taste words on our tongues. I write more
poems for him. He gets excited over snow and spiders and stars
and trucks. He reminds me to play, to look. He reminds me that
I used to want to be a writer.

The dream is back.

I go to the library and take out every book I can find about
writing and writers. I read books and books of poetry. I join
another creative writing class. (I still do not tell a lot of my friends
I am doing this.) I begin to study literature. I buy a typewriter. I
am going to be a writer, I am.

The man who says he loves me finds my poems and tears them
into tiny pieces. Hides the car keys so I cannot go to class. I hide
my writing and the books I am reading underneath the bed. I steal
time to write.

✧   ✧   ✧

I am typing at my kitchen table. My son is six, old enough to play
outdoors in the yard without me, and his new brother is sleeping.
So I have time for my poems. The window is open. I overhear my
son and the little boy from next door.

"What's that sound?"

"My mother's typing."

"What's she typing?"

"Her poems."

"Oh, yeah. My mother says your mother thinks she's gonna
be a writer. She says she's a weirdo."

"She is not. Your mother makes cookies. My mother makes
poems. So?"

My cheeks burn red. I don't know whether to cry because my
neighbour thinks I'm a joke, or laugh because my son knew what

to say. Maybe it is just a silly dream and people are laughing at me. But I keep typing.

I leave the man who says he loves me. I have no money, no education, no job and two children. I am on welfare. This is my life? I still want to be a writer but I become a file clerk in a government office. I write funny poems for retirement, birthdays, baby showers. *It's just this little thing I do.*

I quit my job, enrol in university. Here is a way I can justify reading, reading reading, writing, writing, writing.

I put poems and stories in envelopes and send them away to try to get published. The answers come back: no, no, no thank you. We like your work but no, no, no. We don't like your work, no, no. Then one yes! I publish one story. I even get paid. Then no, no, no.

After eight years of no, one morning the phone rings.

"Are you the writer of the manuscript of poems *Toes in My Nose?*"

"Yes I am." No one ever really called me a writer before.

"We would like to publish your book."

I cannot speak. This must be a joke. A wrong number.

"Hello?"

She tells me this three times. I am going to have a book of poems published! I hang up. I must be dreaming. Maybe I am dreaming my dream came true. No, I am awake. I laugh, I scream, I cry. I phone my mother.

I hug my sons, and we dance in the kitchen.

In 1987, I graduated from university with my English degree and published my first book of poetry. Now, over ten books, two plays, commentaries and articles for newspapers, radio, television and film writing. From there to here. As I said, sore toes and sweat.

But that is not why I started writing: to be able to say, look what I have done. I write because there are songs to sing and stories to tell, and there is music overflowing inside. I write for women and children. Wait, that's not honest. For the woman and child in myself. In hopes my writing will reach the hearts and minds of others. Or even an other. Connection. Meaning. I write to celebrate, rage, lament, explore, question. To order. To maintain sanity. To keep loving the world even though I don't love what happens in it. To pray. All of this and more.

My work has taken me from Belize to Baffin. The Himalayas. Africa. I am writing and loving my work. I am living my dream. But the dragons are still there.

## NAMING AND TAMING THE DRAGONS

I think everyone dances with dragons, although we may call them by different names. They are connected to the past and they live in the present. I could give them fancy names, drawing from myth, but I prefer to call them into the light by who they really are.

## THE WARPED-TIME DRAGON

I learned to find time to write between the rinse and wash cycles. In the time it took for supper to cook. Early in the morning before the house was up. After an essay was finished. It meant learning to work in bursts, revising in bursts. I am still waiting for the children to leave so I can bring my attention to that collection of short stories that will take much concentrated time. Or is that just an excuse because I don't know how to claim the time I have now? No. Maybe. But now, also, it is harder to find time.

On the road means away from the desk. Exhaustion upon return. Publication means someone coming to me and commissioning work. There are letters to answer. These are good problems to have, but they mean taking paid work, and sometimes putting off the work I really want to sink my teeth into. Can I risk working for two months on something that will never see the light of day when I know the other project over here will bring in money?

This is one of the fiercest dragons, the one who can snatch time, or warp it, so that I am fighting for the balance in my life's rhythm that is healthy to my soul and psyche. Here I am now, writing this, at five-thirty in the morning. Before I leave for three weeks. Before the house is up. Before the phones start ringing and life intrudes. I am greedy. I love my work, but I will not surrender my life to art. I do not believe one has to live tortured to create. I have enough of that to draw on to last a lifetime.

Then there is what lack of time can do to the fuel supply. How to learn to say no. It will not all go away if I do less. Or will it? I need to reclaim time and space. To not burn out.

I want contentment without complacency. Health. Inner peace, not discombobulation. The Warped-Time Dragon can warp the soul.

To the Warped-Time Dragon I say: I have learned how to focus. To find the steel-trap moment when nothing and no one can keep me from my task of completion. I have discovered patience — the body of work will be born when it is ready to be born. I have learned to trust in the process. Good ideas will not be lost forever because of warped time. They will re-emerge in another form, another story, and there is no such thing as too late to begin. I have learned that the dishes can wait. That if I sacrifice my work to my family, I suffer. And vice versa. I know about priorities. And despite all your efforts to quiet me, I will speak in the cracks of space and the leaks of time.


## THE GUILT AND WORRY DRAGON

Guilt and Worry are two heads on the same dragon. This is the Waste-of-Energy dragon. This dragon sucks out good energy to replace it with poison — even without motherhood as the central argument. It goes something like this:

In order to write, I make choices. I am not a victim: I chose this path. Which means I chose to embrace work that almost always guarantees no financial security. In the past, to buy time to write, I gave readings and taught workshops. I travelled away from my children often to do this. Left my children, to be with other children. Talk about big-time guilt! And I maintained a standard of living that most times did not reach poverty level. No car. No home. Sometimes an almost empty fridge. But the phone would always ring, just in the nick of time to keep me going. I'm a single parent going to school who wants to be a writer. I am a single-parent poet. Are you crazy? Maybe, but happy crazy. Isn't a happy mother better than a mother who is a file clerk and hates what she does? I am a good mother. Right. How come the dish soap is in the freezer again, Mom?

To the Guilt and Worry Dragon I say: Look at my children, they are doing okay. They are fine young men with coping skills. They have learned I cannot always be there. They will not expect a woman to wait on them hand and foot. Besides, I have done the best I could, always. If my best is not good enough, there is nothing more to say. I accept the consequences. I regret only that I did not start sooner on the path to becoming who I am most fully. And I will not worry about all I cannot do, feel guilty for what is undone. I will not waste my energy and annihilate myself.


## The Money Dragon

I have no pension. No salary. I get royalties twice a year. I am a best-selling author, and that means in an average year I make about eleven thousand dollars from writing. That's very good in this country. Funny, isn't it? I made more twenty years ago, as a file clerk, before I was a BA, MA poet. I thought that if I was published I would make a living. Wrong; I make a living by doing lots of other jobs. Good thing I can talk. How many stories have not been written while I wrote a speech? *We don't have a budget but will you ... ?* Of course. Everything is a worthwhile cause. Did you see the smile on that kid's face? Did you read the letter from this woman who bought the book? There is no dollar value on this.

To the Money Dragon I say: I am what I am. I do what I do. I have learned how to live on little. I have not given up, despite you. I did not start writing for the money it would bring. I am helping other writers demand payment for work. I am learning how to negotiate tougher deals with publishers. But I will not let you stop me. When I give freely of my time, it will come back to me. But I will not always give freely. I have learned discretion so dance yourself into a corner and count your coins, Money Dragon. I will count my blessings. I have not starved, not yet.

## THE DRAGON OF DOUBT

This dragon inches its slimy, scaly body over the empty page and looks up at me. Who do you think you are? Why do you think you have something to say? You're not good enough. This dragon has grown weaker over the years, but it comes back whenever I approach a new form. Okay, so you know how to write nonsense poems for kids. Big deal! What about a real book? I happen to value children's literature; I think it is just as important as adult literature, if not more so. Are you afraid of your adult voices? No, but I need more time. Excuses. Excuses.

To the Dragon of Doubt I say: Stick around. You make me strive harder, push more, dig deeper. But would you wait until I at least finish my sentence before you nag so much? I have learned how to fail — I do some things better than others. I have limitations. Accepting this is liberating. I have learned that the only competition worth entering is the one with myself. I may not have had role models when I was a kid, but I have found them. They speak to me from books. I meet them as I travel. Anyone who survives in this world and keeps the spark of the creative alive inside is an inspiration. I know I'm not the best writer in the world; I am just trying to be the best I can.

## THE CRITIC DRAGON

This is different from the dragon of doubt because it exists *out there*. When you finally release your work to the public, there is a public to deal with. For me, the Critic Dragon manifests itself in two ways.

First, there is the almost swallowed-up feeling that comes when you have some sort of visibility and success. You think it's what you want as a writer — after all, how can a book be a book if it doesn't get read? How can it be read if people don't know about it? But visibility equals vulnerability — especially if you don't wear masks, if you put your true self out there. I live with myself every day and know how imperfect I am. When I receive applause for what I have done, I have a moment of *yeah, I worked hard, I'm glad the work is appreciated*. Then I cringe. It is only my work. Only a part of who I am. All those children give me love because I make them laugh. Women confide in me because I have been honest in my writing. It is humbling. It is an enormous responsibility. I am not worthy. Sometimes, a good response can make you critical of yourself. Overly critical. Hypersensitive. Is this what is meant by fear of success?

Then there are the real critics, I mean the professional ones. You realize you can work for years on a project and in two paragraphs (or lines) someone can dismiss your work. The Critic Dragon can kill and wound, especially if it's on a day when your Dragon of Doubt has reared its head. But I go searching for the Cheerleader Dragon, who can dance the critic away. *Why don't you just grow up and realize that in the real world not everybody is going to like you or what you do?* Right. People like you better when you have potential than when you have actually achieved, or won awards. At least, on bad days, that is what I feel. Truth is, Critic Dragon, there are more people who are supportive than there are people who try deliberately to wound. Besides, you have a right to your opinion. Besides, you were right, that was a good point you made about the second act. Besides, go write your own book. I would love to review it when it comes out. I will try to be fair, too. And, you don't hurt me for as long as you used to. You take yourself much too seriously. I will not let you make me do the same to myself. I will take my work seriously, but not to the extent that you can ruin my day. Well, I'll give you a day. But not a week.

To the Critic Dragon I say: Thanks to my inner critic, I have learned to stay grounded, not to get caught up in images of who others think I am. I know the media are useful but I don't trust the superficial world of hype. I have an ego, like anyone, but I will check in to see when that is where I am coming from. If it is not the true space, then I am on the wrong track. Thanks to the professional critic, I stay honest. Work harder. Get tougher. Form my own opinions. I have learned not to write for you or even for an audience who might like what I do, but for the reason I started for — my joy in the act of creation. And I have found mentors and teachers and people angels who sing louder to me than your loudest roar.

There are other dragons, other issues, but they may all be one and the same. Something that tries to steer you off your path. To burn you before you claim your act of creation. How do you dance ahead in the fire with the dragons, and transform them?

## DANCING AHEAD WITH HEART

Sometimes, embracing the dance and transforming the dragons means using fighting words. Certainly it means finding voice. It is a struggle — there is always a danger with fire-breathing dragons. But the fire is where the passion to create and commit is contained. The dragons we each of us have travel with us. It is a marathon dance. But a dance.

Years ago, when I wrote *Sleeping Dragons All Around*, I thought I had written a book about a young girl who tries to tiptoe past sleeping dragons to get to her cake. She stubs her toe, the dragons wake up, she confronts them and, in the end, they share the cake. I thought it was about being afraid in the dark. In a way, it was. But now I see something else.

I see a young girl who is in the dark and afraid. She is silent. *Shhh! Shh!* are her only words. She finds her voice and banishes the dragons. You bold and brutish bursten-bellied beasts, you brash bunch of bedraggled dragons, you gobblers, you thiefs, you you you! The dragons shrink, then slink away until she invites them back to share the cake. But she is the one doing the serving and deciding how big a slice they get. In the end, she says: *The cake is dee-lightful dee-dragon dee-licious/We dance in the kitchen/ We don't do the dishes.* A children's book? Yes. But it was the best form to say what I had to say at that time in my life. It was me, the writer, trying to find voice; to find the courage and faith to dance with the dragons in the fire I had chosen.

It is a courage I must find every day. Courage. Cour-age. Coeur-age. From the root cor — heart.

May we all live our lives dancing ahead with heart.

# BARBARA DACKS

## RISKING BUSINESS

### FINDING A NEW CAREER AND IDENTITY AT MID-LIFE

*I*t's hard for me to believe, but there it sits on the table — *Legacy*, a real magazine. In fact, a red banner crossing the upper right-hand corner of the cover reads, "1996 Alberta Magazine of the Year." After only seven issues — the Western Magazine Awards Foundation's selection for overall editorial excellence. Judged by editors from *The Globe and Mail*, *Chatelaine* and *Western Living*. I guess I really am a publisher. And since this is a private-sector, regional, cultural heritage magazine — read that as temporarily non-profit, although not by intention — I am also a circulation, marketing, advertising, business and distribution manager, as well as an editor and writer. I did set out to publish a magazine, but I never consciously decided to become an entrepreneur. Somehow, I've ended up doing both.

Not that I operate this business totally alone. I work with a creative, dedicated designer and have a staff of volunteers to help me. My husband, Gurston, does everything from proofreading to dealing with wholesale distributors to selling ads to stapling in inserts and sorting magazines for mailing — after a full day at his real job. Erna, a former colleague, helps edit in the evenings after work. Friends (new and old) appear at distribution time to label and stuff magazines. An ever-increasing list of writers, editors and photographers, many of them complete strangers, people who've called or shown up at my door, contribute on a voluntary or barter basis — free ads for stories. And I count on Marianne and Mable, two women I had never met before I embarked on this wild adventure. Marianne sells ads for me on commission, but also devotes countless hours and immeasurable energy to brainstorming and collaborating on marketing, even though she receives no financial reward for her efforts. Mable appeared at my door early last December like a guardian angel, responding to my request for a student field placement, though she'd recently graduated from the community college business management course. Although she has a full-time job, she comes to my home two evenings a week to organize my chaos.

Through the process of creating this magazine and this business from a spontaneous idea, I have connected in a powerful way — with the people around me, with more than twelve hundred subscribers and thousands more readers, and with something in myself that I didn't know was there.

While I am setting out to tell the story of how, as a woman of fifty, I started my own publishing business, I realize it's more than that. It's a story of engaging in the business of taking risks. Of how, in the process, I have not only connected with other people, but overcome a personal barrier of my own — my sense of being an outsider, an observer trying to figure out the rules. I've learned to leap into the abyss, act now and either figure out the rules later or carve out my own! I have learned to trust and rely on other people when I sense the shared commitment and vision that will drive them to devote their skills and experience to my enterprise. It has touched something in them. But I have also learned to trust myself, in my ability to accomplish what I set out to do.

I have learned that I do have to follow some rules of standard business practice, apply business plans and principles, weigh project costs, revenues and trends — crunch those numbers — to survive. However, I have also learned that in this venture — this business of taking risks — not all my decisions are answerable to the numbers.

The decision that changed my life came to me late one afternoon in May, two years ago, as I stomped along the dirt paths in the ravine near our home with my dog, a black, shaggy, standard poodle named Allie.

I'd just received a telephone call telling me that the quasi-governmental heritage journal I'd edited for the past five years had been cancelled due to withdrawal of government funding. As I walked, I found myself becoming angry — not because I had to find another freelance contract, a career path I'd chosen almost twenty years before, but because I was convinced people wanted and needed a heritage magazine, and I wasn't going to get the chance to develop the potential of the journal I'd been working on. I don't know the exact instant when, or where or why the idea came to me. But by the time I'd climbed the wooden steps back up to the road, I'd decided to launch my own magazine. I'd already named it *Legacy*. I could see it clearly in my mind's eye — full-size, glossy cover, splashes of colour, dramatic photographs. It would report cultural heritage news, explore ideas, contain great stories, art and poetry. While people expected a heritage magazine to be about historical preservation, and only about buildings and sites, at that, I was curious about what was being done right now, today, that would endure and become tomorrow's heritage. I wanted my magazine to reveal what gave Albertans a sense of place, what defined this place for people who lived here. I had no idea how I would do it — and if I had known then how much work it would be, I'm not sure I would have proceeded. I don't regret my decision; the good days have been euphoric and they far outnumber the dark, depressing ones. But while my own experience proves that privately funding and publishing a cultural heritage magazine is possible, only time will tell if it's truly successful as a business venture. And over time I am learning to redefine "success."

I started out true to form — trying to figure out the rules. Having been a freelance writer/editor for close to two decades, a kind of hired pen, I'd worked as an independent contractor and felt pretty sure I could handle the editorial side of magazine work. However, I had always relied on the people who hired me to take care of the business side: paying the bills, deciding on the other contractors, handling the circulation, distribution, advertising, marketing. Actually, I wasn't even sure what all the different aspects of the business side entailed. So, on the advice of a friend who observes and studies business for a living, I signed up for a couple of business seminars.

Good move. But not because they gave me easy, instant answers. None of the information, guidelines and materials seemed to apply. Magazines and publishing weren't even on the list of possible business choices. I listened and asked questions and concluded — uneasily, unconfidently but intuitively — that these weren't the rules I was looking for. The seminars did teach me something — that one size does not fit all.

I knew about the Banff School from talking with friends, artists who had attended or taught workshops there. What I didn't know was that the school offered two-week and three-week seminars on magazines as part of a regular Banff Publishing Workshop. Now, twice in one week, people suggested I look into it. Can't ignore signals like that, I figured, so I picked up a brochure. It seemed more like what I was looking for; it would tell me how to do this right, I thought. Of course, to go, I'd have to apply and be accepted, so I didn't allow myself to count on it. I sent in my application just at deadline — thank you, goddess of the fax machine — and waited.

Those business seminars had suggested planning and development strategies involving a pile of forms and tables and charts. Not quite my style, ever. But the synchronicity of hearing about a magazine publishing course that just happened to have an impending deadline, so I would have to act quickly and decisively, seemed right. Pretty vague way to start a business, yet it fed rather than diminished the sense of excitement, the vision that has led me into this adventure. If I was turned down, then this wasn't the right direction for me, or my timing was off, or perhaps the whole idea was too crazy.

I received my acceptance in the mail. Okay, I thought, maybe this is the right way to go. But now I took a hard look at the cost — $2,400! A pretty steep fee for something that might not pan out, for someone who was effectively unemployed. The letter mentioned the possibility of grants and scholarships — would I qualify? Again, I thought I would apply for them; if I didn't get financial support, well, perhaps I'd better rethink my options. I still felt that peculiar mix of anxiety and euphoria, that sense of standing on the edge of a precipice, but I couldn't help hoping someone or something would pull me back so that I'd have an excuse not to take the next step forward. Then, maybe I could retreat to the safety of contract work, the routine I was familiar with, instead of acting on this mad whim.

Again, though, my new "business" seemed to be unfolding. I received both scholarships I had applied for, and I had no more excuses to fall back on. I'd have to go. While I was not yet confident of what I was doing, I was beginning to learn to trust myself, to take steps as they were presented to me. And the Banff course turned out to be the crucible I needed.

Sometimes a small, unexpected moment reveals more than any amount of planning and thinking and talking. Each solstice, winter and summer, I join two friends for an evening of celebration — burning what we need to be rid of, reading runes, taking stock, contemplating changes in our lives. That summer solstice, I sat somewhat amazed and just a tiny bit skeptical of a message of the runes telling me of a spiritual journey and difficult challenges. Then one of the women shared with us a simple technique she'd seen at a conference, a technique that demonstrates someone's level of concentration and focus. "I'll hold this pencil,"

she said. "Now focus, really focus, and break it with your finger."
I couldn't. My mind couldn't stop the thoughts swirling round as
I stood there, trying to concentrate. I have no doubt that I'd snap
that pencil easily now.

I arrived at Banff as an outsider. I knew no one else in the course
(some of the others had signed up in twos and threes). I had not
been sent for professional development by a major publishing
house, as most of the other participants had been. I was from
Alberta, while many of the others were from Ontario (more
specifically, Toronto). And I wanted to start my own magazine,
not advance my career or expand my position within a larger
organization, as most of the others did. I was also, I should note,
more than a decade older than almost all the others, and many of
the faculty, for that matter. Would I end up feeling like Brown
Owl leading a Brownie pack, or would the age lines blur? It didn't
look promising. But Gurston had tucked a card into my backpack;
it showed a boy of about eleven in a lifejacket, sitting in a canoe,
smiling tentatively at the camera. It read, "The trick is to be brave.
Even if you're not, pretend to be. No one can tell the difference."

I had no chance to act like an outsider once the course began.
During the two weeks, as we attended lectures in the morning
and worked in four groups of six in the afternoons and evenings,
we were to create a magazine — all phases of it. We were to have
a simulated cover and prototype pages, plus marketing, circulation and production strategy and plan — all for senior publishing
executives who would fly in for a daylong series of presentations.

Our group clicked. We worked well together despite varied
backgrounds and differences in age, lifestyle and career goals.
Intense? We survived on few hours of sleep. Assignments were
daily and detailed, requiring computer spreadsheets and collabo-
ratively written drafts of headlines and outlines. Basic rations of
cafeteria faux food and faux coffee almost did us in, until we
discovered we could fast-hike to town and indulge in good,
inexpensive, interesting meals, or at least nip out each morning to
a café tucked into a corner of the campus and get a jolt of caffeine
from really good coffee. We laughed — a lot. Told friends and

family back home it was like being in a combination cult and Outward Bound camp. I did feel disoriented, and not once did I feel certain that I could go out and replicate in the real world what I had done during the course.

On the last evening, after the presentations were over, when we sat in the lounge laughing, talking about our re-entry into the real world in the days to come, one of the senior publishing executives asked me what I was planning to do next. "Launch my own magazine," I replied, a bit overwhelmed by a near-lethal combination of adrenalin and Scotch. "When?" he asked. "December," I answered, although I haven't a clue why I picked that date. "You mean, a little over a year from now," he said. "No, in four months," was my answer. "That's impossible," he said as he shook his head. "Watch me!" I couldn't believe the words had come out of my mouth.

Gurston and Allie came to pick me up the next day. I was full of the course, the people and our presentation, and nattered on almost without catching my breath until we stopped at Red Deer. It was then that Gurston told me the news he'd withheld until I finished the workshop. Two weeks earlier, he had enjoyed a long, lingering talk with a couple of our friends at a neighbourhood party. The occasion had been particularly memorable for the gentle warm night, and the rare opportunity to spend time with these two, as we all race around so frantically that we don't usually see one another. Then, only a week ago, the man — in his mid-fifties, athletic, slim, seemingly easy going and sunny by nature — complained of shoulder and chest pain after a long bike ride. Hot baths and massage didn't help, and his wife decided to take him to a doctor the next day. He died in the car on the way to the physician's office. Heart attack or aneurysm, Gurston wasn't sure. The memorial was to be that night.

I was stunned by the news. I could not contemplate the pain and loss our friend felt as she sat in front of us during the service. This was the real world. I could observe and wait to figure out — what? If I was going to publish a magazine, I'd better just do it. On our masthead we list a contributing editrix, *Vita Brevis* —

Latin, for "Life is short." Our first issue rolled off the presses in January 1996 — five months, almost to the day, after I left Banff.

Since the day I said out loud, with more bravado than sound mind, that I was going to publish my own magazine, I've been involved in one long, almost continuous surprise party — a party I seem to have thrown for myself, to celebrate my fiftieth birthday. Gurston shakes his head as we talk at the end of the day (often the days don't end until close to midnight), and comments that I've surprised him once again. Friends say the same — it never occurred to them that I would be capable of, or even interested in, doing what I have been doing. The truth is, I'm more surprised than anyone. I had no idea that I possessed some of the strengths I seem to have.

My progress from chronic and somewhat cautious observer to risk-taking entrepreneur has been a process of almost daily changes and small steps, and a roller-coaster ride of emotions. As I look back on what I have done to throw my comfortably routine life into such disarray, I realize that the changes probably began more than ten years ago. I set the stage then, surprising myself with the way I chose to spend my fortieth birthday.

A party would have been easy, predictable. I love having friends around me, all of us together to share the good times. Gurston asked if I wanted one but I declined, the words out of my mouth before the thought crossed my mind. I wanted to spend the day by myself — to see if I liked being alone with only me for company. It sounded weird, felt strange, yet I knew I was testing myself.

Gurston dropped me off downtown. I wandered through the public art gallery and strolled across the square to commercial galleries I'd never visited before. I walked from shop to shop like a tourist. Looking around, seeing the city through the eyes of a visitor, I hiked along a dozen blocks and then down towards the river. Since I'd moved here more than ten years earlier, I'd been fascinated with the High Level Bridge, a turn-of-the-century landmark that spans the North Saskatchewan River far below. I'd always wanted to cross it on foot. So this day I did, and rewarded myself with a glass of wine at the café at the south end.

It doesn't seem all that exciting in the telling, yet it was a turning point for me. I enjoyed my own company, my time alone. It was a memorable birthday. In the last year and a half I have had to spend a lot of time in my own company, and I have had to rely on my judgement "of the moment." That birthday was one of the first times I was really conscious of how satisfying, how important it was for me to learn to become "self-centred" — that is, to focus on myself, my needs, nurture myself, all in a positive, healthy way. Not to exclude the needs of others, but to become self-reliant.

When I first started doing yoga, the teacher asked us what our goals were in taking her classes. I thought about what I would say as each person around the room gave her answer, and I happened to glance down at the sheets we'd received about hara — the centre of our being. I realized that it meant two things to me: finding a balance — planting my feet firmly without tilting too much towards the future or leaning too much on the past — and learning simply to "be here" now. I remembered that goal again only a few weeks ago, when I spoke with a friend who told me she had recently expanded that mantra to "be here now — and enjoy." That's my next goal, I think: to remember to not only experience the moment, but look to capture the essence of the pleasure at its heart.

I've mentioned the solstice evenings with my friends. For the last five years my runes have indicated changes, transformation, spiritual journey — and have cautioned me to stop trying to control them, and learn to respond to what is presented to me.

Now, that's been another huge issue. I am a control freak. Probably an asset for someone setting up her own business, yet — major lesson — while I am ultimately responsible, and have authority to make final decisions, I cannot control the results. When I applied for my Goods and Services Tax number, the official I spoke with suggested that I was in the same category as farmers. Now I see why: something akin to a natural disaster, or at least the vagaries of the marketplace, always seems to interfere with my plans, and I have to learn to react quickly or my business won't survive.

In some ways, the past year and a half is a blur. In other ways, it is crystal clear where the turning points have been and how I have had to struggle against my natural (or in some cases learned) inclinations to make tough decisions. And that brings me to another big hurdle I've had to overcome: one that has to do with relationships.

Conflict avoider — that's me, big time. I still subscribe to the notion that confrontation isn't the best way to handle situations where people don't see eye to eye. But I wear different glasses now, and both my field of vision and my ability to see have changed.

On at least three occasions, people with far more experience in business have offered me unsolicited advice about how to improve my "product." I have to be tougher, they suggest, in relationships with people with whom I have contracted or am dealing on a commission basis. "This is a business," one asserted, "not social work." The message: learn to be more assertive. Well, I've learned that they are right — and they are wrong.

I still have to trust my intuition about people, and I have had to learn to combine that with a new-found ability to be self-centred, to see my goals clearly and take responsibility, take action. Yes, the goal is business success, but the measure of success is more than the financial bottom line. And the journey there may be more convoluted, circular, meandering, than I first thought. Along the way I may have to let other people push the limits of their ability, and I have to recognize when, through no fault or intention or lack of will, they cannot meet my expectations. Then it is up to me to find some way that they — or I — can bail out gracefully.

I believe that, to be successful as an entrepreneur, I will have to become the lead actor in my play. I don't mean to be a prima donna, with all the baggage that carries. I just mean that I must not wait for others to take action, or responsibility.

Recently, a business consultant told me his definition of an entrepreneur: creative, lateral thinker, problem-solver, short attention span, enthusiastic, hard worker. I don't know if I fit all of his description, or part of it — or any of it, some days. But I seem to be caught in the chaos of living it. I can't live in my head, dream about doing it "someday," wait until I get everything right. I am in the moment. I have to keep taking risks, with people, with the magazine, with my sense that I can make this happen.

One odd thing about this process of becoming an entrepreneur — it's still extremely difficult, perhaps impossible, for me to plan or predict where it will lead. It evolves. Back to reading the runes again. Last summer solstice, I dipped my hand into the cloth bag and grasped a cool, smooth porcelain tablet from the jumble — the rune Raido, meaning journey, dark passage. The challenge is set for me: When the water is deep, become a diver. I am heading towards completion, ultimately towards a new birth. Strange words for a woman entering menopause. Or perhaps not.

The sense that this is a birth has surfaced before. After the first year of publishing *Legacy*, of changing my life so dramatically, I was overwhelmed. Should I continue, I wondered, or should I shut the whole thing down? Had I embarked on a path I couldn't follow? If I did stop publishing, close the doors of the business, was it a failure? Had I failed? A friend came to my rescue. He patiently, gently guided me through a complete business analysis, helped me gather all the information I needed to develop trend lines and projections for the next three years, and a way of measuring not simply profit (and loss) but changes and trends, so I would have a way of basing my decision on what was actually happening, not what I was afraid (or hoping) was happening.

"What if," I asked him, "what if I decided to shut it all down now? It would feel like a death. I would probably grieve for everything I hadn't been able to accomplish." He let the words sink in for a while, and called me later that evening. "Think of what you are doing, what you have done, as a birth," he advised. "Forget the image of death. You have given birth to four issues of a magazine that didn't exist until you created it. Those issues live on, and even if you decide to close the door on this enterprise, they will continue to exist. Nothing will change that."

I love that idea. Here I stand, a woman at mid-life, choosing this new identity as my mid-life crisis. Perhaps all that energy, that ability to truly "give birth" that has diminished in my body, is being channelled into this "new birth," as the runes predicted.

There is another relationship that has been important in all this, yet it remained unrecognized for a long time until my mother brought it to my attention. A few months after I published the first couple of issues of *Legacy*, and turned my life upside down, my mother called from her home over three thousand kilometres away. "You know, I never realized before that what you are doing is very much like what your grandmother did at the turn of the century," she suggested.

I look like my grandmother. I was close to her. She lived with us as I grew up, and after my father died — I was eight years old, my sister only four — she cared for us while my mother worked. In a brass frame, sitting on a mahogany side table in my living room, I have a photograph of my grandmother. She is a young woman standing proudly on the steps of her first store in Canada — Belgium Dry Goods, reads the sign. She's not from Belgium, but on her journey from Eastern Europe she crossed through that country. The people and place charmed her, so she borrowed the name and kept the feeling. And she went on to succeed: two stores, hard work, iron will. She had come to Canada with practically nothing, but she was determined to become a businesswoman and create a new life. Not an easy life, but her journey. And I am like her, in countless ways.

"Isn't it strange?" my mother continued. "With your university degree and professional experience as a writer, you're following in her footsteps." I'd come full circle, we reflected.

Each year, in the dark of winter, I follow a ritual. I light a twenty-four-hour memorial candle for my grandmother on the anniversary of her death, and I spend the day thinking about her. As this transformation has unfolded, as I have become more and more an entrepreneur each day, I think about her more often. Our relationship has been renewed.

I cannot succinctly sum up what I am doing, but my life is flowing swiftly now, and the currents are strong. I guess I have dived in and accepted the challenge my rune presented me. I cannot even say where I am heading. But the swimming is exhilarating.

# CAROLL DIANNE GANAM

# A STRING OF PEARLS

## FROM MOTHER TO MOTHER

As I muse about myself as mother, I become aware of how my story begins with my own mother's story, and how her story is sourced in her mother's. I find something vaguely comforting in this lineage of mothers influencing daughters who in turn become mothers, in the realization that there is a continuous line of women who came before me. A great crowd of mothers sits on the fringes of my consciousness and, although they are not individually known to me, I sense their comforting presence.

I know very little about my mother's mother and her mother before her — only that my great-grandmother lost a daughter. In 1910 my grandmother, Sarah, a teacher, came to Canada from Ireland with her husband, who was also a teacher. What motivates people so powerfully that they leave their country and clan to venture forth into strange and unfamiliar territory? Grandpa was not a Catholic, and family rumour has it that he fundamentally disagreed with the politics of Ireland. No one knows what motivated Sarah. In those times, I doubt anyone considered what she thought. It was likely assumed that she would do as her man did. I have wondered, however, about her life and her character, and this wondering has shaped my life, forged some part of my therapist curiosity.

Sarah became ill with "consumption" soon after she arrived in Canada, and was bedridden for most of my mother's growing up. Did she take on too much, believe she could handle more than she could, and as a result become crushed by the burden of it? This is a female tradition in our family. Sarah died when my mother was just nine years old. Today, I wonder if my mother's life struggles and her martyrdom had their roots in her own early loss. In her adult life she recreated this separation of children from their mother, this time re-enacting the story from the other side. Separation of mother and child has been a theme through at least four generations of my family. No matter where we are, who we are with, there is always, for every generation, the ache of someone missing. But I will get to that.

My mother, left motherless at nine, was parented by a loving but demanding father who expected her to mother herself and her younger brother, a diabetic. She worked hard at home and at school, as well as at piano and ballet lessons arranged by her father, who wanted her to be a proper lady. She was carefully sheltered. I sense that this was partly due to snobbishness or class-consciousness on my grandfather's part; he raised his child in some image of propriety he carried from his Irish tradition, a sensibility not shared by his neighbours in small-town Saskatchewan.

Grandpa had aspirations for Mother. She was to finish school with sufficiently high marks to win a scholarship to the University of Dublin. She was to return to the homeland and be a scholar. Then she was to marry a nice, suitable Irish man, be well off and live in the old country, where political rationality would have returned by then. Eventually the family would be reunited and would live happily ever after. My grandfather had mother's life laid out for her and, had it not been for my father, perhaps all would have been as he wished.

As a result of her upbringing, Mother was incredibly naïve. Having learned to take direction from her father, she could be readily influenced by any other decisive man, especially if she saw him as able to take care of her. Although she was cultured and brilliant, appreciated subtleties of human behaviour and wrestled intellectually with the complexities of moral values, when a conflict or dilemma presented itself in her own life, her well-developed mental capacities held no sway; her dependencies and emotional neediness dictated her course of action.

So it was when she met my father. He was twenty years her senior, already the father of four children, still married to the woman he had married twenty years earlier. None of these realities interfered with my parents' pursuit of each other. She saw in him an older, dashing, worldly, fun-loving man who drank and smoked and played the piano, a man who presented an opportunity for her to be rescued from the expectations of her father. He left his wife for her, taking two of the children, barely younger than my mother.

From what I can gather, during the years before my birth my mother came to share my father's sophistication. Our house was a raucous party place. Mother was physically very beautiful, and men swarmed to her like bees to honey. She was also caring and kind, and genuinely liked people. While she was being showered with male attention for the first time in her life, she was also forming relationships with women for the first time since her mother had died. She developed lifelong friendships with many of the women who lived on her street. Unbelievably, even my father's first wife became one of her friends.

## My Beginning

My parents had seven years together before I, their first child, was born. Why my mother wanted to have children, I am not sure.

Perhaps it was because most of the women on her block were having children; it was the forties, it was the thing to do, the way things were supposed to be. It would be a natural extension of playhouse reality. I imagine she pressed my father into having more children, eventually wearing him down. In any case, I arrived, and things went badly from the start. First, my mother had breasts that could not feed me. Then she nearly killed me by leaving me on the seat of the car while she went into some store, with the car idling, the faulty exhaust system pouring carbon monoxide inside. When she returned, I was blue. She rushed me to the doctor and after he had resuscitated me and assessed the situation, he advised her that she was starving me. He told her to put me on a bottle, which she did, and I reportedly became the cooing, delightful child she had hoped for. A subtext of my life began at this time, however, a voice in the back of my head, a tension about trusting, about caring and not caring.

And the voice:

*I'm dying here. I'm not sure I want to be here anyway. I've been here mere weeks and already I think coming was a mistake. It was warm and cozy where I was, but it's freezing here, and I'm always starving. That witch puts me to her nipples and I think there will be that silky nectar. A few drops and then it stops. Suck, suck, suck and nothing comes. Bubbles in my stomach. I think I'll die from the pain. I've been screaming and screaming at her. She doesn't do a thing about it. I'm beginning to think there's no point in howling. Should I give up? Something is wrong. I'm fading out. Oh, now she's screaming. The old man in the white coat puts something over my mouth. His hands are rough. Now he tells her I am all right, but he says she's starving me. She says she doesn't know what to do. Give her a bottle, he says. How could you not know that, he asks. Yes, I scream, stupid woman, how could you not know that? She's picking me up. She's rocking me. She's cooing, soothing. I want her to hold me like this for ever and ever. I hate and love her ... love and hate ... how can that be?*

## THE SEPARATION

Perhaps my near death then was an accident. Perhaps the starving was due to ignorance. But how does one explain her leaving me and going off with another man when I was not yet six? By that time there were two of us; my sister was born eighteen months after me. The man Mother left us for was younger and less emotionally mature than she was, but I think she needed a man who didn't want or know how to father her. She told us repeatedly that she had never meant to lose us. She had thought she could come back and take us, once she was set up and my father had gotten over the shock of her leaving. My father, however — perhaps out of parental concern, perhaps out of viciousness — did not support her request for custody. The case never went to court, so perhaps she did not actually fight for us. Although she wept over her loss, she did none of the things a mother intent on having her children would do.

I have spent much time trying to understand my mother. In her time, women did not leave their children, and when they did they automatically forfeited any rights or claims to them. I am sure Mother felt she had no hope of regaining us. Losing us was such a huge price to pay that she had to hang on to what she had purchased with her freedom. To admit that her new relationship was not such a great buy would have been too devastating for her, so she lived in the illusion of its adequacy for forty years. She could not leave the man, so she martyred herself with him.

My mother's leaving when I was five started a period of great turbulence in my life. I felt as though I was both my own and my little sister's mother. I did not do either job very well. We were shuffled around from place to place, while my father continued his party lifestyle. When we were with him, my sister and I were left in the care of strangers; we had numerous housekeepers, often couples with children of their own who, in return for free housing, cared for us. Some of them were mean, and therefore we sometimes lived in fear. Eventually, when I was eight, my older half-sister realized that things were not good, and intervened and implored her mother to take us in. Yes — my father's first wife, the one he had left for my mother, agreed to take in two little girls, because she had a heart of gold and could not let us suffer the consequences of our parents' mistakes. Although we became foster children in a child welfare system that did not seem to care about us, we were finally given some stability. The horrors that might have happened didn't. Even so, it was very difficult, particularly initially, as we found ourselves living with strangers in a faraway place, on a farm with no amenities — a harsh contrast to our previous city life.

And the voice:
*I can't do this. I can't. I must. My God, it can't be worse than where we were. I won't let the little one see me upset. I can be brave. I can print now. I tell Mother not to worry. I will write. My God, I'm mothering both of them. Words, hurried, frantic, rushing over themselves, tumbling through my head. I can't make sense of it. I can't think straight. I must. She's putting us on this train bench. I'll do as she says. I'll be brave. Hold the little one. She is so small. Her black lashes curl against that little cheek. Gently, baby, gently. We will sleep. Mother says the train will rock us to sleep. Mother smells so good. I won't cry. I'll smile at her while she tucks the blanket under my chin. Don't leave me! Shush, little one.*

After the initial visit to my father's first wife, my sister and I spent three unstable years being shuffled around from one household to another, cared for by various hired caretakers overseen by the child welfare system. Eventually I learned that my father's first wife and her new husband had kind hearts. While I lived with them, from the age of eight to sixteen, life was orderly, predictable and fair. I learned that, if I followed the rules, there would be no trouble. I was a model teenager; I was afraid to be otherwise. (I had to go through the adolescent stage of discovering myself and deciding what was important to me much later, in my thirties, but for me that was a safer time to do it.) Thanks to this "other mother" in my life, I was shown a path that could take me where I wanted to be. I owe her a huge debt of gratitude. Her capacity to mother someone else's child influenced my own decision to adopt one. But I will get to that later.


## GROWN-UP MOTHERING BEGINS

It was twenty years since that train ride. I was twenty-five years old and had been married to the right man for seven years. With him, I did not feel lonely. I was ready to be a real mother; enough years of school had been completed, enough money banked, a suitable home started. I became pregnant, and with this pregnancy came the promise of a family where mothers and children were never separated, where they lived like a grove of California redwoods, indestructible, together, for ever and ever. Three months of excitement, anticipation, longing. Then the ecstasy retreated to doubt that I could do it right, and with these doubts came the red spots of failure, darkening, staining, tarnishing the hope. Days later, mountains of anxiety and fear later, the hemorrhaging came. That life, that promise, extinguished. At that moment I crystallized my sense of myself as incapable of mothering, incapable of sustaining the life of a child.

And the voice:
*Hopeless, this is hopeless. I don't trust I can be enough, love enough. I could never give a child what it needs. How dare I even try? No child could survive well with me. I didn't do a good enough job with my mother, with my sister. I'm not enough to be a mother. Life is wretched, I am a wretched woman.*

Tormented by the knowledge that I had learned not to trust myself, I went into a deep depression. On a mountaintop in California, in a Gestalt growth group, I worked on this. Mothered by a crone-therapist, I was asked to surround myself with all the important people in my life, and the issues I had with them. Not surprisingly, taking care of others was a major issue for me. The

crone asked, "Where would you put a baby?" There was no room.
I pushed everyone back through my tears, but I could not move
my sister out of the circle that surrounded me. She was my baby.
The crone said gently, "You started that job at five years of age.
No wonder you were not able to be a good enough mother; you
were only a child yourself. But now you are a woman, and you
have all it takes to be a good mother."

Something in that experience freed me of a burden of shame,
of the unconscious belief that I couldn't be good enough. I
conceived a few weeks later. Three months of excitement and
anticipation, three more of joy and loving, three more of contentment. My son's birth was the climax of my experience to that
date. In the moment I held him for the first time, I knew that I
truly loved for the first time. In a heartbeat, I tied my heart to his.
But in that same instant I knew that I would have to separate from
him someday, and I believed I might not survive the pain.

And the voice:
*Oh my God, look what I've done now. That shell I have to protect
me, the one that lets no one really inside, I cracked it wide open this
time. Look at his little toes, little fingers … this one, this child of
mine, is going to open me wide. There's not one place I will be able
to hold back, not any escape door with this one … my God, I could
be destroyed with this one … but he is so precious.*

I was a shaky mom, I must confess. I needed someone to show
me that my son wouldn't die, that this baby I so loved wouldn't leave
me that way. I turned to the woman who had taken me in when my
mother left. She had helped me survive; she could surely make sure
that he too survived. She came on the bus in the cold of winter,
battered suitcase at her side, having ridden all night. She came
without question, already grey-haired and gnarled. She saw my
anxiety, warmed his blankets in the oven, made me tea, and for the
first time in the twelve days since his birth, I slept.

Then began the best period of my life. My son surely was the
most precocious, adorable, handsome creature ever born to any

woman. For three months I was totally happy at home with him. Then, gradually, I began to feel restless. I no longer wanted to sleep when he did. My sixty-hour work week, which had been so fulfilling even up to the week of his birth, began to call to me. Yet I would not leave him. I knew about the impact of mothers on children, about the effects of primary separation. I vowed that I would never foist that kind of psychological catastrophe on my precious boy. But in the afternoons he would sleep and I would cry. I didn't want to have coffee with my friends any more. I didn't want to read alone. There wasn't a closet left to clean. I wanted to work, to contribute to society in a significant way, and I felt guilty for having these desires.

And the voice:
*Heartless woman! Had a child and now can't stand it twenty-four hours a day. Real mothers can. They want to. Mothering is not a part-time occupation. I know what it was like having a mother who left me. How can I even think about it? Maybe I didn't deserve a baby. Selfish woman. I can't leave that child for a moment.*

My analyst friend and mentor came to visit. I could never hide anything from him. My tears explained my unhappiness and my words explained why I couldn't do anything else. My friend gently pointed out that I wasn't a lot of good to my son crying while he slept, anxious for him to waken so I could feel needed. I went to work one day a week after that, while his father stayed home with him; I would have trusted no one else. We did this for three years, during which I had six more miscarriages. I was called a habitual aborter by my gynecologist. I think that every time I got doubtful about my capacity to manage the enormity of motherhood, I would lose pregnancy. I know the first miscarriage after my son's birth was related to my fear that I could never be a good mother to another child. While I felt I was doing a fabulous job with my boy, I did not believe it possible to love anyone else as much as I loved him. Subsequent children would be shortchanged, and this wouldn't be fair. My pregnancies aborted at three or four months; two occurred the day after I felt movement.

Very recently, some twenty years after these miscarriages, I was doing energy work. When the healer passed her hands over my abdomen, I felt waves of pain crash through me and I began to sob uncontrollably. I saw fetus after fetus dropping from above me, almost like a red waterfall, and in my trance I saw them flow down through the earth, soiling it red. My healer indicated that women carry each others' experiences through generations. Our energies are connected. She thought I had tapped into the age-old pain of mothers losing babies, sometimes through choice, sometimes through violence. At my next session I was timid as she began working, but this time, as she moved across my abdomen, I began to feel joy; tears of celebration ran down my cheeks. This time the fetuses turned into angels. This time there were only seven of them. This time they were my babies, and I knew they were all right.

But then, twenty years ago — when I was miscarrying time and time again, tormented by thoughts of inadequacy, unable to get my body to trust me — there was another way. My husband and I started adoption proceedings. Almost immediately after we were approved, my daughter was conceived. It was as though my body realized that I was serious about being a mother for a second time. There were no episodes of spotting, no anguished weeks of worry. My son had survived, in fact thrived, and I could do it again.

I knew, on the fine spring morning when my daughter was born, that I could love her as much as I loved my son, just not exactly the same way. I sensed that, in our shared femaleness, we would know a closeness that would be different from what I had with my son. I cried tears of joy. As I held her rosebud mouth to my ready breast, I felt a connection and a peacefulness about us. I was a calm, happy mother with her, not the anxious, unsure mother I had been with her brother. She, in turn, was a calm baby. I saw in her gently mellow nature the girl child I had been before the rawness of life had knit the coat of wariness I wore. I had no worries about her. I understood her. I knew every pore of her being and knew she was fine. I vowed to protect her from callous experience, to ensure that she would not have to develop a shell to hide in.

Precisely twelve months after my daughter's birth, a much unplanned, unexpected second son arrived. No fanfare; no spotting. It was as though I had finally got it right. All my inside energies were lined up, heading in the same direction. If my husband had not had a vasectomy before I brought this third one home, who knows where I would have stopped? This last one was a spirited, mischievous child. Had he been my first, I would surely have been overwhelmed; I might have labelled him "difficult," felt like a failure. But not now, not after two success stories. This I could deal with. His father slept with him on the floor, hour after hour, patting his back. His sister, barely a year old, cuddled there, patting him too. I would often think how lucky we were, how privileged we were. I was grateful that I was not a single parent struggling for money, for survival; grateful that I had a partner involved in parenting his children, equally giving, supporting, loving, nurturing.

## THE CHANGE

We thought we had stopped having children then. However, when our second son was five years old, my husband and I went to a Third World country for the first time, and I came back changed. I saw children in the streets, orphans, eyes glued shut with the pus of blinding infections. I saw jeepneys left from wars, the only homes many of these children would ever know. I saw brown liquid running in the ditches, and realized that this was all the water there was. I soon reached the point where I could not take in any more, could not absorb it. I stumbled back to our hotel, our island of unreality, and sat mute and distant on the edge of the king-sized bed. The face of a child with eyes glued shut by pus, with running sores under her nose, would not leave me, and I wept.

We tried to bring back one of those homeless children, but the local government's position was that the orphans could not leave; they needed their heritage, their culture. My husband and I argued, "Their average lifespan is seven years," but they said, "We have our policies." We had only three weeks there, and we believed that when we returned to Canada, we could arrange an overseas adoption. We were wrong. The end of that story, however, was the beginning of another: our adoption of a Canadian child considered hard to place. We chose our fourth child because of that Third World experience. We had to try, in some small way, to make a difference.

Our second daughter was almost five years old when she came to us. She had been through two adoption breakdowns, and had been in a psychiatric unit for six months. Here, my greatest challenge as a mother, perhaps even as a woman, began. Much of it is not a happy story. I was trying to ensure that this traumatized child moulded herself into what I thought she needed to be, to have the life I had in mind for her. I tried to impose my unconscious belief that she needed to behave, think and act a certain way to compensate for her feelings of unworthiness. I projected my own dynamics onto her; I didn't recognize that what I really wanted was to protect her from the consequences of her ravaged childhood, as I had done for myself.

It was no coincidence that I had adopted a girl of five, the age I was when my mother left me. I tried to make sure she didn't make any mistakes, hoping this would protect her from the harshness I had experienced. But my efforts brought havoc to our family life. Our three other children encountered behaviours from both their sister and their parents that they had never experienced. I, who had never before raised my voice or spanked a child, was sometimes a raging tyrant. My obsession with teaching my new daughter, helping her, correcting her, meant the other children were denied the time and patience I had always had for them. My husband had no idea how to intervene effectively. At times he tried to support me, and at other times to challenge me and our new daughter. Mostly, though, it was a drama between the two of us, while the others were an anxious, helpless audience.

The voice was frenetic during those years:
*I can't do this, I'm not a good enough person. If she would only do what I say! When I was in her place, I figured out the damn rules, I didn't fight them. Why won't she figure them out? What does she think will happen? I won't give up on her. But I'm a fool, I should have known love wouldn't be enough. It's as if I'm handcuffed to her, I watch every word, every move. She can have a good life, but she has to learn not to lie, not to be slow, not to be nasty, not to leave her homework undone. My God, I'm losing my mind over this. Can this be good for her? for me? for any of us?*

The other children coped, as children will. In the final analysis, we are considered a success story. But we all had to go to places inside ourselves that we would rather not have gone to. And I learned, in time, that I could not impose on my adopted daughter my idea of the life she should have. I know I transferred many of my own issues, rooted in my abandonment by my mother and my efforts to create security for myself, to this child. It would have been much better if I had done more of my own healing before she came.

## SEPARATING BEGINS

When the stage of my children's leaving home descended, it was wrenching for me, as I knew it would be. Yet I am gradually learning to trust that we can find new ways to be connected, even living under different roofs, with different people moving into the inner circle of their lives.

Perhaps my first-born's wedding symbolized this transition most dramatically. I should have felt only joy that day, but I dreaded it. I remembered that fleeting moment, twenty-three years before, when I first held that squalling red bundle and knew that, if I gave myself to this tiny creature, I would be locking myself into a commitment to love more deeply than I had ever loved before. In that moment I had also known that I would someday lose him, and that the pain of letting go would be much worse than the pain of childbirth. And now he had given himself to her. During the festivities I was well-behaved, the gracious mother of the groom, but later after too much wine, tequila and brandy, my veneer of propriety slipped and I raged at my boy, now a married man. "It's okay," he told me.

And the voice:
*It is NOT okay. I hate this universe, the goddess who gave me this child to love, to grow, to nurture, and now takes him away. I will NOT be good about this. This is more than my spirit can bear. I cannot let go, I will not handle this gracefully. I cannot say goodbye one more time. I feel my heart is being ripped right out!*

I wept shamelessly on his arm, as he held me, and suddenly something shifted in me. Suddenly something was wildly funny. I began to laugh, and so did he. Then his father was there, taking hold of me gently while I told him, "She is in his heart, but I *am* his heart." Fortunately my son married a wonderful woman, and she has taught me lessons about sharing that I desperately needed to learn.

My eldest daughter has always been my soulmate. I bounce myself off her and she, like the best mirror, tells me what she sees. I rely on her clarity, her knowing me and loving me; she is a mothering woman. Perhaps she was required to mother too soon; she was just one year old when her brother was born. Mothering seemed instinctive to her as she talked for him, cuddled him, absorbed every ounce of him. Her gentle, loving nature did crust over during the struggles in the family, but through her own hard work, that crust is being chipped away and her loving, happy spirit is re-emerging. I love that we are friends now. I want nothing more from her than she already gives.

My youngest son is leaving as well. He appears angry, but he assures me that behind the anger is his need to step back from the family, to discover who he is as his own person. And I know that I must stand back and let him do so. If I can do this now, it will be the beginning of his realizing that he can be who he needs to be, and that I will be there, but I will not be there when he needs me not to be there. But my anxious heart asks how long it will take for him to know that I will love him in any shape, form or presence he may take. What I wish for him doesn't really matter. It is his life.

As for my youngest daughter, she now lives with her boyfriend. She tells me what is in her heart and mind, and in that way she is close. I am grateful that we have a good relationship. In exchange for the scars we both carry, we have been beautiful gifts in each other's lives. She knows she has a mother who loves her and is there for her, and I have a second daughter. Our struggle was about the right each person has to be herself, and the obligation parents have to respect that. I still hurt from the pain all of us experienced through learning this lesson, but I am also proud of us.

In the end, each one of my letting-goes shows me that I am not the little girl who had to cope with separations that overwhelmed the capacities she had. I have support from old and dear friends, from a husband and even from that little sister, who is now a wise woman. I revel in knowing I need no longer be crippled by loss. Somewhere along the way, I even learned that I can mother myself, that I am no longer dependent on the strength of others. But at each stepping apart I still need to work with myself, stay conscious, see the natural, healthy process occurring and trust the foundation upon which the relationship is built. My children take pains to remind me of this, and for that I am grateful.

## GOODBYE, MOTHER

It is fitting that, as I come to the end of this reflection, I have a goodbye to say to my own mother, who died recently. She taught me things I never wanted to learn, but she also taught me many things of value. From her I learned patience and tenacity. I could have given up on her, but that was too frightening a thought; I needed instead to understand her and what effect she had on the person I am.

The most important thing she taught me was the power of feeling loved. She made it clear that her leaving was not because she didn't love me, and she made sure I knew that none of the tribulations I experienced as a child were my fault. I can say, with gratitude, that she never once yelled at me, never once lost her temper, never once made me feel I wasn't perfect. Sometimes she thought I needed to be a little clearer in my thinking about this or that, but she thought I was beautiful, wonderful, brilliant, and she was very proud of me. She taught me I was lovable. I am ready to say goodbye to her now, and to take her place as the old woman in the family.

And the voice:

*Mother, you left so suddenly. Christmas Eve you laughed, ate hungrily at our last fondue. I see your eyes, bright, happy, as you sat surrounded by all those you loved, always gracious, never demanding. But the next day, Christmas Day, you begged off dinner. "Too tired," you said, "I've just exhausted myself; I need a quiet day." I have forgiven myself for not dragging you to the doctor. I know how you hated hospitals. I saw the little helpless girl you became every time you had to be in one — angry, defenceless, pleading to get out. That Christmas Day, I gave you the present you wanted. I did not persuade you, drag you, mother you out. Did I do the right thing? They say you died gently, quietly in your sleep that night, of congestive heart failure. I think you were wise to do it your way. No heroic efforts, no forced life shoved into your veins, your throat, through plastic tubes. I am glad it was gentle. You were not the type to argue against death, against anything. But you didn't say goodbye to me. How could you leave again without a proper goodbye? It has taken a while, but now I feel you near, sweet dear lady, mother of my wisdom, mother of my gentleness. Be peaceful where you are. You are cradled again with*

*your mother and the mothers who came before her. I know you wait
for me.*

## And Now

Although I know there is much more to learn, I feel the mantle of
experience draped round my shoulders, I feel the core of mothering inside my womb. I came from generations of mothers and I
will influence generations of mothers. I am heavy with this, but
not dissatisfied. My children and I, along with their father, are
like pearls on a necklace. Each generation a new string comes
together, added to the strings that were there before. We are each
distinct but I am aware, not of our separateness, but of the kinship
among us all, those who came before and those who will come
after. I see these strings of pearls threaded by mothers in their
stories of the past, and through mothers yet to be born, their tales
yet to be told.

# TONI SUZUKI
# LAIDLAW

## LIVING THE
## CONTRADICTIONS

### A LIFETIME
### OF EXPERIENCES
### WITH MEN

As I think about what I — a woman, a feminist, and a heterosexual — want to say about men, I feel torn. I live in a culture that has privileged men, just for being men, for centuries, and that remains saturated with this inequity. A large part of my professional life has been devoted to exposing the repercussions of this lopsided view of the world. Through teaching women's studies and feminist psychology, I've absorbed many insightful descriptions, analyses and critiques of male cultures and behaviours, and even contributed a few of my own. In my work as a feminist therapist, I've learned from my women clients the devastating effects that male violence has had on their lives, often taking years to overcome. Nonetheless, I continue to value, respect and love many individual men, most of whom I've known personally. Some of the deepest feelings I have about men are rooted in my lived experiences with them — the men I've actually known and interacted with throughout the course of my life.

During my formative years, men, as a presence in my life, were rare. This is because males are the exception rather than the norm in our family. The few that do belong generally arrive through marriage rather than by birth. Only one of my many cousins on both sides of the family is male. Men in our family also have a propensity for dying young. Neither of my grandfathers was alive when I was born and two of my four uncles left the world before I was five. I grew up in a household that had a single male — my father. Since he was the one man I was close to throughout my childhood, he had a profound influence on my life. And because I was only twenty-six when he died, my memories of him are precious.

Dad was a warm, even-tempered, gentle man who had a witty, offbeat sense of humour. He was a very social person who enjoyed people enormously. He was also that rare human being who didn't have an arrogant, duplicitous or unkind bone in his body. His many interests in life ranged from cooking to delving into the origin of words. He also loved to drink and did so steadily throughout his adult life, dying at fifty-eight from cirrhosis of the liver and complications from late-onset diabetes. But unlike many heavy drinkers, he was never mean or unkind. I don't ever remember seeing my dad angry. In many ways, he behaved more like an older sibling than a father — a kind of second child in our one-child family.

He was the cable editor at a major newspaper in Toronto where he was admired for his strong editorial skills. He was also well liked because he was so amiable and easy to get along with. In spite of his many talents he had no interest in advancing his career. Born in 1909 to a wealthy family in Japan, he was the youngest of three children; from birth, parents, siblings and servants catered to his every need. Like many men from privileged backgrounds, he simply assumed that this care would continue throughout his life. Since he was content in his job, he saw no need to move beyond it. My mother, who came from a far more deprived background, both emotionally and materially, found his indifference toward success infuriating.

Dad also had no interest in practical matters involving money. Despite the fact that his family had lost all its wealth as a result of the war, he seemed to assume that cash, like care, would simply materialize whenever he needed it. By default, the responsibility of making ends meet fell to my mother. Unfortunately, her own childhood experiences meant that she had as little knowledge about handling money as he. The thought of creating a budget or making sure that bills were paid at the end of the month seemed beyond them both. Because Mom had had so little in the way of beautiful things as a child, she couldn't resist them as an adult. "Always buy the luxuries; the necessities will look after themselves," was her personal motto. This meant that we literally alternated between "feast" and "famine" on a fairly regular basis. We also moved many times while I was growing up, in part because they couldn't pay their bills. By the age of fifteen, I'd gone to eight different schools. The strain of such a chaotic lifestyle had a significant affect on my parents' relationship. They married, divorced and remarried again before they finally admitted defeat and separated for good. Their lifestyle also had a profound affect on me. Even as a child, I often felt that I had to be the one "adult" in the family. The only constant I could count on was their deep love for me.

My cultural background is unusual — I am the product of a father who was half Japanese, half Scottish, and a mother who was of Polish /Jewish/ American origin. Because of this, I identified with other "outsiders" from a very early age. I was born at the beginning of the Second World War and began elementary school in 1944. During those early school years, it was not unusual for some classmate to label me a "dirty Jap" or a "dirty Jew." To my parents' great credit, I remained proud of my unusual heritage. "Remember that you are our very own little United Nations," my father would lovingly reassure me when I came home angry and upset by school ground taunts. "You represent the world's future." And I believed him.

Deeply proud of his Japanese heritage, my father taught me how to use chopsticks long before I could manipulate a fork or knife. Throughout my childhood, he regaled me with stories of his life as a young boy growing up in Japan and with tales of his ancestral background. (We come from a long line of samurai warriors, which may account, in part, for my fierceness in defending my principles and the people I love.) After the bombing of Pearl Harbor, when Japanese Canadians were subjected to harassment, recrimination and degradation, he made the painful decision to officially change our last name from Suzuki to his mother's maiden name of Laidlaw in order to protect me. I was three years old at the time. When I married for the second time, many years after my father's death, Auntie Nettie, his older sister, presented us with my great-grandmother's silk kimono, which her women friends had made for her sixtieth birthday. I asked my aunt why the kimono seemed designed for someone very young, and she explained that a sixtieth birthday is particularly significant for the Japanese. It means you have completed one full cycle of life and are entering your second, beginning once more at childhood. I have decided that for my sixtieth birthday, to honour my father and my Japanese heritage, I will reclaim the name he so generously gave up during my first childhood. Officially, I will become Toni Suzuki Laidlaw.

Dad also taught me to question the limitations society places on people because of race, class, religion or sex. I remember a discussion the two of us had when I was twelve, about the lack of women editors on newspapers. Although my mother had been a freelance journalist during the war, there were no women on the editorial desk of his paper. I thought that, when I grew up, perhaps I could be the first. He was very encouraging. He dismissed as ridiculous the prevailing view that "hard news" was something men had to handle, whereas women were better suited to "soft news" like social events, advice to the lovelorn and fashion tips. From his perspective, this effectively eliminated an enormous pool of talent, including my mother, from the editorial desk. However, his main concern was that I find a job that made me happy.

When I was sixteen, my parents, my aunt and I drove to Washington D.C. for a short visit. My mom and aunt went off to shop, but Dad was eager for me to see the American capital. Since we had just missed the bus tour, he decided to hire a cab to drive us around. A young black soldier in uniform had also missed the tour, and Dad invited him to join us. We spent a wonderful afternoon with a cab driver who showed us all the sights, giving us detailed information and answering our many questions. When we finished the tour, Dad invited the soldier, Tony, to join us for dinner before he caught his train back to his posting in New York. We set out in search of a good restaurant, but after we tried three places where we there was "no room" it slowly dawned on us that we were being refused because Tony was black. Tony suggested we go to dinner without him, but my father wouldn't hear of it, and we ended up at a corner café where the food was forgettable but the company was wonderful. I was furious about the way Tony was treated, in uniform and serving his country, but I also felt enormously proud of my dad. In his gentle and determined way, he made sure that a memorable day became a memorable evening for us all.

My last special memory of Dad was on my eighteenth birthday. He took me to dinner at our favourite Chinese restaurant in Toronto to celebrate my coming of age. As always, he was gracious and entertaining throughout the evening. He had beautiful manners, the kind that reflect care and respect rather than habit or protocol, and I was the focus of his undivided attention. Over plates of scrumptious food, we reminisced about my childhood and discussed plans for my future, including attending university in Montreal. Throughout the evening I felt valued, appreciated, supported and loved. As we were leaving the restaurant, I overheard the people at the next table whisper, "Isn't that disgraceful? He's old enough to be her father!" While it no longer surprises me that a man's attentiveness toward a woman is simply assumed to be sexual, it saddens me. To this day, when I see an oriental man who is about the age my father was that night I want to cry. I will always miss his company.

Over time, I have come to realize that my father has been the yardstick by which I measure all men. On the negative side, I have little respect for those who are financially irresponsible, and I feel uncomfortable around people who drink excessively. I also value ambition in a man, provided it's not the focus of his life. On the positive side, I have no patience with men who are superficially charming, egocentric and self-serving. I like men with no hidden agendas who are not underhanded or intentionally manipulative of others. I am also attracted to men who are gentle, humorous, non-violent and affectionate. My partner Eric is like this, which lends credence to the view that women marry their fathers, or in my case, the best of their fathers.

Since I had had little contact with boys as a child, my only interest in them during my teens was as potential boyfriends. My taste was pretty typical of females of my generation: I thought that Montgomery Clift was gorgeous and that James Dean's petulance was sexy. At fifteen I fell in love with Ron, the eldest son of an upper-middle-class family who was a year ahead of me in school. Neither overly popular nor particularly sociable, Ron behaved like an outsider, a rebel of the James Dean variety, which I found very appealing. He even owned the requisite black leather jacket. Pressured by him, and finally feeling I had no choice, I lost my virginity at seventeen. This first sexual experience, like that of so many of my women friends, was truly awful. It also resulted in an unwanted pregnancy and abortion. While both my parents and Ron were supportive of my decision, my attitudes toward sex were strongly coloured by this early experience and its consequences. My relationship with Ron ended shortly after the abortion. It would be some years before I felt truly comfortable having sex again, and even longer before I felt secure enough to express my own sexual needs. When I last saw Ron some years later he had sacrificed his leather jacket and rebelliousness for pin stripes and conventionality. I think he was even a member of his local

Chamber of Commerce. I still dream of him occasionally, much to my conscious surprise.

At twenty, I moved to Alberta to marry a young man from Western Canada whom I'd met at university in Montreal. Ed had completed his degree and was beginning a new job. I had finished one year of university and planned to continue my education in Calgary. My husband's background was very different from my own. His was the classic traditional family. He lived in the same house throughout his childhood and adolescence. His father was a civil servant who hated his job and his mother was a stay-at-home mom who baked, knitted and did needlepoint. My in-laws enjoyed playing cards and bingo and they often went to church on Sundays. My own parents' lifestyle couldn't have been more different; they enjoyed opera, classical music, jazz and theatre, and loved private parties, fashionable nightclubs and late-night bars. My mother rarely cooked, never baked and took up knitting only when she had grandchildren. She always held a paying job. The only time my parents saw the inside of a church was at weddings and funerals. My husband preferred simple rather than exotic food and physical rather than literary or artistic activities. He seldom drank. At the time, his background, lifestyle and interests represented the stability and conventionality I so sorely missed in own family. My marriage to him was, in large part, a rejection of my parents' lifestyle and values.

Within two years I had dropped out of university, given birth to two baby daughters and become a full-time mother. Because Ed's job involved working with people, he preferred not to socialize when he was at home. Being new to Western Canada, I had no friends of my own, so he was often the only adult with whom I interacted for weeks at a time. When we did go out, it was with his colleagues and their wives. Even now, when I think of those parties, I get a knot in my stomach. The men talked mainly about their work and the women talked mainly about the men or their children. I was used to my parents' parties where talk centred on world events, books and politics. (There was the occasional piece of inside gossip about some famous person which never made the news because in those days, it was considered extremely unprofessional, not to mention in very bad taste, for journalists to write about the private lives of public figures.) The gatherings that I went to with Ed seemed alien in comparison, and I felt completely out of place. Even when Ed and I spent time together as a family, we did things that Ed enjoyed. I don't remember ever going to a movie or a concert during our marriage. I do remember camping with two small babies in a snowstorm. It would be thirty years before I could be enticed back to the woods to sleep in a tent again.

My self-confidence, which, in hindsight, was more bravado than genuine, began to erode. I can pinpoint the first instance to our honeymoon. My mother had lent us her car, and when I drove, Ed was clearly nervous. He even slammed his foot on an imaginary brake a number of times. His behaviour really annoyed me. Driving was something I had done since I was fifteen and I was good at it. Finally, feeling totally frustrated, I told him that if he was as concerned as he seemed about my driving, he could take over. Rather than reassure me, he happily complied and continued to do so for the rest of our marriage. Within three years of our honeymoon, I was too nervous to get behind the wheel of a car. Over time, I also lost confidence in my ability to interact socially. It reached the point that at social gatherings, unless I knew someone well, I secretly hoped that no one would come over and talk to me. To this day, I still feel uncomfortable at gatherings where I don't know people, although I've become very adept at hiding it.

While I dearly loved my little girls, over time I found it difficult to spend most of my days interacting exclusively with children. There were limited activities in the house to keep me engaged and involved. After four years of marriage, I was restless and unhappy but didn't have the insight to understand why. I had a faithful, responsible husband with a good job, and two wonderful children. We had our own house, which was one of my most cherished dreams. I had found the security and stability I had longed for when we first married. Yet I became more despondent with each passing month. What was wrong with me? When I tried discussing my feelings with Ed, he felt threatened and withdrew. Because I had no close friends, I went to a counsellor who told me there was nothing wrong with my life and sent me home. Finally, to avoid sinking further into depression and lethargy, I decided I had to help myself. I'd learned to do this as a child living with unpredictable parents, and it was critical that I do so again. It meant that I had to take an honest soul-searching look at the person I'd become. The person I once was — sociable, optimistic, energetic, curious — was slowly being buried, perhaps forever. This shocking realization snapped me out of my inertia and into action. Within a year I was back at university, completing my degree; within two, I was separated from my husband.

When I reflect on my first marriage, I can see a number of things that led to its inevitable collapse. Some had to do with our differing backgrounds and expectations, some with our lack of shared interests. However, the most significant problem for me stemmed from my willingness, even eagerness, to sacrifice myself for a sense of security. I wanted a life that was stable at its core and, rather than developing that stability within myself, I looked to my husband and marriage to provide it. In return I embraced the conventional belief that a good wife sacrifices herself for her partner's vision of their life together. If this meant giving up my own needs and interests, so be it. As I look back at that painful time in my life, I feel sad for the young woman who was so eager to please others at her own expense in order to feel secure. However, I am also proud of her determination to make the changes that were needed, and her strength to carry them out, even though they caused great distress to those she loved the most — her children.

With a few important exceptions, sexual attraction has not been the main focus of men's interest in me, or mine in them. When I was younger I found this both reassuring and upsetting. Some of my friends have suggested that I've never been very adept at picking up sexual cues. I remember how stunned I was to discover that a man I had known for a year had a long-standing attraction for me; I had absolutely no idea. It's probably also the case that I rarely send out sexual cues, even when I want to. While I was at a Feminist Film and Video Conference in Amsterdam many years ago, I developed an enormous crush on an Australian filmmaker with green hair. I thought I was flirting outrageously. I later discovered that no one else was aware of my signals, including the filmmaker.

Not being an obvious object of male desire has had its advantages. Unlike many women, I have rarely been sexually harassed. My worst experience, which happened when I was in my forties, involved a federal politician whom I had known, along with his wife and children, during my first marriage, before he entered the political arena. He phoned my office one day out of the blue, to let me know that he would be visiting my city on behalf of his political party, and asked if I would introduce him to a well-known academic colleague of mine. Prior to this contact, we had neither seen nor spoken to each other for over fifteen years. On the last evening of his stay, he invited me out to dinner. We had a pleasant meal together, catching up on news about our families and mutual friends. At the end of the meal, he asked if I would accompany him to his hotel, where he had some material he wanted to give me. Once there, he offered to take my coat before he collected the papers. As soon as my coat was off, he pushed me onto the bed and threw himself on top of me. I tried to push him off, telling him I wasn't interested and asking that he please stop. He seemed genuinely surprised, as if he were unused to being refused, and continued to hold me down, insisting that we both wanted it and what after all, was the harm? I asked him again to let me go and struggled until he finally released me. As I fled the room, I barely remembered to grab my coat and purse. I still feel angry when I think of the incident, and furious on behalf of his wife, whom I liked a great deal. When he was defeated in a later election, I was elated.

My experience with the men I've been close to is also in sharp contrast to the picture I encounter in my work. I have maintained a small private practice in feminist therapy for a number of years, primarily working with adult survivors of child sexual abuse. My female clients are a constant reminder of the devastating consequences of violent male behaviour. I can't listen to their stories of abuse without being profoundly affected. Each time I read of another man murdering his wife, each time I hear a story of child abuse, each time I see a picture of a battered woman, I am outraged. I have to remind myself that not all men are brutal, that many are as loving and supportive as my father was, as Eric is today.

Even when male physical aggression is carried out in a playful way, I'm uncomfortable with it. Eric and my nineteen-year-old stepson, David, "horse around" together quite often. When they do, I feel like an unwilling bystander who is observing an ancient male-bonding rite passed on, from father to son, for generations. What's the motivation behind this kind of behaviour, my psychologist self asks. Was the purpose originally to develop and practise combat skills? Is the desire to show off physical prowess based on some kind of primitive need for female approval? Are they trying to reassure me that I will be protected in the event a male from another cohort invades our territory? Even though I know they're having fun, I resent their presumption that they can simply invade my space. I also can't escape a nagging fear that one of them will get hurt. It's at these times that I yearn for solitude or the gentle companionship of women. My good friend Sue thinks this sportive physical contact between fathers and sons is an experience that would also be beneficial for girls. She feels it would make them more confident about their bodies, enhance their strength and help them develop physical courage in a safe environment with a trustworthy person. She's probably right — she usually is — but I still feel unsettled by it, particularly given men's historical record of violence.

My close connection with the women's movement has, from time to time, forced me to do some serious reflecting about my personal relationships with men. I remember a discussion at my house in 1970 — long before I married Eric — where a feminist acquaintance accused me of not being genuinely committed to the movement because I still associated with men. I disagreed with her but I felt defensive. After all, if I really believed that men were the problem, why would I spend time with them? Why wouldn't I consciously choose women as lovers, as she was suggesting? By associating with men, was I actively complicit in my own oppression? At that time I was willing to accept intellectually the prevalent feminist view that all men were oppressors, but at a personal level it didn't feel right to lump them into one homogenous group. I knew there was a difference between "men" as a category and particular men such as those I chose to associate with, but I didn't know how to justify my contradictory feelings and beliefs.

I had a similar sense of incongruity a few years later. At a dinner party, a good friend argued that a woman living in a patriarchal society could never have consensual sex with a man, since the man, by definition, had more power. I was delighted by the observation, considering it a brilliant insight into women's sexuality in a patriarchal culture. Based on my own experience, however, I knew that in reality this wasn't always the case. Once again I felt torn between theory and lived experience, although I chose not to say so at the time. As feminist analyses developed over the next decade, the differences in women's experiences became the focus, more accurately reflecting the complexities of our lives. So it is with respect to men.

In 1974 I accepted a teaching position at Dalhousie University, first in the School of Education and then in the Faculty of Medicine, where I am today. During my twenty-five years here, my experiences with male colleagues have generally been positive, and I have developed good working relationships with a number of male faculty. The extent of their support has surprised me somewhat since my commitment to feminist scholarship and to confronting sexist practices on campus is well known and not universally applauded. Even a few male administrators have actively encouraged my research activities, providing academic and financial support.

However, open identification with feminism in the university is always risky, and I've had difficulties from time to time. As Paula Caplan describes in her book, *Lifting a Ton of Feathers*, women, and particularly feminists, face a number of problems in the academic environment because of the pervasive maleness there.[1] In my experience, the majority of male academics resist change, and they have no difficulty finding others on campus who actively support their attempts to maintain the status quo.

At a university senate meeting in the early 1980s, for example, a feminist colleague and I, who were members of a presidential committee appointed to develop sexual harassment procedures for the university, brought forward our recommendations for the senate's approval. Although they had been vetted by virtually every group in the Dalhousie community over a laborious two-year consultative process, a prominent senior professor in senate characterized them as fascist and my colleague and I as Nazis. We were both appalled that he equated our democratically developed procedures with the evils of Nazism in order to undermine our proposal and further his own political agenda. I was personally hurt, as well, since this was a man I had worked with on a number of university committees, and our relationship had always been congenial. I'd also worked quite closely with his wife, an artist, in producing a television show about her and her work. Ultimately the professor's position did not prevail, but it was distressing to see the extent of his support in senate. Since that meeting, we have not spoken to each other again.

One of the worst experiences of my academic career happened just a few years ago. I was one of two guest speakers invited by a prominent psychiatrist to give keynote addresses to an educational conference at a provincial mental hospital. The focus of the conference was sexual abuse, and the other keynote speaker was a psychiatrist who worked with trauma patients in a hospital setting. He presented his material on the first day and I presented on the second. Because I was unable to attend his sessions, I was unaware that his position on child sexual abuse was that it was uncommon, that people who claimed to have been abused as children suffered from organically based psychiatric disorders and that feminist therapy was not only bogus, but dangerous. What I quickly did become aware of was his hostile attitude toward me. While I presented my paper, he talked to his neighbour and made obviously derogatory gestures such as rolling his eyes. When my talk concluded and the moderator invited questions, he immediately rose to the microphone and monopolized it. Rather than challenging my position, he patronized me. Because my research was qualitative rather than quantitative, he dismissed it as bad science. He called me naïve and misguided. With each assault I tried to address his criticisms calmly and rationally, but he clearly wasn't interested in anything I had to say.

The forum concluded with a panel involving both of us. One of the people from the floor asked about success rates with adult survivors of child sexual abuse. The psychiatrist acknowledged that his were minimal but claimed this was because abuse survivors were borderline personalities who are notoriously hard to treat. When it was my turn to comment, I said that many of my clients were originally diagnosed as borderline personalities, but that when their abuse was finally acknowledged and understood to be the major source of their distress, they were able to begin the healing process. I added that if health care professionals applied the methods of therapy that I and others used, as outlined in my presentation, while it may take some time to complete therapy, the recovery rate was excellent. At that point, the physician exploded in anger, becoming extremely aggressive verbally and attacking me personally. A number of people in the audience were visibly uncomfortable, but none of the hospital psychiatrists, including the one who invited me to attend, intervened. Only one elderly male community psychiatrist publicly came to my defence.

Still not satisfied with his public outburst, the psychiatrist continued to attack me within earshot once the conference was over. At that point, I walked over to him and stated that, if he had something more to say about me, would he please say it to me directly. He told me that I was a danger to the mental health community, and turned and left the room. The only psychiatrist to approach me was the organizer of the conference. He minimized the other guest's behaviour, claiming that he was merely acting in the spirit of academic give-and-take, and quickly left. A group of social workers and students then told me that the visiting psychiatrist was simply reflecting the views of the most influential psychiatrists at the hospital, including the organizer. Anyone identified by these men as feminist was treated with disdain. With shock I realized that I had been intentionally set up. This was a classic example of the sort of tactic an old boys' network uses to discourage unwelcome female intruders into their bailiwick.

Although I had maintained a professional demeanour throughout the meeting, I left the hospital feeling angry, upset and used. Instead of returning to my office as I'd planned, I went straight to Eric who held me while I cried. Next I called my friend Sue, who also teaches at Dalhousie, and who has been a strong source of support since we first met in 1974. She dropped everything and spent the afternoon listening and consoling me. She supported my feelings about the incident, making the important point that had the situation been reversed and it was I who was being abusive, the organizer would certainly have intervened and condemned my behaviour. This helped me regain a much-needed perspective. That evening I phoned my close friend Cheryl in Edmonton. She also let me vent my anger and gave me much needed validation and support. The experience at the hospital was an important reminder that I still need to take steps to protect myself in environments that may be hostile to feminists. It also reinforced how crucial it is to have a personal support system in place when things do go wrong.

There have been other comments made by male colleagues over the course of my professional career that were unjustified and inappropriate, but not all were vicious or even unkind. I joined the Dalhousie faculty in 1974 as Toni Johnston. When I completed my Ph.D four years later, I decided to revert to my maiden name of Laidlaw. At the next faculty meeting the Dean announced congratulations to Dr. Toni Laidlaw on the awarding of her degree. An elderly distinguished professor who was sitting next to me at the time turned, and with a gentle smile said, "My congratulations, also, to Mr. Laidlaw."

I've had a variety of experiences with men as a result of teaching a class on gender socialization for many years. One of my most memorable occurred during my second year at Dalhousie. Toward the end of term, I invited a speaker from Gay Alliance to make a presentation to the class. When he left, one young student disclosed to the rest of us that he was gay. He received a very positive response from almost everyone, with the exception of two male class members were who shocked and distressed. Over the course of the year they had come to know this student well and liked him a great deal. Having grown up in small towns where homosexuality was considered both a sickness and a perversion, they couldn't integrate their positive experiences of him with his newly disclosed sexual orientation. The remaining members of the class decided to stay on while the two students tried to sort through their conflicting feelings. After some time talking it out with everyone, they finally understood that their fears were unjustified and that they needed to seriously re-evaluate their negative stereotypes about gays. I valued their frankness, their courage to share their feelings honestly when they knew that the rest of the class felt differently, and their willingness to be open to what others had to say. That long evening we all spent together is one of my most treasured memories as a teacher.

I once had a police officer in class who, during the first month, challenged everything. Over time he became more receptive, partly because he had two daughters and was able to see how their gender could negatively affect them, particularly when it came to work options. However, he was unwilling to extend the analysis to his wife's situation. During the second term, while we were examining the prevalence of male violence, he experienced a personal breakthrough. In his written journal for the class, he talked about his father's violent behaviour towards him when he was a child. By the end of the course he understood the connection between his father's brutality to him and his own difficulty in expressing affection or showing vulnerability. I was hopeful that these insights would act as catalysts for change in his life, including improvement in his relationships with his wife and children.

I can't end this reflection on men without acknowledging their importance to me as friends. Over the years, I have developed a number of very special relationships. One is with a partner of a close friend. A few are with friends I've had since university. Others are with men I've met since moving to Halifax. While these men are individually very different, they share a number of things that are important to me. They enjoy the company of women. They are professionally active, politically progressive, intellectually curious and highly creative. I love spending time with them because, like my father, they are men who embrace life fully. And when I'm with them — as when I was with my father — I feel valued, appreciated, loved and supported.

All in all, my feelings about men are filled with contradictions. As a feminist, I have used gender as a category to make visible women's unequal relationship with men. But I also recognize the limitations of categories, and the dangers they create by simplifying, homogenizing and falsely dichotomizing the complexity of human experience. As a psychotherapist who has worked primarily with women who are adult survivors of childhood trauma, I am very aware of the destructive power of men. But I also recognize men's vulnerability and pain. There are aspects of masculinity that have been, and continue to be, objectionable and dangerous. There are particular men who behave in objectionable and dangerous ways. But I know many others who reject the destructive trappings of their gender and consciously choose to live as caring, productive, non-violent people. These men affirm my belief that change is possible. Together, we envision and work towards a more tolerant and compassionate society, one that both respects and values difference.

I know my dad would be proud.

## ENDNOTES

1. Paula J. Caplan, *Lifting a Ton of Feathers: A Woman's Guide to Surviving in the Academic World* (Toronto: University of Toronto Press, 1993).

# D I
# B R A N D T


## C A R I N G
## M A G I C


*MY RELATIONSHIP*

*WITH JOAN*


*I* came to Joan in 1986, in the middle of a profound crisis. In my mid-thirties I suddenly
didn't know who I was any more. I had just finished
writing *questions i asked my mother*, a dramatic, rebel-
lious challenge in poetry to my strict, separatist
Mennonite upbringing. The manuscript was at the
publisher's, and I was in terror about the reception
this book would receive in my home community
and my own family. I had written myself, outrageously, out of the culture, and felt suddenly exposed, lost, cast adrift. Several other major crises
had converged at the same moment in my life: an
unexpected pregnancy and abortion, a marriage in
crisis and serious finanical worries. I was a graduate
student with two young children and an unsupportive husband, and my university fellowship was
about to run out. My world, as I'd known it, seemed

to be falling apart. I was in shock. I couldn't eat or sleep. I could barely breathe. I began fantasizing suicide daily. I was afraid to be alone; I worked hard to arrange my life so I wouldn't ever have to be. Outwardly, I appeared competent, cheerful, warm. Inwardly, I felt completely in darkness, in a body that was slowly fragmenting, shattering, going numb.

I didn't understand what was happening to me. All I knew was that I was slowly edging toward death. This made me feel very sad and also guilty: I was the mother of two wonderful daughters, ages ten and seven, whom I loved deeply. I had enjoyed taking care of them so much when they were younger. Now, I suddenly couldn't seem to take care of them, or anyone, or anything any more. I couldn't really talk to my friends about it, though I sometimes tried. I didn't understand what was happening to me. I had suddenly lost my knowledge of how to be in the world, and in my own body.

After I understood how close to death I was, that I was ready and, yes, willing to die, I decided, on the advice of a friend, to try one last desperate thing: find professional help. I was extremely afraid. My husband had been telling me, abusively, for years, how "crazy" I was, and had threatened many times to call a psychiatrist and have me "locked up." He enjoyed staging scenes that would make me feel "crazy," much like the husband does to his wife in *Gaslight*. It was a joke with him that the wife in this film reminded him of me. It took me years to understand that it was he who was a lot like the husband, and that this film was about cruelty, not about craziness.

I had heard of electric shock and mind-altering drugs, and could think of nothing scarier than falling into the hands of doctors and psychiatrists who might try these things on me. The friend suggested I try private counselling and body work, and recommended Joan, warning me, however, that she was an "angry feminist." This sounded like a good thing to me, someone who cared passionately about women and women's experiences and rights. I didn't know what body work was, but it sounded important and comforting and wonderful. I called her and talked to her briefly on the telephone. She sounded kind and gentle and caring. I thought, if this doesn't work, or if she tries to hurt me in some way, I will kill myself.

The first time I saw Joan, she let me talk for three hours. I remember we sat in her living room, filled with green plants and a fat, lazy, orange cat named Casey, and as I talked I watched the sun go down through her big corner window. She listened quietly to my long litany of worries, nodding occasionally and handing me tissues when I seemed overwrought. When I was finally done, she said, "There's one thing I didn't understand in your story. You keep saying you're stupid and incompetent, and yet what I heard was a woman who is very talented and hard-working, and coping amazingly well in an extremely complicated and difficult situation." Her comment caught me completely by surprise. I was ready for any number of put-down responses, of the kind I'd grown up with and was used to in my daily life. I was not prepared for recognition, acknowledgement, encouragement. Especially I wasn't prepared for her deep understanding of the material and emotional difficulties of my situation. I was trying to complete a graduate degree while living in an abusive marriage in which I had very little access to money for child care and household maintenance, and yet was expected to do most of the work. At the same time, I was trying to prove my seriousness as an academic and do feminist work in an institution where women students with young children and woman-centred research, at that time, were generally distrusted and often overtly discouraged.

Joan agreed to see me three times a week for a few weeks, then twice, and finally once a week. Many years later she told me how scary it was to work with me those first months: how fragile I was, how close to death. One false move could have sent me into a suicide spin. For my part, I was surprised and grateful to have found someone who was willing to listen to me at last, a woman who reminded me of my own mother sometimes and yet behaved in significantly different ways. For example, she didn't try to protect me from my pain. Rather, she pushed me firmly, gently, toward and through it. We had to proceed slowly. There were so many tangled threads in my life to untangle. There was so much healing to be done. For another thing, she didn't seem to be afraid of men, even abusive ones, or of power. She actually believed it was possible for women to have self-directed, independent lives. And even more amazingly, she seemed to have an endless array of strategies at her command to help me figure out how to get control over my own life, and to be empowered as a woman.

The body work was crucial to my healing. I was very good at disappearing up into my head or even going out of body altogether, when feeling scared or threatened. The massage made that impossible and unnecessary. Every session provided important links for me between what was going on in my head, my feelings and my body. In one of the early sessions, I told Joan I felt as if my feet weren't quite on the ground, but rather floating several inches above it. I'd had a scary dream earlier that year in which I had no feet at all, just wooden leg stumps, and no heart, just a hole in my chest. I'd written these images into a poem, but they remained with me existentially. Joan said, "Well then, let's start the massage with your feet today, and see if we can coax them to touch the ground again." I thought, "Hey, I didn't mean it literally," but then was immediately fascinated by this kind of literal mind-body connection, a simple, magical correspondence that I knew about from writing poetry, which is after all a profoundly embodied way of being in language.

Another time she listened to me describe something and then said, "How does your stomach feel?" To my surprise, I saw that I had been clutching my stomach while talking. So that became a clue for us in the body work that week. One time while reliving a particularly painful memory during massage, Joan suddenly said, "Is there something your eyes don't want to see?" I realized I was covering my eyes tightly with both hands. I was amazed to find how eloquent and expressive my body gestures were, quite apart from my conscious intention. I began feeling a new respect and understanding for my body, which I had been taught to hate and denigrate and silence when I was growing up. (I was anorexic for several years in high school. This was before the medical term for this disorder had become current. I was attending a boarding school at that time and no one was watching me closely. At home, I would have had to eat whatever was served, so the anorexia was a kind of move toward self-determination. I started eating again, at age seventeen after I graduated from high school and left the Mennonite community, with great trepidation, but also with a huge sense of freedom from the restrictive rules of home.)

I remember other details of those first weeks and months of meeting with Joan. Because I was so near death and in grave danger psychically and physically, I was alert to every nuance and gesture in her voice and body. In return, I found her to be absolutely attentive to both what I was saying and how I was feeling. There was often a discrepancy between my words and feelings in those days. I was defensive, for example, about my "bad" marriage and in denial about my husband's abusive behaviour toward me, and yet at the same time obviously distressed and needing help. Joan never argued with me, never criticized me, never pointed out my faults, never once gave me the sense that I "deserved" to be treated badly, as I had grown up to believe. She had a way of challenging my views that I found extremely compelling. Instead of saying, "That can't be true," or "You're wrong about that," she would just look at me with eloquent disagreement in her eyes, while at the same time physically offering support and encouragement, for example, leaning forward sympathetically or reaching out to touch my hand. This was a direct reversal of the kind of behaviour I was used to in my family, where people would claim to love me in words, but then behave cruelly. I was used to sparring with people intellectually, while submitting emotionally and physically to criticism and abuse. Joan's silent war with my intellectual defence mechanisms had the effect of gently disarming me: I remember it was like laying my weapons down carefully, slowly, one by one.

Joan often acknowledged my artistic giftedness, saying how delighted she was to be working "in collaboration" with the poet in me. I often heard her say to other people, later, how wonderful it was to work with women artists, and how important she thought creativity is to the healing process. This was an important issue for me: I had grown up with the designation "gifted child" and received lots of encouragement and acknowledgement for it from teachers and relatives. But this encouragement came with all kinds of emotional punishments and deprivations attached. I have a twin sister, and my mother often interpreted my academic awards and prizes as an affront to this sister. My father, on the other hand, often interpreted my achievements as a threat to his authority. I grew up feeling emotionally abandoned by my mother, criticized by my father, and envied by my sister and brother, and sometimes classmates. I felt my "giftedness" as a kind of curse on everyone, including me. I thought I was doomed to intellectual achievement, but because it hurt everyone's feelings, I needed to atone for it endlessly. I identified a lot with the David Helfgott character in the recent movie, *Shine*, who suffers deeply for a similarly confusing family message around creative achievement.

There was also the twist of having grown up in a separatist religious peasant community, in which intellectualism was paradoxically revered, feared and scoffed at. For women, it was something that belonged only to grade school: we were expected to give up whatever independent thinking we'd acquired around the time of puberty, and learn to practise, literally, submission and obedience to our fathers, brothers and husbands-to-be. I left that community at age seventeen, and married an unconventional, fun-loving rebel artist who believed in me as a writer long before I began to believe in myself. He taught me how to be an artist, how to take emotional and imaginative risks, how to play, how to locate myself in the artistic community and to thumb my nose at critics and detractors. I thought I had moved as far away as I possibly could from my Mennonite upbringing, but Joan often pointed out to me, in those early years of our working together, the ways in which my marriage had duplicated old family dynamics after all. I came to understand that despite his early encouragement, my husband was now "punishing" and threatening to abandon me for becoming an independent, successful artist, and that I was duplicating old family patterns in punishing myself.

The unspoken message Joan gave me from the beginning of our work together was that as an unusually sensitive and also creative, intelligent woman, I needed extra attention, extra care, extra emotional protection, certainly not less than other people. I also understood quickly that she wasn't going to engage in an intellectual power struggle with me. Whenever she inquired into something I knew a lot about, perhaps more than she did, instead of becoming defensive and hostile the way my father would have done, and the way my husband, and also university professors, tended to do, she gave me quick acknowledgement and went on to something else, as if to say, "Oh, you already know about that, well, then, we don't need to talk about it. Let's move on to something else." I also appreciated, deeply, the way she resisted trying to define my healing experience for me. There was a complete lack of therapeutic jargon in our work together. I never felt like a "client," and she herself refused that term, preferring to call the women she worked with just that. She left the naming of the healing experience almost entirely up to me, often asking me to put the massage experience into words at the end of the session. This kind of trust in my ability to name my own experience gave me a huge sense of power and imaginative freedom.

Another of Joan's unspoken messages was that she wouldn't challenge or push me toward making changes more quickly than I was willing or able to. On the other hand, she never let me get away with simply listing problems. I remember she would listen to me and then say, "What do you want to do about that?" And I would think, startled and surprised, "Oh, you mean I can do something about it?" It was such a powerful permission to begin revisioning my life, and a dramatic reversal of the paralyzing messages I was used to, such as "Don't be so ..." and "You mustn't ..." and "You're far too ..." In fact, because I was living in such a destructive marriage and because I was so near death, I was able to make changes quickly and profoundly. Sometimes Joan offered simple suggestions about self care, which seem self-evident to me now but were often startling and wonderful then: relax and slow down; go for a long walk; go home and take a long, hot bath. Often these suggestions were accompanied by a touching little gift, such as a few bath beads or an audiotape of birdsong. Other times, though, she responded strongly and advised immediate action, responses that taught me how to recognize serious dangers more clearly. This feedback was crucial and necessary: having lived in crisis for so long, I no longer felt it as such.

One time I told Joan about a conversation I'd had with my husband, in which he said, "If I had a choice between you not getting through this crisis and dying, and getting through it and leaving me, I'd choose you dying, because I love you so much." I replied, "Well, why couldn't I get through it and we could work through our differences *and* stay together?" But inside, I thought to myself with a sort of chill, "My husband wants me dead." I remember when I told Joan about this, she did not advocate sympathy or understanding for him, as she sometimes did. She took my alarm very seriously, and expressed grave concern for my safety. After that, we began strategizing steps toward marital separation, even though it would put me in a precarious situation financially, and would probably cause him to accelerate his negative behaviour toward me. I also knew it would upset everyone in my family, including, of course, most directly and importantly, our children.

Gradually, I began to feel safe with Joan, to breathe easier, and to eat and sleep again. I started feeling healthy and joyful, more so than ever before. My writing expanded in scope and depth. I remember those first years of therapy as a wellspring of creativity. Poems and ideas flowed out of me and onto the page. There was a lot of public acknowledgement for my writing, which terrified me but also inspired me to keep going. I was so relieved and happy to be truly alive, at last, and to have found such a powerful, creative ally in Joan. I used to walk by her house at night, sometimes with my dog Maddie, my other best friend in those days, marvelling at the healing magic I felt emanating from the house, from Joan.

The massage combined with counselling was deeply comforting. I had always craved touch, and this was a safe, non-sexual kind of touching that I hadn't ever known as an adult, and not nearly enough as a child. It was absolutely wonderful to make constant connections between talking and acting, and thinking and feeling. It was great to begin to wake up all the cells of my body, to stretch out into my real self. One time I said to Joan, "I feel much too big and much too small at the same time." And she said, "When you find the right space to inhabit, neither too big nor too small, the universe will open for you." It was a powerful promise. I believed in it utterly, and I have found it to be so.

There were many forces conspiring against the sorts of changes I was beginning to make in my life, changes that moved me toward a healthy and independent life. My husband tried every method of sabotage and seduction he could think of, including occasionally physical violence, to intimidate and stop me, before we finally both understood the marriage was irrevocably over. My family carried on its usual judgmental behaviour toward me. I'd been the first to leave home and break a lot of the restrictive rules of the community, to their dismay. They, on the other hand, tended to treat me as a scapegoat for whatever went wrong in the family, generally. (Joan once pointed out that I suffered two months of depression before and after every Christmas family gathering — an observation that led to a Christmas boycott of my family for several years, while I was renegotiating my relationship with them.) Moreover, I was in the middle of a difficult programme of study with very little income to support myself and my children, and no guaranteed job prospects at the end of it. My life continued to be unmanageably complicated for several more years after I began counselling with Joan.

Many times, later, women would ask me, "How did you manage to go through a messy divorce, earn a Ph.D, write several award-winning books, and raise two children as a single parent, all at the same time, on a freelance and part-time sessional instructor's income?" I couldn't have done it without Joan. She was my closest friend and support for nine years, sharing most of my significant life experiences over that decade. She gave me the kind of detailed, careful mothering that I'd needed and never had. Her concerns ranged from little things such as noticing how poorly I was dressed in the middle of winter and lending me a scarf to walk home in cold weather, to big things such as helping me strategize custody and child maintenance legal proceedings, and helping me organize my doctoral dissertation plans. And through it all, lovingly, caringly, stroking my body into greater ease and self-awareness during massage.

In 1989, after three years of therapy, I suffered a spinal injury in a car accident. Joan suggested I attend a yoga class for injured backs. The first time I went, the first simple yoga pose I tried, I went into a very scary, powerful hallucination. The room seemed to be spinning … the floor was caving in … I was a little baby … I was sliding into the earth … there was dirt in my mouth … there were black wings flapping over my face … I was dying. This frightened me so much, I probably wouldn't have gone back if it hadn't been for Joan. She comforted and challenged me as usual, suggesting I talk to my instructors about the experience. I did, and one of them offered to give me free individualized yoga lessons for the rest of the term. I am grateful to Sheri Berkowitz of the Winnipeg Yoga Centre for those months of closely supervised, caring yoga instruction, in which I learned how to circumvent some of the terror I encountered in that initial yogic experience and to cope with the kind of healing energy released through yoga.

That hallucination was the beginning of my remembering the extreme, shattering violence that happened to me when I was a baby. Because I was so young when it happened, only a month old in the first instance, and less than a year old in the second, it took us several years of creative therapy to uncover the details of what actually happened: oral rape, battering, strangling, severe beating. During these years I continued to have mysterious, terrifying, unidentified hallucinations during yoga and sometimes during massage, only slightly less terrifying than that first one. I have written about the actual remembering of these traumas extensively elsewhere (particularly in *Agnes in the sky*; *mother, not mother*; and *Dancing Naked*). What I want to say about it here is that I was extremely lucky to find a woman healer with enough wisdom and resources to be able to recognize the signs of deeply buried trauma, and to help me unearth it the way we did. I'm aware of how indebted we both are to the revolutionary feminist therapy movement that was happening all around us in North America in the 1980s, which provided us both with information and support. I was also lucky to find a therapist with whom I felt such deep rapport. We were alike in many ways: we both had two daughters and were divorced; we both had worked in the academy and were doing freelance work outside it; we both had a creative bent; we both had grown up on prairie farms; and so on. Most importantly, we liked and admired and understood each other.

Two little moments among the many, many profound moments of caring I experienced with Joan stand out. One blustery winter day I came to her with a bad cold. She looked at me and said, "I don't think you need therapy today. What you need is several days in bed, and someone bringing you hot soup." I looked at her in some desperation. There was no one who could bring me hot soup. And who would take care of my daughters? Who would earn the money while I lay around in bed? The next morning I did let myself go back to bed after taking the children to school. Suddenly, there was a knock at the door and there was Joan with a big hearty steaming bowl of homemade minestrone soup. She had walked over to my house in the snow between therapy sessions — we lived in the same neighbourhood, about fifteen blocks apart — to deliver it.

The second moment is the time I came home from an evening yoga class with a mysterious rash all over my back. My body was beginning to release its terrible secrets, but not without hysterical warning signals. I called Joan, and she said I could come over right away, even though it was ten o'clock at night. I remember that massage session, because it was dark instead of sunny outside the massage room window, and the light from her lamp cast such a different glow than I had grown used to in that peaceful, lovely room. I remember it mostly because I was so touched that she would see me at ten o'clock in the evening. I was blown away by such attentive, prompt caring, which seemed to go far beyond what I was paying for, and was something I'd never experienced with anyone before.

After I'd recovered the abuse memories and done a lot of healing work releasing the early trauma stored in my body, through massage, creative visualization and voice work with Joan, and of course yoga, I decided to tell my family about it. I carefully planned a separate meeting with each of my sisters, my mother and my brother. I decided it didn't matter how they responded; the main purpose of these visits was to give them information. It might take them awhile to absorb and understand it, much less acknowledge it in some way. This turned out to be good protection for me, since, in fact, my story, because of its extreme, unthinkable violence and the early occurrence of it was a terrible shock to each of them. It was also a horrifying indictment of members of our family: I was essentially accusing my uncle, Peter Janzen, of sexual assault and attempted murder, and my father, Henry Janzen, of grave physical assault, causing serious emotional and bodily harm, all without legally provable evidence. (My uncle was at this time estranged from the family, and had a history, I discovered later, of known sexual violence. My father, on the other hand, was deceased but had been a well-respected man in the community, a man I loved deeply.)

I think they didn't all believe the whole story, and indeed, it has taken them (and me) a decade to even begin to understand it, but each of them listened carefully. Immediately after that, the emotional dynamics in our family changed dramatically. It was as though something got released in everyone, quite beyond anyone's conscious volition.

By far the hardest challenge was telling my mother. She had rejected me emotionally from an early age, and I was sure her abandonment of me had everything to do with my early trauma. My mother is very intuitive, and even though she had no way of knowing about the assault by my uncle (she was in hospital at the time), she would have sensed its effect on me and no doubt understood it as simply something "wrong" with me. I was used to her overt denial of my feelings and needs, and the prospect of her negative response to my story was simply unbearable. Joan suggested I invite my mother to come for a joint therapy session, so I could feel emotionally supported while telling her, and so my mother could feel emotionally supported while listening. My mother was willing to come and drove the one hundred kilometres from her village to my house, and we walked together to Joan's. I'm sure she had no idea what was in store for her. During the telling, my mother was completely silent. Every once in a while, Joan would gently cue her to make a response. Sometimes she would gently cue me to add another detail or explain something further. I know that was a difficult afternoon for my mom, but it was the beginning of a profound change in our relationship, a change that couldn't have happened without the kind of gentle, supportive mediative work Joan performed with us that afternoon.

The other truly difficult telling involved Rosie, my twin sister. She and I had hardly spoken to each other since the publication of *questions i asked my mother*, five years earlier. Because she lived in Toronto, far away from Winnipeg and our rural Mennonite community, she had missed most of the social drama of this scandalous event, though it had frightened her enough at a distance to withdraw almost completely from me. Because it was one of the first books written by a Mennonite woman in Canada, there was no milieu for its reception in either my family or the community. The Mennonites, used to practising public silence as a separatist community, responded for the most part with shock, horror and judgement. For my mother, it was a time of public humiliation and shame. As for me, I felt extremely hurt by my twin sister's abandonment of me at a time when I was going through so many difficult life changes. We had always been very close sisters and friends before that, and shared most important experiences with each other. I also knew the stories I had to tell implicated her in some way: surely she was present when they happened. Could some version of them have happened to her, as well?

Rosie agreed to meet me at a coffee shop near a subway stop in downtown Toronto. We chatted awkwardly for a moment, then I told her in as much detail as I could about the process of remembering the two abuse traumas and my therapeutic recovery from them. I talked for nearly three hours, during which time she listened attentively, but hardly said a word. After I was done, she said, "Thank you. I see my train is going to come in a few minutes, so I have to go now." I was flabbergasted, but reminded myself over and over that she probably needed time to make a response.

A few months later, Rosie called me and suggested we try a mediated conversation as a way of beginning to communicate with each other again, since we both felt scared and angry and hurt. Somehow, we agreed, all the painful misunderstandings of the family had landed between us. I was thrilled, and suggested Joan. This was a risky idea for her, since she didn't know Joan, and it would mean coming to Winnipeg by herself for a weekend. However, she took the chance and came.

It was a dramatic, tense weekend for us. We orchestrated all our time in advance — who she was staying with, how many meetings we'd have with Joan, how much time we'd spend with each other alone between sessions. Thinking about it now, I remember two things most vividly. The first is how frightened we both were to enter into that deep hurt space between us, where we shared the unspoken, preconscious memory of severe infant trauma. We think now that she was not assaulted the way I was, but that she was there witnessing my uncle's crime in the deeply empathic, intuitive way of an infant, a terrible secret to have inscribed in anyone's unconscious memory. The other thing I remember, in the brightest colours so to speak, is the intense love we felt between us, sitting there in Joan's living room. The years of estrangement fell away between us as we talked our way gingerly through the most painful parts of our relationship and our relative positions in the family. By the end of the weekend we had talked through the years of engrained denial and projection and avoidance strategies, circling around the unspeakable event, back to the deep, primordial connection that only twins can know.

My younger sister, Carolyn, meanwhile, had become a social worker, specializing in abuse issues in families. She and I had always been close. I was ten when she was born, and remember playing with her and taking care of her as one of the greatest joys of my childhood. She was supportive to me throughout my years of therapy, even though, like the other members of the family, she was unprepared for the surprise and scandal of having a writer in the family, and often participated, as we all did, in the family scapegoating pattern that was so deeply engrained in us. It was Carolyn, in fact, who had helped me approach the threshold of remembering what had happened to me as a baby, by calmly discussing the possibility with me, during a long walk through Assiniboine Forest.

Last summer, we celebrated my mother's seventy-fifth birthday. My sisters and I organized a party, and invited her friends and closest relatives. About eighty aunts, uncles and cousins came, along with many young children and grandchildren. This was about half of our immediate extended, Mennonite family, not counting second cousins, great aunts and uncles, and so on. It required seriously creative planning on our part, this party: we wanted it to be fun and celebratory. We didn't want "preaching and praying," which Mennonites tend to practise, even at so-called parties. We didn't want any sanctimonious lies about our family to be said publicly by anyone. We wanted everyone to notice how beautiful and talented and adventurous and lively our mother had become in her old age. We wanted to be ourselves, and yet somehow bridge the impossible cultural gap that existed between the relatives and us. We were among the first generation of children in our traditional Mennonite community to break out of the strict religious separatism that had characterized our culture for centuries. We understood, suddenly, in this moment, how complicated it must have been for our mother to straddle these two worlds. We wanted to celebrate our birth family's being together, even though we hadn't been in the same room since our big family fight several years earlier.

The fight had been over the family farm "corporation" —

who owned it after our father died, who controlled it, who was given information, who wasn't — but it was also, profoundly, about the skewed communication and scapegoating patterns in our family. I was the person who instigated it, as the most scapegoated of the children, with Joan's encouragement and support. But my two sisters joined in, enthusiastically, once they understood what the quarrel was about. They had both gone into counselling not long after I did, and were also learning how to negotiate creative changes in their lives. The fight went on for about three years and involved a legal investigation, and many family meetings, conference calls and letters written back and forth. I even talked them all into coming for counselling with Joan at one point, though my only brother and his wife refused to come after the third session, during which my sisters and I challenged him on his judgmental, manipulative behaviour.

This brother, Harvey, who lost a lot of privileged ground in this fight, sold his share in the farm and left the community and the family, without any attempt at open communication or resolving our differences. He had been experiencing severe health problems due to extensive exposure to pesticides, and has since been involved in his own healing work in Alberta. Our mother felt cut in two: after that she was forced to have two Christmases, two Mother's Days, and so on, since we sisters refused to meet with our brother. All the relatives, we were sure, had heard about the fight, and highly disapproved of us, Mary's selfish and "worldly" daughters, for carrying it out. Several people told us during the quarrel that we shouldn't be pursuing it because it would "kill" our mother. This didn't make sense to us: we didn't understand how challenging everyone to tell the truth would kill anyone, much less our mother. In fact, even though it was a difficult process for her and the rest of us to go through, we reflected later that she seemed younger, healthier and livelier after that than before, and we certainly felt that way ourselves. I can also say, proudly, that despite her conflicting loyalties regarding the quarrel about the farm, she took a brave, feminist stand for her daughters' rights to information and shares to the land.

Planning the birthday party wasn't easy. Each of us, we found out later, even our mother, experienced acute psychic pain and fear and scary dreams the week before. But ... we did it! We rented an elegant old house on the Red River in Winnipeg for a sunny day in August. We organized an art show. This was my idea; I wanted everyone to see that I'd come by my scandalous artistic nature honestly, that we're all artists in our family, even though I was the first to practise it professionally! The children and grandchildren exhibited paintings, drawings, photographs and handmade guitars. I brought copies of *Agnes in the sky* and *Jerusalem, beloved*, my least controversial books in family terms, and a painting with one of my poems in it. My two daughters, Lisa and Ali, now twenty-one and eighteen, brought paintings, drawings, sculptures and a handsewn satin designer dress. Our mother, with a little coaxing, exhibited half a dozen of her spectacular award-winning quilts. Our brother and his family drove sixteen hundred kilometres to attend and participate. We performed several songs in four-part harmony, Mennonite style, in both German and English. The grandchildren, who didn't learn German or singing in the Mennonite villages the way we did, tried gallantly to keep up.

None of us anticipated how much fun it was going to be. For us, for the relatives, and most of all, for our mother, who was, after all, the heart, the centre, of this gathering. The grandchildren were delighted to see each other again after the long separation following our feud, and each contributed a little anecdote about Grandma for the occasion. Mark and Andrew, the nineteen-year-old identical twins, performed a lyrical version of "Feeling Groovy" by Simon and Garfunkel for Grandma, because, they said, she may be old but she thinks and drives like a teenager. My favourite moment in the party was when we sang, "How do you solve a problem like Grandma Maria?" adapted playfully for the occasion from *The Sound of Music* by our three-year-old niece, Rachel. There was pure pleasure in our mother's and all the aging aunts' and uncles' faces as our voices swelled into the choral finale, "How do you hold a moonbeam in your hand?" We had thought our mother would veto this song in advance, because of its irreverent lyrics celebrating the disobedient, stubborn Maria's lively spirit, but she didn't; she loved it. There's a lot of Maria in our mother, besides the name.

My other favourite moment was seeing Joan there. I had invited her to attend, but wasn't sure if she could come. Seeing her among my relatives, most of whom I hadn't seen in years, made me feel suddenly as if the day was complete. So much healing had happened in our family since those traumatic days when I was nearly dying and after, when it seemed every week unearthed yet another serious crisis or quarrel for me to go through. It was wonderful to see my two mothers together in the same room that day, surrounded by flowers and gifts and song. I understood how my nine years of being mothered by Joan made it possible for me to renegotiate my troubled relationship with my sisters and my birth mother, and how all those years of hard work by all of us had translated, finally, into this afternoon of fun and love and joy and celebration.

It seemed magical then, and I think it is. Thank you, Joan. I love you.

## Endnotes

1. Joan Turner is a therapist in private practice in Winnipeg, Manitoba. She is a former associate professor, Faculty of Social Work, University of Manitoba, and a former owner of a women's bookstore, Bold Print Inc. She has edited three collections of essays and other writing: *Spider Women: A Tapestry of Creativity and Healing* (J. Gordon Shillingford, 1999), with Carol Rose; *Living the Changes* (University of Manitoba Press, 1990); and *Perspectives on Women* (University of Manitoba Press, 1983), with Lois Emery. Her essay on body work, "Let My Soul Soar: Touch Therapy," which includes a brief section on working with Di Brandt, appeared in Cheryl Malmo and Toni Laidlaw's *Healing Voices: Feminist Approaches to Therapy with Women* (Jossey-Bass, 1990).

# JEANNINE
# CARRIERE

## *IN THE SHAPE OF*
## *HER EYES*

### *RECLAIMING*
### *MY METIS CULTURE*

*I*f I am to write about the place of culture in my life, I must first define what culture means to me and explain how it has had an impact on who I am. My definition of culture encompasses an identification with a set of norms and values. It also encompasses the community to which I belong. I didn't understand the significance of these attributes of culture until I realized, as an adult, how much had been taken from me at birth, through adoption. What was imposed on me in childhood was the expectation that I would adapt to a set of norms and values that, while working for my survival, did not feed my soul with a knowledge of my place in a history of family, community and the universe. Reclaiming my culture was a significant rite of passage I undertook as a young woman, but it certainly didn't eliminate the painful journey that was necessary for me to find myself. Today, I am still defining who I am: Jeannine Marie Carriere, a Metis woman defining myself in a world that wants to define *me*. Thank you, Creator, for making me a rebel!

I was born in 1952, in St. Boniface, Manitoba, in the heart of Metis country, an area once known as the Red River Settlement. I was adopted at six weeks of age by the Aubins, a French Canadian family who were small farmers in the town of St. Adolphe, situated along the temperamental Red River. Back then, St. Adolphe was still home to a number of Metis families: the Delormes, the Courchenes and the Carrieres. These Carrieres were probably distantly related to me, but I didn't know that as a child.

I don't remember much of my early childhood, but I do remember that when I was five years old an angry boy from next door said to me, "What do you know? You're just adopted anyway!" That was the first time I felt afraid and lost, because I didn't know who I was any more. When I asked my parents what it meant, I was given a common, kind explanation — that I was special, or some other gibberish. They underestimated my curiosity and my imagination, and they also underestimated my shame at being different from any other child I knew in St. Adolphe.

Grade One was extremely scary for me. I remember my mother bringing me to the convent school, and me cringing behind her print dress as she introduced me to the nun who would be my teacher. It was the first time I had met so many strangers; other children and nuns were everywhere. I felt like running but my legs were like jelly. When I saw my mother's print dress getting smaller as she walked away down the hall, I felt alone as I never had before. I sat in my seat, uncomfortably, and smiled nervously, but I thought that day would never end. I don't think I spoke much that first year. (I made up for it later!) The nuns in their black robes frightened me. The smell of the convent was distinct, a mixture of floor wax, detergents, chalk and other "nun" smells; it's a smell that has never left me. Only those who have walked on those holy, waxed floors know what I mean. Many years later, as a social worker, I walked into a renovated convent to attend a meeting. The smell was still there!

In Grade Two I started piano lessons. My parents didn't own a piano so I was forced to practise at the convent, and my instructor thought I would learn better if she smacked my fingers with a ruler when I hit the wrong note. Like a good pet I learned the tricks, but after six years of lessons and playing at community concerts and so on I cannot, today, play the piano. I hope the knowledge is saved somewhere in my memory banks, but I am not optimistic. Learning through fear is not a positive experience.

In Grade Five I made friends with two boys who were foster children and lived across the road from us. Ah, finally someone I could relate to! They happened to be Metis. Later that same year Sister Marie informed us that Metis people were somewhat slow, and that the rest of us had to be patient. I remember how hurt I felt for those two boys.

Life in St. Adolphe was not particularly eventful. Winters were long and cold, with only Christmas to look forward to. The danger of spring flooding always brought excitement, and sometimes a temporary move. Summer was a time of easy living for me, as it was for other children. From age six onward I was the only child at home, so I lived in my imagination. I ran through the bushes with my dog, and climbed trees and pretended I was flying to exotic countries. My adoptive parents were not wealthy, by any means, but we always had food, grown in a large garden that usually supplied vegetables to half the town. My father, a meat-and-potatoes kind of man, also ensured that we had plenty of meat from butchering our own animals, or wild meat from his hunting trips in the fall and spring. Yes, life was somewhat predictable — until one summer evening when I was twelve.

There I was, in my yard, painting my wagon. Today's twelve-year-old girls wouldn't dream of doing such a thing, but hey, I was a country girl. I pulled all kinds of cargo in that wagon, and it needed a paint job. I heard a car driving down the road towards our house. In those days we knew every car in town, and this car belonged to no town person. I kept watching as the car pulled up near me, and a teenaged girl got out of the car and came towards me. She was very pretty, with long black hair and big dark eyes. She looked familiar but I knew she was a stranger. She asked, "Are you Jeannine?" When I replied that I was, she announced that she was my sister Suzanne. My whole world changed with that announcement. I lost everything and I gained everything. It was as if something inside me shifted and I felt connected. I belonged again. No, let me rephrase that: I felt as though I belonged for the first time in my life.

My sister looked like me, just darker. She told me that I was the youngest of a family of twelve who had been separated by the Manitoba Children's Aid Society when it was deemed that my birth mother could no longer look after us because she was too poor. There are many of these stories in Aboriginal communities across Canada: stories of lost children who are now grown up, who may or may not know who they are, where they are from and who their people are. These lost adults undoubtedly feel a sense of disconnection and a great sense of loss. Although their grandmothers wept for them, they disappeared into a "child welfare system," or abyss — many never to return.

I was very fortunate to be found by my sister and to connect with my family of origin, as painful as this has been at times. Once I had an honest definition of who my family and community were, however, I needed to reclaim them as mine, and to redefine who I was. This process of reclaiming my family and community took years. We Aboriginal women in this country have been defined by everyone but ourselves. Through legislation such as the Indian Act, we became unclassified attachments to male partners. Through the historical events of colonization, we lost our rightful place as respected, equal members of our traditional societies. Through residential school, we lost our gifts of nurturing, kindness and other parenting qualities. When we fought against the laws and practices that oppressed us, we were criticized by our male leaders as troublemakers, as angry and untraditional. There was a lot to be angry about. We were beaten and degraded more than other women, and lost our self-confidence, self-esteem and sense of self-determination. When we began to heal, we fought back and reclaimed our place as women with gifts, visions and strengths to give back to our communities. As well, we began reclaiming culture as part of our healing.

For a long time, I was an angry young person, hell-bent on destruction. You see, my fairy-tale reunion with my family didn't turn out too well. When social workers found out that my sister and I had reconnected, she wasn't allowed to visit me any more. However, no one told me that. When I was thirteen, she just disappeared as mysteriously as she had come. The abandonment I felt was so painful that I spent the next few years trying every drug available, drinking and engaging in other dangerous activities such as careless promiscuity. My relationship with my adoptive parents was very strained, and I rebelled against just about everything. When I was sixteen, I dropped out of school and left home.

At age twenty-one I finally found my sister again, in Winnipeg, in what we used to call an Indian bar. From that point on we were never separated. I also met the rest of my family — what was left of them by then. Three of eleven siblings had died from alcohol-related illnesses or accidents. It wasn't until mid-life that I began to use my anger to fuel my own healing process, a process that involved healing the wounds of three generations of Metis and First Nations family members. With my surviving siblings I faced the damage that "child welfare" had left behind: anger, hate, alcohol and drug abuse, criminal activity, violence and a great overall sense of loss. We all have our ghosts — memories we'd rather forget, stories untold to our children because they are too painful. Over the years we have shared some of these; we have laughed and cried together.

They call me the lucky one: I had a running chance, I was adopted. I was lied to about my birth family by my adoptive parents, but I was lied to out of love. That makes a difference. In spite of that love, however, I still tried to destroy myself. I believed that somehow the loss of my family was all my fault, that

I was a bad child who deserved to be abandoned by her birth parents.

For most of my life, I have tried to punish myself for wrongs I didn't commit. I wasn't lovable enough; I wasn't thin enough, pretty enough, smart enough — all those guilts that young women in most societies experience in some way or other. If you mix these insecurities with being a mixed-blood woman, not quite "Indian" enough and not quite "white" enough, along with a constant feeling of displacement inevitable after adoption, there's plenty of material for lifelong psychotherapy!

I was a victim, ready for anything or anyone abusive, and abuse found me — twice through marriage, and a few other times with so-called friends and lovers. Physical, mental, emotional and spiritual abuse — I went through it all. When the abusive relationships ended, the self-blame would begin, and I would binge on food, alcohol, drugs and more relationships to keep filling the void, the big black hole that wanted to engulf me. I was afraid that if I was alone for too long, or if I stayed straight — sober and clean — for too long, I would simply disappear. The hole would swallow me and I would be in another space in time. There was no core for me to hang onto. I had an internal mechanism to survive, but there is a difference between surviving and really living. Since my recovery, I have spoken to many other past addicts and users of various substances; they know what I mean.

I believe now that women have a different survival mechanism than men. Women have a voice within, a spirit who will save us if we let her. Clarissa Pinkola Estés calls this the "wild woman," the woman who runs with wolves. Many of us fight against her for a long time before we are quiet enough to hear her speak to us. This inner spirit is the one who tells us right from wrong. Her comforting voice prays with us, speaking from the experience of many grandmothers. We all carry her within us, this spirit woman. It's what makes us different from men. It's what medicine men recognize as a force to be respected during our moon time. It's the core from which we gather strength to give birth, to love our children unconditionally until it hurts, and from which we give without expectation of anything in return. This is woman's centredness, grounded in universal principles, although white, yellow, black and red women experience it in different ways.

The privilege of the colour white has separated us from each other in the circle of women. Herein lies yet another problem. Until we reach a balance in the universe, this wedge will endure and our circle will be incomplete and out of balance. It is imperative that this balance in the valuing and empowering of all women be restored. For it is the women in most cultures who heal themselves first, and from their healing comes the healing of children, of men, of communities.

When I was seventeen, my birth mother died. At that time I had met only my sister Suzanne. I hadn't yet had the opportunity to meet anyone else in my family. I remember hearing the announcement on a radio newscast while I was on my way to Grand Beach, Manitoba, with my boyfriend and some other friends. I listened to the details in silence: "Adeline Carriere died in a car accident, driving down the wrong side of the Trans-Canada Highway near St. Pierre, Manitoba." This was where my sister Suzanne had lived, in a cruel foster home. I felt numb listening to the description of the accident. "She was with her son." A man I hadn't met yet, my brother. I didn't flinch a muscle. I didn't cry. No one in the car knew this news had anything to do with me, and I didn't tell them. I struggled to feel something beneath the numbness, but I couldn't. I didn't know these people. It made no difference to me.

I have two pictures of my birth mother. In one she is about thirty, standing in front of "the shack," as my brothers and sisters call it: a two-room, part log, part paper structure. It was in this shack that we were all conceived, though not all from the same father. My mother looks pregnant in this picture and there is no doubt she was; she had twelve children who were at most two years apart. Once in a while, I look at this black-and-white picture and I try to find myself. My mother looks Indian, and I can see most of us in her eyes, in the shape of her eyes. We are a rainbow of people otherwise, some dark, some fair. Some of my brothers and sisters are very proud to be Metis; some are not. When they speak of my mother, I still hear the pain in their voices, especially in the voice of my eldest sister, Jean.

Jean was only sixteen when "the welfare" arrived to take away our mother and place all her children in foster homes and group facilities. According to Jean, my mother was pregnant with me and very ill at the time. Jean had already quit school to help look after her younger siblings. When the family was split up, she was considered too old for the foster care system, and was forced to go to work, cleaning houses and looking after other people's children. My heart aches for her when I think of how she must have felt on her own, away from all her sisters and brothers and her mother. She tried to stay in touch with our mother, however, which was lucky for me. One of the biggest gifts Jean gave me was to tell me that my mother refused three times to sign the adoption papers, until the doctors and social workers eventually convinced her that she would never be able to be a mother to me. They told her that she would have to let go of me, just as she had let go of all her other children. It was after this that she began to do some serious drinking. When she and my brother got into the accident that was fatal for her, there was alcohol involved. What a tragic ending to a tragic life!

It took me years to forgive my mother. I finally did so when I heard some grandmothers speak at an Indian child-welfare conference in Winnipeg. These old women spoke of adoptees who had returned home, their grandsons and granddaughters; one said that these children had never been forgotten. I thought about my mother and what Jean had told me. My mother, apparently, had never forgotten me, and she had loved me and wanted to see me. I imagined her picking up the phone many times to call me, but hanging up when one of my parents answered. I thought about all of this as the elders spoke and I began to cry. I had always thought of my own losses, my own pain. I had never placed myself in my mother's pain. As soon as I did, I had to forgive her. By then, I too was a mother.

My daughter, Robin, was born just before I turned eighteen. I wasn't a very good mother at first. I still wanted to party with my friends and do the hippie thing. I was living in Toronto, having hitchhiked there with my boyfriend, Robin's father. Although we played with Robin and looked after most of her needs, I didn't take parenting too seriously at that point. When Robin was two, we moved back to Manitoba and I began to resolve my difficult relationship with my adopted parents. My mother did a lot of child care for me. I was still disconnected, doing drugs and feeling depressed. I entered college for something to do, and after graduation I asked Robin's father to leave. He had been unsupportive to me while I was in school, and had continued to abuse me emotionally. When I realized that I could support myself, I knew I didn't need him any more.

While I was working at my first job after college, something happened that was quite magical for me: I found my roots and made a connection to where I belonged in history. Quite by chance, I was hired to work for the Manitoba Metis Federation as a researcher in land claims. I got the job because I was fluent in French, not because I was an expert in land claims research. From time to time my job included translating archival material from French to English for the purpose of analyzing it in relation to a land claim. At that time I was still somewhat uncomfortable describing myself as Metis. I wasn't even sure I was Metis. I knew my mother was, and so were my siblings, but what was I, the adopted daughter?

Another part of my work as a researcher was to look at archival material to establish how the expropriation of Metis lands had taken place. We had already developed a list of speculators who had been busy buying up Metis lands in the 1800s for corporations such as railways, banks and so on. These archival documents were easy to recognize after a while, because the same signature would appear on the bill of sale and the land title deed. This was the case for most of the 1.4 million acres the Metis had lost in Manitoba. My mother's maiden name, Carriere, appeared time and time again, and I was always distantly curious when I

saw it. One afternoon, as I flipped through the microfilm, a name
came up that changed my life — Augustin Carriere, my grandfather. A bill of sale was written with his name and lot number, and
the signature of the land speculator, Donald A. Smith. My grandfather's signature was a large "X," as he was illiterate. By making
this mark he had signed away 240 acres of prime land in the city
of St. Boniface, now a prestigious French Canadian neighbourhood on the banks of the Red River. This land would be worth a
small fortune today.

I sat staring at the document for a long time, and then I cried.
All of a sudden, there was a connection for me. The poverty, the
child-welfare involvement, the family breakdown, the deaths —
these were consequences of that signature, and I was connected
to it. Finding the document with my grandfather's name on it was
the moment when I linked my personal life to a political reality.
I had a place in history. I was part of a culture. We had a land base
that had been stolen from us. Our language, our music, our stories
— these were mine too. Pride swelled in my heart, and although
there was also sadness, I claimed this too. I was determined to
make a difference in my community from that point onward. I
would devote the rest of my life to promoting my people's
interests and taking my rightful place in the world as a Metis
daughter of the Red River.

Once I reclaimed my heritage and culture, I had much to learn
about customs, traditions, family history and Metis history. I
have spent most of my adult life working in the Metis community
and I am still defining who I am as a Metis woman. My culture,
for me, is more than being part of an ethnic group. I am a woman
who is a mother. I am a social worker in Western Canada in the
nineties. These aspects, too, are part of my culture. It is all
interconnected. Every event in my life has made me who I am,
and finding my roots has helped to define me further.

In the past few years, I have begun to learn more about my
connection to my First Nations ancestors. My grandmother, a
Sioux, was apparently a healer, a medicine woman. I'd like to
think that she has influenced my personal and professional

choices. The cultural and spiritual teachings of the First Nations have also been helpful in my own healing and recovery. I pay great attention to the teachings of the medicine wheel about how I should strive for balance.

In my work with Aboriginal women, I have often tried to help them find their own connections to family of origin, to history and to the political context in which Aboriginal people have been placed within this country. It is remarkable that, once they do this, they let go of a lot of guilt and blame that have been hampering their personal growth for years. As women, we tend to blame ourselves for all the wrongs of the world. Why do we do this? Perhaps because we are the nurturers, the mothers, the foundation. One of the hardest lessons for us is to realize that unless we become healthy ourselves, as individuals, we perpetuate the disease of others. This has been a powerful teaching for me. The hurt of one is the hurt of all.

I have a lot to be thankful for, and every day I try to remember to thank the Creator for all my blessings. I have had an extremely interesting life. I have been blessed with finding out who I am, my roots, my place in my family and my place in history. I continue to make discoveries every day. I have reclaimed what was taken from me. What was never taken was my inner spirit, the spirit of my mother and the medicines of my grandmother. I read a powerful description of one woman's connection to her female ancestors: she saw herself standing on the shoulders of her mother, who stood on the shoulders of her grandmother, who stood on the shoulders of her great-grandmother. It was a vision that made her feel strong. I can see myself in this same vision, and I feel the power of it in my own life. And I feel blessed, too, because I can look up and see my own beautiful daughter, standing on my shoulders.

For all of these gifts, I say *migwetch* — thanks, many thanks.

# SOLEDAD GONZALEZ

## *CASTING OFF*

### *AN IMMIGRANT STORY*

*T*hirty-five years ago, on a hot November evening at Chile's small, crowded Santiago airport, I quietly listened to an ardent speech from my
mother, whose quivering voice rose in an effort to
drown the sounds emanating from the loudspeakers. I had never grown used to her public displays
of emotions, which seemed to be meant for everyone else but me. The discomfort I felt made my
small adolescent body rigid and unresponsive.

"I'm sorry I can't give you something to take
with you, my sweet daughter. All I have is advice.
You are going to a strange country and I don't know
if you realize what a big change this will be for you.
When I was fifteen I just let things happen to me.
That was when your father and I got married. But
you are wiser than I was. You are taking an enormous leap to the north. The best advice I can give
you is that you learn the language well enough to
read the original works of famous American and
English writers. You are a very lucky girl."

Her words were as foreign to me as the language I was suppose to learn. At fifteen, books had not yet entered my life. And when they did five years later, while my first daughter practised gentle somersaults within my belly, it was the Russian authors who awakened my curiosity. At the airport, my mother's words felt empty, meaningless. Just another variation on the drill I had been hearing from my relatives and friends during the months leading to that confusing, timeless summer evening.

"Take advantage of this opportunity" ... "Work hard, don't be lazy" ... "Make the most of this great chance" ... "Be good to your uncle and aunt. They are such good people" ...

Wasted words. These advisors had no way of knowing that from the moment I was told that I would be joining my uncle's family for two years while he studied abroad, indifference had become my refuge. Years of drifting from relative to relative, after our parents' bitter separation, had taught my three brothers and me that we must be glad for any opportunity that came our way. We also knew from experience that any objections or signs of fear would meet with criticism. Who were we, after all, to look a gift-horse in the mouth? Upon hearing the news of my forthcoming journey to some unknown place, I succeeded in hiding my anxiety but failed to provide my family with the expected signs of gratitude. By that time, they had grown as used to my peculiar reactions as I had to seeking refuge in indifference. Indifference to the nocturnal visits by our uncles to their young nieces' beds, indifference to our father's routine electro-shock treatments, to our mother's drunken scene, to the hostility of the two feuding families. In the turbulent, unpredictable world of adults, apathy became my comforting raft.

For weeks, my oldest brother had patiently tried to get me interested in a map. "Look. This is Chile and that's Chicago, all the way over here in another continent. You are going to one of the biggest cities in North America, the city of gangsters," he would repeat, letting his eyes wander through a confusing maze of lines and drawings. But my attention was focused on my brother's tender efforts to deal with his own feelings. "My little sister," he would say, solemnly folding the map. The sadness in his thoughtful eyes, which seemed to come from something ominous about my future, something revealed by the map, only added to my fears. Yet I sensed that if I spoke what was really in my heart, if I begged him to go in my place, he too would have echoed what everyone else was saying about my good luck. The fact that he, like the rest of my brothers, had not been chosen to go because he lacked child-care and domestic-work skills, was never mentioned. After all, my contribution in labour to the families who took me under their wing was another excellent opportunity to practise the role to which I had been born.

After glancing once more at the group of waving relatives and noticing my oldest brother leaning against a pillar with his hands in his pockets, I walked into the steel bowels of a machine that took me above the clouds, transforming forever my limited reality. Up to that point, my life had been shaped by profoundly contrasting surroundings: sea and mountains, forests and deserts, poverty and wealth. I was accustomed to extremes. In fact, I was born to them, since my relatives represented opposite sides of Chile's intense political and social climate. My father's people solemnly observed the Christian Democrats' credo while my maternal family eagerly followed the Communist doctrine. But none of these extremes had prepared me for the torrent of events that began the moment I stepped on foreign land. The sudden opening, without my touch, of an airport door leading to a city of bitterly cold winds, the likes of which I had never experienced, was a sobering taste of things to come.

Within hours of leaving my country, I found myself immersed in a sea of tall, blond, blue-eyed strangers whose confidence and beauty intimidated me. Though their type was a minority among my people, I had often heard their look described as the preferred one. "My cousin had such a beautiful baby. You should see him! Blond curls, fair skin and beautiful blue eyes." Except for the blue eyes, two of my three brothers had fitted that description. During my childhood I had become the protector of the youngest one, who, like me, was dark and "common."

A couple of years ago, at least three lifetimes after my departure from that muggy airport, my mother and I looked back with the compassion and grace of two grandmothers who know better than to ignore old ghosts. She acknowledged that she had loved my brothers best, but not only because of their looks. "I was taught that male children were the preferred ones," she said in a quiet voice, "especially if they were fair. I felt as though I had to love you secretly." I was immensely grateful for her courage in admitting what I had always suspected.

As I settled into the new land, I began to feel even more deficient. I saw my inability to understand the language instantly as a sign of my stupidity. Disorientation engulfed me like a fog, and during the day the feeling was aggravated by the absence of the mountains which had been my cradle and my compass. Each night I went to sleep thinking I would wake up feeling less of a misfit. My memories of those first months in Chicago are now a collage of moods and situation.

*... The school bell rings. Students grab their books, get up and go as others come in. I stay sitting, wondering where everyone has gone. One of the students says something, pointing to a door across the hall. I get up and walk to that room. When I walk in, the teacher looks at me and says something in a loud voice. A roomful of heads turn towards me. My cheeks burn. Is it possible that in this country students move from class to class and teachers remain in the room, not the other way around?*

*... My long straight hair is a novelty for the girls at school. They touch it and ask to practise their braiding skills. I am ecstatic to discover that we have things in common. I relax as they comb and tease, turning me into a fashionable girl with a hopelessly tangled balloon on her head. The beauty sessions become language lessons "Say this: boys ... cute ... sweetheart ... kiss." Their laughter is no longer hurtful. They want to learn from me. "How do you say 'I love you' and 'Kiss me' in Spanish?"*

*... Slow-motion images on television of the president being shot, his wife trying to climb out of the car, the car speeding off. I strain to understand. The president's wife is now walking along the coffin. She shows no feelings. Was she reprimanded for trying to leave her husband's car? Did she, also, find refuge in indifference? The images get played over and over again. My aunt and uncle grow impatient when I ask too many questions.*

*... I'm bathing my two little cousins when my concentration is suddenly interrupted by my uncle's persistent looks. Although I saw his silhouette standing by my bedroom door the night before, I had talked myself into believing that it had been a bad dream.*

*... At the museum, surrounded by the works of famous painters, I feel overwhelmed by guilt for being the "chosen one." By rights my oldest brother should be standing in this room, since his life has been steered in the direction of art, following the steps of our paternal grandfather whose fame has been a blessing and a curse. I hold my grandfather's ghost responsible for my father's perpetual melancholy and for his inability to rise above the colossal shadow. Back home I was been more forgiving of this grandfather at nightfall, when my grandmother played the piano for him as his presence was made known to us by the squeaking of the old, dusty furniture.*

These moments were permeated by a single comforting thought: it was all temporary. And so, even though I suffered from perpetual homesickness, two years elapsed faster than I had expected. By the end, some of the "strange" things were almost familiar. My words made sense to others. I could appreciate winter days, ice-skating and vanilla milkshakes. I had learned the value of each coin and no longer paid by holding out money hoping the storekeeper or bus driver would take the correct amount.

My memory was full of details that I had saved like a squirrel for my brothers. How was I going to describe the brilliant colours of the autumn leaves in a way that sounded believable? Would they think I was boasting if I told them that I could understand Elvis Presley? How much could I share with them without making them feel bad for not having been the "chosen ones"? Maybe they would feel better if I told them about some of the mistakes I had made. Like the day I used a word I had often heard at school, which I thought meant "Great!" in front of my uncle's lively American dinner guests. They had a hard time keeping a straight face while explaining to me the exact meaning of "fuck."

Feeling genuinely grateful to my new friends, and firmly committed to keeping in touch, I began to collect pictures, addresses and souvenirs of a life that would soon be a past adventure. My excitement grew as each moment lessened the space that kept me from my brown-skin people, my mountains, my sun. Then one day, approximately three weeks before the scheduled departure date, I received a letter from my father reminding me that I still had no home to which I could return. Although they were living in a new apartment, his new wife had proposed that I stay in the United States and finish high school, which he thought "was an excellent idea, especially since very few people have this great opportunity to go abroad ..." etc., etc.

After experiencing feelings of shame for assuming that some relative would surely provide me with food and shelter, my old friend indifference came to my rescue once more. This time, I began a conscious process of forgetting about all the things I missed. Tucked into a dark, useless corner, my homeland ceased to be my point of reference. A friend of my uncle and his wife, a single mother with three small children, invited me to live with her and I had no choice but to accept. I was unable, once again, to feign gratitude. Instead, I secretly questioned her motives for welcoming a foreigner into her home. I could not imagine what I might be able to contribute to the apparently untroubled life of this American stranger named Liz.

With time, as I stopped living in memories of my homeland, my new family became the source of unexpected gifts and pleasures. I watched, amazed, while adults listened to children, invited them to give their opinions and even enjoyed their company. My ideas and beliefs began to matter. Under the protection of my gentle guardian, I learned trust. It seemed to me that every member of my new family was protected by an invisible sacred shield, and that one had somehow been bestowed upon me. Consequently, my actions took on new meanings, which often caused me to reflect on what I judged to be my state of total crudeness.

The earliest understanding of my "coarseness" came after receiving a box of chocolates from Liz on Christmas day. During my childhood, chocolates had been a luxury that our family could not afford, so this delicacy had rarely come my way. Like on the day a neighbour, in an effort to impress my aunt with whom he was in love, had taken me to a very exclusive candy store, inviting me to pick anything I wanted. Feeling the pressure of having too many choices, I pointed to a pile of chocolates in front of me, which, to my great disappointment turned out to be lemon peels covered with bitter chocolate.

Receiving a box of chocolates on Christmas morning from my new family seemed like a dream from which I might suddenly wake up. This thought caused me to rapidly disappear into my bedroom, before anyone would notice. Within a short time, I had silently finished every piece of sweet from the box, and after stuffing the empty container under my bed, I quietly returned to the living room. As I walked into the room, I caught a fleeting glance from Liz which jolted me into awareness of what I had done. Stung by remorse, I perceived myself as a barbarian who had yet to learn the ways of civilized people.

But this, and other moments of self-condemnation, did not last long. The multiple lessons I received from my guardian and her children were delivered in ways that were much less painful than those to which I was accustomed. Their messages were free of judgement and reproach, free of hidden resentments passed on for generations. Problems were not broadcast to the four winds, nor were they a matter of family honour or a sure sign of my mother's "wild ways."

Within this caring environment I learned to trust people's sincerity when they remarked on the things they liked and admired about me. This new gift sustained me through the painfully slow process of making friends with myself and with the new world around me. My efforts to forget about my homeland were made easier by the nurturing I received from the strangers who became my second family. Their way of life was a contradiction to what I had learned about "the insatiable American way." Although the abundance around me often stirred uneasy feelings of guilt, my guardian, a secretary, worked as hard and steadily as any woman I knew. Her lifestyle was modest. She drove an old, dilapidated car unlike anything I had imagined an American would own. But I was never made to feel I was a burden, though she received no financial support from my family. Her kindness and that of her friends, who accepted me as a member of the family, transformed my impression of the "Ugly American."

The metamorphosis that was taking place within me coincided with one in American culture. A new generation, the baby boomers, had began a movement that spread like wildfire. Shedding conventional beliefs, they defied traditional values, challenged authority, spoke of ending injustice and repression, and denounced government policies at home and abroad. For the first time since my arrival I felt that, in spite of our differences, we spoke a common language. Their causes were themes from my daily life during childhood, especially when my maternal grandmother was my most constant guardian. Like many of her friends, my grandmother divided her time equally between her domestic duties in the morning and "the Party" in the afternoon. Before we learned to read, my brothers and I already knew The Internationale and most of the songs from the Spanish Civil War, which we sang at the endless meetings to which our grandmother carted us almost daily.

During those days of immersion into North American life, all my memories were on hold. The homeland, with all its content, was safely tucked away while my attention resided in the present.

I spoke only English, stopped answering letters from home, never read in Spanish, and seldom had contact with other Latin Americans. Having abandoned my family, I had also rejected my culture, deliberately ignoring the transformation taking place throughout Latin America. It never occurred to me, at the time, that my grandmother's values had a profound influenced on the way I was shaping my reality. With experience, I discovered that her vision, courage and strength, for which she had adopted the label of Communist, could also have been called feminism.

Shortly after my high school graduation, at the age of eighteen, I married a tender man whose desire to build the nest he never had was equal to mine. I had been prepared, from an early age, to get married at that point of my life. It was the expected step into adulthood. But as a small token of my defiance, I ignored my relatives' instructions to "marry well," by which they meant "marry a doctor or a lawyer," and took pleasure in letting them know that my young husband was a struggling filmmaker whose riches were not in the material world.

Into this climate of personal and social change, my husband and I brought two baby girls, one year apart. As their lives became my life, my cravings for home began again. I longed for my mother's advice, her nurturing, her confident ways. When my ignorance as a mother paralyzed me, I summoned the memory of the women in my family. Daily, hourly, I yearned to share with my kin the pleasure of my little ones' smiles, first teeth, first steps, first days at school. The delights of motherhood became eclipsed by feelings of isolation. Memories of home returned, persistent, incessant, plunging me into a deep depression.

Following a doctor's suggestion, I returned to Chile in 1972 with my new family for a visit. We were received with all the affection and tenderness I had craved. Shortly after our arrival, I knew the doctor had advised me well when at the street market my frozen spirit began to thaw at the sight of mouth-watering foods and the sound of vendors shouting, boasting and tempting. If up to that point I had doubted my sanity and questioned my desire to live, especially since my father had taken his life the year before, the trip served to confirm that there was a place on earth to which I definitely belonged.

The country's mood was vibrant, promising, yet fraught with conflict as Chileans participated in the first freely elected Socialist government in the world. Music filled with hope and ethnic pride replaced the traditional sentimental songs about broken hearts and impossible dreams. Countless volunteered their time, travelling to remote villages throughout the country to implement innovative social programmes, much to the displeasure of a strong opposition. In Santiago, people gathered nightly at the crowded coffee houses to share their political views while rumours of an impending military coup spread. Every so often the foreboding words "Djakarta is coming" would appear scrawled, in red, on a city wall.

I cherished each moment of our brief three-month visit. Against my will, we returned north, back to Boston. An intense feeling of dissatisfaction once again overtook me. The impotence I felt at having to go back turned into a profound rejection of North American people and their culture. Arrogance began to plague me without mercy, as I daily found proof of my cultural superiority. Then one day, standing in front of a store window, deep in thought as I searched for yet one more fault in my surroundings, I was brought back to the present by the sensation of warm liquid running down my leg. I looked down to meet the indifferent eyes of a big brown dog who calmly put his leg down and walked away wagging his tail. I don't remember how long I stood in the middle of that yellow puddle, but I do recall that, once I came out of my stupor, the streets of Boston seemed friendlier.

On September 11, 1973, a year after our visit, a military government overthrew the democratically elected government of Chile. Thousands disappeared, were imprisoned or killed, as human rights ceased to exist. My family, already partly disintegrated by their own neglected demons, dispersed in search of safety.

What took place in my homeland was more than I could fathom. Every day that passed shed new light which connected American involvement with the tragic events taking place in Chile. Every day was, for me, one more day of shame. My heart became heavy with the thought that I had paid taxes to the very same government that had made this bloody nightmare possible. The marches of my childhood, the songs, speeches and endless incomprehensible discussions to which my grandmother had exposed us, surfaced with new meaning, adding pieces to the historic puzzle and taking me one step farther from my embryonic state.

My marriage, likewise, soon collapsed. The long process leading to the final breakup was not unlike the one experienced by most women who marry young and full of illusions only to discover that love was not what the poets and troubadours professed. I had never been warned about the immense effort it took to keep the demanding little cherub satisfied.

Before marriage, love had been uncomplicated. My first significant experience had came at the age of ten, when I fell silently in love with a boy who lived with other children under a bridge near my grandmother's house. This boy, who never answered questions, would come to our door in the early afternoons to eat leftovers my grandmother saved for him. He would take his bowl of food and sit at the top of the stairs of our rundown apartment building, eating noisily, as I secretly watched him through a crack in the door. Since I was assigned to hand him the food, he and I often exchanged glances, but we never spoke. If we passed each other in the street, he would look away. But if I turned around, I would catch him watching me. With time, I looked forward to his daily visits and to his animal smell. I admired and envied his freedom, the dignity with which he refused to answer questions, the pride in his eyes when he took the food from my hands without a thank-you. Then one day he stopped coming. When I looked for him under the bridge, all the street children were gone. Only their dogs remained, roaming, looking lost. A year later, while participating in a school performance for a reform school, I became aware of a pair of eyes that stared insistently from the sea of shaven heads and brown overalls. I did not recognize the clean face of my nameless love until later, when I was on my way home. Perhaps, in my romantic illusion, I was unable to accept the fact that he was no longer the proud, free spirit that I had worshipped.

At the age of twenty-seven, when my marriage ended, I was still trying to sort out this question of love. I left my husband and, since I had not yet learned that life was possible without a man's protection, migrated north to Canada with my two daughters, to join the man who would later become my son's father. We settled in Prince Edward Island, and all its beauty was not enough to soothe my troubled spirit. The isolation began to erode my fragile commitment to a lifestyle I had not consciously chosen. Until that point, I had more or less drifted, taking what came my way without being clear about what I really wanted. My new companion lived according to his wishes, making most of the decisions, living his "back to the land" dream. I went along reluctantly, with a gnawing feeling of discontentment. My daughters travelled back and forth from my side to their father's. After our divorce, my ex-husband and I continued to support each other, as true friends do.

The birth of my tender son brought me only temporary relief. I was able to set aside my needs for a while to satisfy those of this little growing person, but the reality of my situation was too powerful to ignore. I felt trapped and dependent on my son's father, and my world seemed hopelessly barren of choices. There was no one to whom I could turn for support. In addition, my alien status was frequently magnified by the innocent remarks of curious, well-meaning islanders: "So ... are you one of them there boat people?" "I just want you to know that we don't mind you people here."

In isolation, books and dreams became my guides, providing me with clues which I learned to decipher by carefully piecing together the images that emerged. One of the most generous dream came to me when I felt almost completely petrified by fear:

*While looking for Carl Jung, I walk into a room full of television sets. There are hundreds of screens, each with the same image: a person's leg, wearing brightly woven boots, keeping time to a beating drum. As I get closer to the screens, the drum begins to resonate within my body like a heartbeat. "Pueblo ... they are Pueblo Indians," I say to myself. The images become enlarged and I am now in the desert, surrounded by red sand and clay, watching men, women and children in ceremonial dresses. They are dancing to the beat of the drum, walking towards each other, forming a circle. Their faces are raised towards the brilliant blue sky, as if searching for something. The sound of the drum becomes more intense. Suddenly a very small figure appears in the sky. As it gets closer, I realize that it is an eagle carrying a live white pony in its talons. The eagle gently descends into the circle of dancers, deposits the spirited pony in the centre and slowly returns to the sky. I am astonished and deeply moved. I say to myself "The people made this happen. But how? How did they do it?" With this question I begin to wake up. When I open my eyes the answer comes, perfectly audible, as if spoken by someone: "Faith."*

Though I had given birth three times, I had never recognized my natural power to perform miracles. I had no faith in myself. This dream was an invitation to be part of the individual and collective faith that would empower me to be in the world. The splendid gift of the dream gave me the strength and confidence to walk through my fears. Struggling with feelings of guilt for once more failing to provide my children with a stable family environment, I left my son's father to start a new life. In a matter of days, I moved to the nearest city, applied for welfare and student loans, found a daycare for my son and enrolled in university. My youngest daughter joined me while the older went to live with her father. I trusted that at some future date, when my children got over their grief and confusion, they would accept my efforts to live with courage as my best apology.

My new beginning was all the more significant in that I was the first woman in my family, of my generation, who left a man without going to another, and the first one to hold a university degree. But the progress was slow. Centuries of colonization had sown their seeds within me, making each steps towards autonomy excruciatingly painful. My determination wavered when I was haunted by financial problems or by doubts about the wisdom of the choices I had made. I feared I would lose the "wonderful earthiness" that was supposed to be such a pleasant part of my character. The most sombre of moods plagued me when I questioned the effect that my lifestyle, full of exams, term papers and other deadlines, might have on my children. I had been taught that only power-hungry women chose this way of life, after going against their natural maternal roles and sacrificing their families on the altar of ambition. All these doubts and fears, as well as the genuine pleasure I derived from being with my children, often inspired me to declare a "mental health day" for all, so we could skip our various schools and relax in each others' company.

Our next move from Prince Edward Island to the port city of Halifax, Nova Scotia, brought my children and me into contact with other misfits from my homeland. Happy to find each other, we turned our gatherings into celebrations with abundant food, music, anecdotes and political discussions. A strong Latin America solidarity network in Halifax supported our efforts to create awareness of the social and political situation in our country. Through this network, we were able to receive detailed news about events taking place in Central and South America, as well as in other parts of the world.

Seventeen years after the military takeover, Chileans regained their voices when elections were held. Their resounding NO to the continuation of military dictatorship was loud and clear. By that time, I had finished my studies and was looking for ways to return home. My greatest dream was to share with the women of my homeland the skills to alleviate the suffering of sexual abuse survivors. I had acquired these skills as a reward for the battles I fought with the menacing shadows of my past, alongside Canadian women who courageously exposed the global outrage of child sexual abuse. I was keenly aware that in my homeland child sexual abuse was still a well-kept secret.

After receiving a work grant, I returned to Chile for eighteen months. Although much had changed, I again found myself mirrored in the culture of my homeland. When I saw my reflection in others of similar shape and skin colour, I felt a rekindling of the life force and a heightened sensitivity such that love seemed more tender, laughter more humorous, suffering more tragic. A powerful sense of belonging surfaced the moment I stepped onto Chilean soil, and kept me walking a fine line between reality and romanticism.

During the first months, I explored the streets thinking of the horrors my people had lived through. After recovering from the initial shock of being met with submachine guns on nearly every corner, I gazed at the uniformed men who held them, their index finger resting lightly on the triggers. I wondered if the ruthless power they had been granted had effectively concealed their feelings of emptiness and fear. I looked at the clumsy efforts to hide the bullet holes around the rebuilt presidential palace. I attended events at the stadium where so many people had been detained, tortured and killed. In the eyes of bus drivers, street vendors and pedestrians I searched for clues of what they had learned to silence during those long, dark years.

On a cold winter morning at the city market, I admired the courage of an old woman who challenged two inquiring policemen to arrest her for selling fresh coriander without a licence. While cheering with the other sellers when the officers quietly walked away, I was acutely aware of having enough money in my pocket to pay for the licence this woman could not afford to buy. Similar feelings of guilt and admiration surfaced daily as I witnessed the ingenious survival efforts generated by the inhabitants of a country that had recently been declared "the Jaguar of Latin America" because of its "economic miracle." With high-rise buildings and shopping malls appearing overnight like mushrooms, a perpetual cloud of smog suspended over Santiago was perhaps the best indicator of the abundant foreign wealth that made the "miracle" possible. But the was not thick enough to hide the growing number of indigents and the widening gap between rich and poor.

Silently fearing that I might never see my aging mother again, I left Chile after eighteen months of savouring and engraving in my heart each precious moment. My teenage son, who had joined me half-way through the project, began to proudly acknowledged his Latin American ancestry. My work had been successful, largely due to the fact that people were open and ready to talk about sexual abuse in ways that I had not predicted. Although I was encouraged to stay since there was much work to be done, I felt the pull of my northern roots and needed to be with my children and grandchildren.

The return to Canada was not as shocking as I had feared, although it took a conscious effort to make the transition between both cultures. Perhaps part of me has accepted the inevitable exile, after thirty five years of living in the north. But I am still divided and still struggle with homesickness. I know I am not unique in this human sentiment. It may well be that the land in which my identity was forged, the ground that was my cradle, will always occupy a larger part of my heart. I am reminded of this when I look at my image in the mirror, when I experience racism, when in times of trouble I seek comfort from memories of Andean landscapes.

One of the few times, probably the last one, that my brothers and I had the pleasure of being together, we discovered that we had very different perception of the past. Most of their childhood memories evoked pleasant images, whereas mine were tinted by melancholy. Though we had a good laugh at the differences, I was secretly convinced that life had handed me a less than fair deal just because I was born female. But that was when I had not yet discovered the strength and solidarity of women, before I perceived the loneliness of men who still do not know how to nurture each other.

For a while, I also attributed the sadness of my childhood memories to my given name, meaning "solitude," which I often thought was a curse. Though solitude has become a good companion, she is not always a welcome guest among Chileans, who seek human contact as frequently as they seek food. For Chileans, nothing can compare with the company of human friends, which is probably the reason why the word "pet" does not exist in our vocabulary. The closest word is *mascota* (mascot). A dog, for example, is an animal that stands by the side of law enforcers, as an enemy of the people, or who roams the streets with others of its kind, searching for food. Rarely does one belong to a family that can afford the luxury of feeding it. Most other animals are simply meals you enjoy in good company, with plenty of wine.

I have often wondered what would have become of me if I had not left my family and my homeland. Women of my generation and social class, brought up among impoverished intellectuals, had even less chance of becoming independent than women born to economic poverty. In our family, our public image, based mostly on past grandeurs, was all we had. It was a woman's sacred job to safeguard this image. My mother, whose dream was to be a writer, surrendered to the call of the muses and failed in her task. After leaving our home for the love of a poet who had as many wives as he had children, she spent the rest of her youth trying to find her voice through him. The brutal judgement and righteous indignation that flared up whenever my mother's name was mentioned from the day she left affected me so deeply, it took me years to understand what she had gone through. Abandoned by her family and cut off from all the sustenance she needed to survive when the world became a reality, she got stuck in mid-labour. Her dreams became mirages. In the last phase of her journey, the one I am now entering, she turned to Jehovah in search of forgiveness for all the times she believed to have let others down. Judging by her devotion to this foreign god, he may prove to be much more compassionate than her family ever was.

There is an Irish proverb that says our ancestors are like potatoes because our better half is underground. For me, this wonderful saying captures the absurdity of taking pride in the accomplishments of ghosts whose achievements permeate our lives from an early age. During my childhood, I never experienced the pride I was expected to feel as the nameless granddaughter of a famous man. And now that my past exists only in the form of images and memories, I can gladly say that my better half is not underground but thriving exposed to all the elements, in the form of my children and grandchildren.

The closer I get to the end of my life, the more I want to live in the present. My identity as a reproductive being, as a childbearer, is slowly disappearing. A great sense of loss haunts me when I remember how fully I enjoyed maternity and the cycles of my body. I am having to forge a new identity as a crone, but if I summon my family spirits for guidance I cannot recall hearing anything positive about growing old. When I asked my mother what menopause was like for her, she answered that she had simply stopped bleeding. No more to it. But I know that she faced this stage alone, without support, and that she endured it stoically, as she had done most things in her life. People of our culture believe menopause is one of those taboo subjects that women should keep to themselves, especially since it represents a step towards old age. Youth worship, which is now being chiselled even more deeply into the Chilean psyche through a North American cultural invasion, was not always part of our values. However, reverence for old age disappeared centuries ago, when the Spanish, with substantial support from the Catholic church, infected the inhabitants of our land with their fear of death.

Perhaps it is right that I should look beyond my culture as I forge a new identity, since old age is an experience we all face, if we live long enough. I hope to share with my children the pleasure of growing old. I want them to know that the spirit expands, becoming infinite, as our material body contracts. That is what my people failed to teach me.

In celebration of the rich life I have lived, I want to become a robust maple tree with audacious autumn foliage, to unburden myself by infusing each falling leaf with memories of the past and thoughts of the future, as I have done in these written pages. My deepest wish is that my last day will find me with nothing but small raindrops, shimmering with sunlight, hanging from each branch, surrounded by old trees and young saplings. When this wish prevails, nostalgia fades away, erasing all boundaries. There is no here, no there, and no homeland to which I must return.

# MARTHA KENISTON LAURENCE

# A THREE-PART COLLISION

## ORGANIZATIONS AND ME

*M*y personal awareness of the destructiveness, for women, of patriarchal organizations began with my appointment to a small, rural, conservative university in Ontario, Canada, in the mid-1980s. The university was applying to the provincial accrediting body for approval of a doctoral programme in social work; it was to be the university's first doctoral programme. Approval was deferred pending the appointment, at a senior level, of a clinician with a research and publication record in the field of aging, since a field of concentration in aging was to be part of the programme. The university favoured the hiring of a woman, because the faculty was extremely short of females. I was recruited. I had never heard of the place, but they made me a very good offer. I was intrigued and figured that I had little to lose, and that it would be an adventure. Naïve enough to believe that the day I needed tenure to keep a job, I had bigger trouble than merely keeping a job, I gave up a tenured associate professorship in medicine at another university.

For fifteen years I had been working in hospitals and long-term care facilities, teaching in a faculty of medicine, and practising and consulting as a clinician and organization development consultant. I was aware of sexist and power dynamics, and viewed myself as a feminist change agent, but it wasn't until I reached my new university that I was confronted in such a way that I had to take direct action. My survival and sanity were at stake. In reflection, I liken my journey to a series of unplanned collisions on three levels: the political — my work for change as an activist; the intellectual — coming to terms with the myths of female equality in light of reality; and the emotional — dealing with some of my personal demons through my own therapy.

## Collision Number I: Political

Three weeks into the fall teaching term of 1989, I got a call from a woman colleague asking me if I had seen the display in the university dining hall. Posted around the walls were the spoils of the previous night's panty raid — an assortment of women's underwear mounted on sheets of newsprint, some adorned with things like ketchup to simulate menstrual blood and feces, and accompanied by commentary and epithets pronouncing someone a whore, someone else too fat, asking if someone took Visa. The vision and tone were assaultive, misogynist, demeaning to women, creating a hostile environment in which to work and eat. A group of us women faculty had lunch and discussed calling the local newspaper, but I asked to make one call to the senior administrators first. There was no one available to speak with me until I said that there was a display in the dining hall and that we would call the local press if it was not removed within the hour. The response from the surprised administrator: if the display was as I described it, it would be down within the hour; otherwise a call to the media would not be out of order. Reportedly, by the time the administrator arrived, a group of offended students had torn down much of the display, and university staff disposed of it.

It emerged over the next few hours that the panty raid had been an administratively sanctioned and orchestrated orientation activity, "good clean fun" to help the boys and girls get with the programme of undergraduate life. (The next day's display, of men's underwear — including the slogan "Larry is a fag" — was vetted for improprieties and presumed to pass muster as more good clean fun.)

About eleven A.M. I got a frantic phone call from the students who had begun to dismantle that morning's display; they had been threatened with charges of destruction of university property if they did not leave the dining hall. By now the student population was at war, some outraged by the panty raids and others defending them. The administration and student leadership were firmly lined up in support of the raids. I collared the president, and he struck a committee to look into the matter.

Over the next month those of us opposed to the panty raids met and organized to address different aspects of the problem by forming an education committee, an orientation committee, and a political action committee. Some male faculty and staff formed a Men against Violence against Women group. A colleague and I called an initial meeting and booked a room for thirty, but the issue had struck a nerve; we had to move to accommodate at least one hundred and thirty. On the other side of the issue were undergraduate participants, residence dons, student services administrators, staff of all ranks, student government and some faculty.

Meanwhile, the president's panty raid committee had become six (four men, two women) and had met sporadically, holding "hearings." I was the first called to a hearing. I took a large male colleague with me, so that I would have a witness. I was assaulted verbally in loud, angry tones for two long hours. The committee's position was that I had sanctioned the wanton destruction of university property; would I sanction the destruction of works at the Art Gallery of Ontario by someone who took offence at a painting? I sent an outraged memo to the chair, protesting that no one should be treated as I had been. The committee's work was, however, to pick up pace.

A month later the campus was still seething. Those opposing the raids reported continuing threats of assault, and taunts that they would be shown "what a good man could do for them." Food fights were a regular feature of mealtimes, and name-calling (dykes, bitches, fags, etc.) was rampant. The students, especially, were exhibiting all the signs and symptoms of harassment: they were scared; they couldn't sleep (thanks partly to routine pounding on their doors throughout the night); they were discouraged and depressed. Some said they were unable to study, to do their work or go to classes, and some even talked of dropping out of university. Yet, it was becoming apparent that there would be no change in the orientation activities. Only the location would be different; in future, panty-raiders would mount their displays in the residence common rooms.

After a month of these Campus Gender Wars, I asked the other anti-raiders if they wanted to break silence and approach the press. They said they did. Initial calls to the *Globe and Mail* indicated that the paper was not really interested, but a small, sanitized piece appeared on a back page of a late Saturday edition. Given this lukewarm response, I contacted Michele Landsberg, a feminist columnist with the *Toronto Star*, who met with a number of the students. She listened, and affirmed them in their umbrage. Her column ended up as a major news story on the front page of the next Wednesday's *Star*. In the following wake of public embarrassment, the university administration made a public statement that orientation activities would be re-evaluated and panty raids would no longer be tolerated.

There were costs to breaking the silence, however. The rage against those who had spoken out continued unabated. The student association gathered signatures and petitions and trooped to the offices of the *Toronto Star*, demanding to be represented in a more favourable light. The original fury about "being censored" turned into outrage about airing dirty linen in public. Nothing in my life had prepared me for the fury on campus about the public exposure of the panty raids, and the resulting castigation in national and local editorials and news reports.

Meanwhile, the rancour shifted more specifically to me. A master's student whose research I had supervised was awarded the university's gold medal at the fall convocation, which was held in the week when the Star's panty-raid article appeared. She named me during an interview for a university press release and was told that my name was not to be mentioned — on orders from above. Even if she was interviewed by outside press, she was not to use my name. In the end, there was no press release; a student's day in the sun was cancelled because of her association with me. In addition to being boycotted, I was openly threatened with everything from a thousand undergraduates marching on my office, to hate-filled and abusive phone calls, to admonishments not to be alone on campus or within reach at night or I would be "taught a lesson." I was derided by some faculty members, and diatribes appeared in the student newspapers against me, Michele Landsberg and others seen as spoilers of good clean fun.

But the sexist, misogynist attitudes on campus were not limited to orientation activities; they shaped student response to more violent, even criminal, acts. A student leader reported, with pride, how well the administration had dealt with a recent rape on campus: the young woman had been sent for counselling service, and the young man had been barred from further orientation events and told not to drink. Why were charges not laid? Well, they didn't want to jeopardize the future career of a young man, did they? This was presented as a great advance over the old way of handling such incidents: the woman would have been held responsible for drinking too much, and for encouraging the young man's amorous attentions, which she had obviously let get out of hand.

On the afternoon of December 6, 1989, I was on the telephone with an organizer for a national radio show where sexist activities had found a receptive audience. Would I go on the programme for a discussion of the Campus Gender Wars, with two women from other universities? I said that I did not yet feel safe enough on my own campus to say anything publicly. In fact, I had declined all media overtures. Perhaps, after the December break, things would have settled down; perhaps I would feel safe then.

Was I exaggerating the real threat associated with all this misogynistic talk? Two hours later, an embittered man shot and killed fourteen women at a university in Montreal. Because they were women. Because they were studying to become engineers.

When I walked into the faculty lounge in the days following the Montreal Massacre, I was acutely aware of the sudden descent of silence. Once, I overheard a senior male professor expressing empathy with the killer, stating that he had felt like doing "exactly that" around this place over the past couple of months. Yet I had only sought equity and respect for women students. I had only sought what the university itself professed to seek. I couldn't understand the hate.

## COLLISION NUMBER II: INTELLECTUAL

Since I had been hired because of the new doctoral programme, I initially assumed that I would be involved in its start-up. It took me at least three years to grasp the reality: now that provincial approval had been granted, the boys whose names were on the proposal didn't want me anywhere near it. I couldn't understand the nastiness, the dismissals and put-downs, the denigration of my own degree and training as obviously inferior, the way I was deliberately excluded from much of the decision-making.

When I came up for tenure early in my third year I was shocked and hurt by the vicious anonymous collegial "reviews" against which I had to defend myself. Since there were insufficient grounds to turn me down on the basis of scholarship, teaching and service, objections were raised to such personal sins as "walking too fast through the halls" and "not fitting in."

Once my tenure was passed, I spearheaded a revamping of the procedures, implementing accountability, if not to the candidate directly, then to the colleagues, and a focus on performance and output rather than mere compatibility. Shortly after the revised tenure procedures were trialed in the department, the faculty as a whole became a certified bargaining unit, and improved procedures were enshrined in a collective agreement. Given the conservatism of this little university, I think the act of certification was a dramatic political departure for most of the faculty; it suggested that the abuses of power were not in my imagination.

I did my first stint on the university-level tenure and promotions committee in the first year of that collective agreement. Although I was aware of the group's struggle with the new procedures, the proceedings confused me. It seemed to me that the same criteria were being applied differently to different candidates. Questions asked in some cases were not asked in others, for no apparent reason.

There was a telltale impasse at the first meeting for senate-level tenure and promotion considerations, when the chairperson asked who would take the minutes. The male colleague next to me said that he wasn't taking them and turned to me — the only woman — and said, "I doubt you are going to take them either." I responded that I had taken more minutes in my life than I cared to remember and I thought it was someone else's turn. Silence reigned briefly, until a dean looked at me angrily and shouted, "Oh for God's sake, TAKE the minutes!" I wasn't quick enough to come back with an appropriate response, but my silence indicated that I would not be bullied. The chair extracted reluctant acquiescence from one of the other faculty, but an administrative secretary — female — was brought to subsequent meetings.

By the time I went on sabbatical in 1991, I was depressed and burned out. The sabbatical provided me with time to reflect on my experience in this organization, to step back and create some distance — emotionally, intellectually and physically — in order to understand the cultural dynamics of the university, to analyze the exchanges between men and women as if from the outside. It was during this fifteen-month period that I came face to face with my own myths, wants and beliefs, my fantasies about equity for women, and compared these to my personal experience with gender politics, and my work as a change agent. In this time I came to know — in my gut, not just in my head — that many men and women would never view some things as I did, and that energy spent trying to educate them was energy wasted. Perhaps most significantly, I had to realize that male identity had been predicated, at its fundamental core, on the premise that men are superior to women, period. No level of brilliance and productivity could counter the early socialization and training that remained at the psychic core of these men. No matter what I did, or what I was, most of the men I worked with would never relate to me as an equal. Intellectually this fact was understandable; emotionally it was hell.

Like many women growing up in the 1950s, entering university in the early 1960s, I had believed that if I got the right credentials and demonstrated my professional mettle, any world of professional practice would be open to me. Over time, though, I had noticed that definitions of performance changed depending on whether the person under discussion was a man or a woman, and was someone who conformed to the status quo or challenged the way things were done. It was a long time before I realized that my very acceptance into the club meant upholding the traditional rules and definitions, which in turn meant maintaining the dance in which women pander to the egos of men.

Of course, I too am a product of my socialization and experience, which taught me that I was not as valuable as a man, and this has affected how I have dealt with my male colleagues. For example, much as I aim to participate as a full and equal member in deliberations, I still struggle with the early training that taught me to worry about offending male egos. I was also affected negatively by the assumption of female inferiority. One of my larger hurdles has been to learn not to berate myself for not seeing sooner that which in hindsight seems so obvious.

As a result of the reflecting I did during my sabbatical, the focus of my work became clearer: my superordinate goal became working for improved opportunities and experiences for women and minorities. This clearer focus provided me with a frame of reference within which to make decisions about how I would work, where I would work and when. Perhaps the greatest clarity I achieved was with regard to the realities in which the work would be done. Applying my knowledge of field theory — the theoretical lens I have used throughout my career of working for change in the care of the elderly — I realized that resistance to change is a normal, logical and predictable human response. Understanding this, I decided to work professionally with women in circumstances similar to my own.

## COLLISION NUMBER III: EMOTIONAL

Theory and experience have taught me that the emotional, intellectual and behavioural parts of the self are inextricably linked to one another. Inattention to one area, in deference to the others, only serves to confound and cloud understanding. I knew that ignoring my fears only served to strengthen them. Also, I believe that as a clinician, I cannot take a client further than I have been in my own work. Therefore, it seemed imperative that I examine my emotional life. At different stages I have used therapy as one way to deal with struggles, to learn to move beyond them. It was time, now, to confront another demon.

The particular demon that challenged me when I arrived at this university was my fear of bullies. I had never been reticent to acknowledge this fear but, try as I might, I could not will a way to overcome it. Fighting and conflict have always scared me and I avoid them if I can. Bullies, particularly because they often strike without warning, scare me into immobilization.

I was confronted almost immediately after my arrival by a colleague who scared me. He was verbally confrontational, hostile, assaultive. He was also big and had a menacing look that frightened me. I came to think of him as a "hit-and-run" artist: he would come up to me in the hall, charge me with some misdeed in strong and angry tones, then peel off down the next corridor, leaving me tripping over my tongue with explanatory gibberish. When I was in my office, I found myself checking to make sure he wasn't in his office or the halls so I could relax. Occasionally my office door would fly open and he would stand over me, accusing me of some transgression, shaking his fist or finger, while I sat speechless at my desk.

These collisions were undermining me, and I felt I was living in a constant state of alert. It seemed like a good time to make use of therapy. I also hoped that therapy would help me deal with the craziness of working in this organization, and with earlier pain. I decided to set out on a therapeutic search through my body, on the premise that we store our pain in our bodies. I found a cranio-sacral massage therapist and psychotherapist who worked with me over a two-year period; it was probably the most effective therapy I have ever done. Then, with my new resolve and my fortified self, I brought my understanding of how to change behaviour to my management of the ranting bully.

I worked out what I would like to say the next time the bully assaulted me in the hall or charged into my office. I wrote it out. I practised it at home until I was ready. The next time he attacked me in the hall, I answered: "If you want to talk to me, make an appointment and come see me in my office; but don't assault me in the hall!" Response: an amazed look. Then he charged into the office of another woman and I heard him yell, "That G—d— bitch!" as he slammed her door shut. The next time he burst into my office, I stood up, interrupted him and said in equally loud tones, "Get out; if you want to talk to me you will make an appointment and we will have a third person present, since I will not meet with you alone." Response: he recovered from his surprise and launched into his tirade again. It took about three runs before my "Get the f— out of my office!" seemed to register. He hurled himself out, slamming the door on his way. I heard him barge into the office of the colleague next door and slam his door, amid oaths reflecting on the general undesirability of my character. But he's been more careful around me since then. More important, I don't live in fear of him, or of most ranting bullies, any more.

The therapeutic principle I applied in this example was, of course, "focus on the process rather than the content of the charge." This required interrupting and stopping an unhealthy exchange from which I could only emerge defeated and power-less. It is difficult, at the moment of peak emotional encounter, to remember that behind every bully there is a scared person. I find this even more difficult to remember as my experience of bullies has progressed from ranting ones to those who are much more skilled and subtle: the porcelain bullies. Translucent and smooth, though vulnerable to shattering, the porcelain bully is usually a woman, engaging in the only effective bullying that a woman can pull off in an organization. Women who rant and roar are usually dismissed as hysterical, and dropped from the influence ring, so female bullies learn to be more skilled. The porcelain bully intimidates and controls through the adroitly placed thrust of the rapier tongue. This is particularly effective because the argument is coated in tones of reason and logic, while the thrust is aimed right at the solar plexus. Although I am still practising catching this type of bully at the moment of strike, my overall comfort with bullies is now much greater than it has been for most of my adult life.

## THE NEGOTIATED PASSAGE

My task of navigating my journey and integrating the pieces of my Self — the personal, practical and political — continues on the personal and professional levels all the time. I expect my growth and development to continue till I die. The sense- making that has arisen out of my three collisions has brought me to a place where my work feels the most centred and solidly founded it has ever been, because it is congruent with my core being. Stronger in my own sense of self, and aware of my thoughts, feelings and behaviours, I can better focus on hearing others. I have learned that, while I work for change for women and minorities, it is also important to protect myself so that I don't get attacked for either my ideas or my ways of doing things. Whereas I once just took risks, I now try to take calculated ones. While sorting out my own experiences, I have tried to identify and develop practices and strategies for myself and others. Not only have I come up with new models and guidelines for working towards change; I have also developed a level of comfort with the negotiated passage of working in an organization. And I am learning to have a good life while doing it. It was my own work and the work I did with other women that eventually opened up a direction and means for working towards change that have enabled me not only to survive, but to thrive.

# BARBARA COTTRELL

## *MORE THAN THE*
## *SUM OF THE PARTS*

### STRENGTH IN
### COMMUNITY

*T*wo of my friends, Jeanne and Linda, were
born on the same day. For some years now,
four or five of us have thrown an annual birthday
dinner for them: a cozy, slightly extravagant affair
with good food and wine and the fun of opening
presents. Every year the wrapping paper and ribbons are more and more adventurous and beautiful
as we do clever things with handmade purple-
swirled paper, or newspaper, or brown paper and
string. It's always exciting to watch, to see which
one of us managed to be creative this year. For in
truth, most of us will settle at the last moment for a
nice bottle of wine, or some pretty, smelly candles
wrapped in something ordinary. But every year one
of us really does well, and every year it's a different
person. I remember the year Jackie found a gorgeous green silky jacket for Linda. It was the most

un-Linda piece of clothing we'd ever seen: lush, elegant, even flashy. Linda, who wears without exception navy blue or beige, giggled with embarrassment. We all shrieked with laughter and demanded she try it on right there and then. What a transformation! Linda beamed, looked lovely and even held her shoulders differently; and she chided us that we weren't to get her used to expensive clothes she couldn't afford. Jackie protested that it had cost a pittance in a seventy-five percent off sale. We all coveted the jacket for ourselves, and wished we'd been clever enough to find it for Linda.

This is our community of friends. We cherish each other, celebrate each other and encourage each other to grow and expand. Today it is a privilege to have a job and a decent income, and we are all lucky enough to be employed in work we love. But our work is bleak: most of us are social workers and community workers of one sort or another, and if we don't see poverty and violence every day of our lives, we're reading about it, thinking about it. We get together to replenish our stock of positive energy. We provide each other with lush green jackets and, more important, the courage to wear them. We strengthen our egos by nurturing each other. It's family, without the family-of-origin baggage we all carry. We have our tensions and difficulties, but we try to resolve them positively, with minimal damage. At the same time that we are transforming ourselves, ever evolving, refreshed, stronger, we come together with a shared political agenda, believing that together we can challenge society in ways we are unable to do as individuals. When we put our heads together, our collective wisdom is vast; when we yell in unison, our collective voice is strong. We spark off each other's ideas, and our understanding deepens, our creativity outstrips our individual potential.

This year, Jeanne and Linda turned fifty. We asked them how they wanted to celebrate and gave them some options: a big crush of a party at one of our houses, a smaller party of more intimate friends, a dinner with, perhaps, a few more people than the usual birthday dinners, or something totally unusual — perhaps bowling followed by a few beers in a pub? It's significant that we asked them to choose. The nice thing about being part of a nurturing community is knowing that you can choose for yourself, and you don't have to fear criticism for the choice. I used to think parties had to be thrown by others as a surprise, and that if this didn't happen it meant no one cared. I dreaded any significant birthday coming up because I assumed it would be a disaster: either no one would pay attention and I'd feel unloved or, worse, my friends would throw me a surprise party. For me, there are few supposed-to-be-exciting things in life worse than a surprise party. Walking into a room and being met by a huge crowd of people focusing on me, when I've been expecting a casual evening with a pal, is a nightmare.

For me the right community is one that encourages me to choose and then respects my choice, one that allows me to be in control, holds me in safety so I can stretch beyond the everyday place where I am comfortable, and bears witness to my growth. Now, at fifty, I know that in my community I can make those choices and have that control. If I want a party, I can choose to have one — I can throw it myself, or I can ask my friends to do it — and if I don't want one, I don't have to have one. I sigh when I think how many parties I have attended for no other reason than because I thought I'd be counted out if I didn't. And then I remember my epiphany years ago: I don't enjoy most parties and I don't have to go to them. If not spending hours in a crush of bodies, trying to think of something to say, is going to mean I'm out of the loop — so be it. If that's my community, I'm in the wrong one.

For in truth, within the limits of our lives, we choose our community — or rather, communities, since each of us belongs to a number. When we asked Linda and Jeanne how they wanted to celebrate their fiftieth birthdays, they decided that they wanted us to bring together people from the different communities they belong to. The birthday fell on a Sunday, and the available and affordable place was a church hall. We made poster invitations on shocking pink paper with creatures holding placards bearing slogans such as *Happy Birthday Linda and Jeanne*, and

*Flash: Fifty and Hot!* These were handed out at Jeanne and Linda's usual haunts: the Anti-Poverty Organization, the Metro Coalition for a Non-Racist Society, the Committee against Woman Abuse. We asked people to bring gifts of food or drink to share, if they could.

We loaded up with extra bottles of pop, wine and juice, with bags of chips and boxes of crackers, just in case people didn't bring enough. But this is Nova Scotia, and people arrived loaded with food and goodies. Young people and old crowded into the hall to celebrate together. Linda's and Jeanne's mothers sent flowers, and were there in spirit as speaker after speaker toasted and roasted their friends and co-workers. In her thank-you speech, Jeanne said, "This is what I want in my life: community. I want the people I work with and for, the people who share my struggle against poverty, to come together and share the milestones, the significant moments of my life." That day, we felt we belonged to a community of communities.

I realize that not all communities are available to us. Sometimes we don't have the money necessary to join certain communities, or to travel to them. Sometimes membership is denied because of who we are, or aren't. Years ago a group of lesbians in Nova Scotia organized a conference — a weekend where lesbians could be together in community. One of my friends agonized for weeks over whether she could ethically ask to attend. Sarah had called herself lesbian for over fifteen years, since she and her husband had separated, and she had lived in the company of women and loved women. But she had never had a sexual relationship with a woman. I talked it over with friends who were organizing the weekend and I knew they had no reservations about welcoming Sarah, but Sarah herself felt awkward and wasn't sure she could shake the feeling of not belonging. In the end she did go to the conference, and she had a wonderful experience. It confirmed for her that this was indeed one of her communities.

For ten years I had the privilege of belonging to a particular rural community. I lived in a very small fishing village on a rugged, windswept peninsula that juts out into the Atlantic Ocean. Built on granite bedrock, with few trees to protect it from the weather, it is at the end of a road: traffic can go no farther than around the two arms that hug the bay in a Y shape. More than one family has moved out, sometimes less than five kilometres away, to escape the incessant wind. There are twenty-four small wood-frame houses in the village, all built by their owners and occupants. The only other buildings are the fishermen's "stores" on the wharves, housing fishing gear and salt fish. There is no school or firehall, no church or community centre. The population has hovered around one hundred for a number of generations, with the same families living there for many decades. Mostly, it's the men who are born in the village and the women who move in to marry them. Over the past twenty-five years some people native to the area have moved out, and newcomers have moved in and been welcomed as part of the community, but most of the villagers are from local fishing families. As fishing has never been lucrative in this area, most of them were born into poverty. Although there are few fishers left, many families continue to struggle on household incomes well below the poverty line.

The lives of the villagers are strictly gender-segregated: women's work is inside, men's work is outside. This means that the women work, for the most part, in their homes. The women paint the inside walls of the house, the men the outside. The men drink and drive around together, hunt and fish together, and sometimes sit in their cars on the government wharf talking together. The women take sole responsibility for keeping their houses spotless and preparing meals. There are few opportunities for them to socialize; there are no support groups, clubs or organizations in the area, there is no Women's Institute or Lioness Club. Apart from the elementary school and firehall in the next village, there are no volunteer opportunities either. The women volunteer at the school only if their children are attending there, and no woman from this community has ever volunteered at the firehall.

Probably the most important skill these women possess is the skill of making do. Somehow, with never sufficient money and with meagre resources, they are able to manage their households. For some, this includes managing the support side of the fishing enterprise: handling finances and taxes, ordering and receiving supplies and making endless phone calls about everything from boat parts to bait.

At first glance you might think the village was a tight-knit community, and in many ways it is. But despite being so physically close, and interrelated, the women live in isolation. They sometimes speak to each other on the phone, but visits are only occasional. I've heard women remark that they haven't seen anyone, other than their husband and children, in days. Every other week or so the women get together to play cards — Bertha is their favourite game — but that too is sporadic.

In the ten years I lived in this village, it became one of my most important communities. I loved the visits I shared with the women, and deeply admired their ability to cope with limited resources and constant stress. In this community, choice is a rare commodity. One day I received a form letter from the Atlantic Health Unit inviting applications for a Community Development Grant. Knowing that this community could certainly use the five thousand dollars being offered, I asked my friend Dolly Blackburn and two or three other women whether they would be interested in applying. I figured that we could think of something to do connected with women's health needs. They all said that they didn't understand what it was about, but were interested.

We called a meeting of the women we happened to see in the following few days, and ten of us gathered to discuss the idea. All the women were enthusiastic about doing a project together, but they were shy and insisted that they had no idea what it might look like. I suggested that we do "kitchen talk" research to find out what our health needs were, then analyze the results of these interviews and take appropriate action. When I explained that the action might take the form of workshops, one woman said, "Barbara, you may want to explain what you mean by that." I talked about inviting a speaker in to help us explore different topics, and the women laughed. A "workshop" to them was the shed behind the house where the men kept their tools and drank together!

In time we received the health grant and proceeded as planned, and during our work on the project we all learned a lot about community. We began by inviting two women I knew by reputation, Georgina Chambers and Anne Bulley, to come to the village and conduct a workshop on identifying women's health needs. Over and over, the women identified lack of money and too much stress as creating dis-ease. The day went by very quickly, and everyone enjoyed it so much that we decided to do another workshop the following month, after Christmas. When Georgina and Anne returned, the women's comfort level had risen and a sense of safety was soon established in the room.

That day began with sharing what good and not-so-good things had happened since the last time we had all been together. I thought I knew these women and their lives, but I was not prepared for the pain they shared that day. Christmas, for many of them, had been a time of misery: more money and energy were demanded than they could give, and their own emotional needs had not been met. They talked of no one sitting down to the turkey dinner they had cooked because "Ben doesn't really like turkey" and "David was having a fight with his girlfriend." One woman said all she wanted for the entire holiday was to see her two-year-old granddaughter open her gifts, but no one in the family would drive her and she didn't have her own car. Others talked of spending the day alone because their husbands had gone drinking and come home only to sleep it off. We also talked of their childhood Christmases, which had often been filled with abuse and pain.

The talking made us feel close, at least initially. What we hadn't paid enough attention to, however, was the fact that although the women lived in relative isolation and rarely had the opportunity to share their experiences like this, they were also closely related. The husbands they were talking about were the other women's brothers and sons. We had created a sense of safety where, in fact, none existed. Some of the women who shared painful secrets that day never returned to the group.

Fortunately, many women did return, and they were soon doing telephone and kitchen-talk interviews. My heart still warms as I recall the beam on Carolyn's face when she said, "I always thought you had to have a college degree or something to do this kind of stuff." Skills learned, confidence built, pride in ourselves: the project brimmed with positive outcomes. Carolyn grew confident enough to apply for a job as teacher's aide at the school. She got the job, and talks now about the difference that having a little independence has made in her relationship with her husband and family.

At the end of the project the funding agency wanted a final report. Still not comfortable with the written word, the women now had enough confidence to state their preference; they chose to make a video report. I show that short video often, especially when I am conducting workshops on new ways to do community development and community-based research. This community experience is having an impact on people outside the community, too.

Seven years after we first began the health project, the women are still meeting. Their second project was on literacy, and it left them with a shared computer and a love of the Internet; they are now a member of the province-wide Nova Scotia Women's Fish-Net and are planning to get together with women from other coastal communities. Today they are working on their third grant proposal. There are still many things for them to learn and practise about community: correcting the tendency to think negatively of each other, and to drop out as soon as there are difficulties, for example. Although we are living in a time when coastal communities are in crisis, these women are thriving together in a way none of us thought possible a few years ago.

Community is never all rosy; we all have our fears and anxieties, and our bad days when we are at less than our best. But if there's trust and safety in our communities, we can talk about our problems. At the fiftieth birthday party, when Jackie gave her public address to Jeanne, she said, "Jeanne is so kind; she didn't indulge in gossip. Notice the past tense. I am proud to tell you that I was the person who taught Jeanne how to gossip. I want you all to know there's probably not one of you we haven't stuck our heads together and nattered about. It's not that we don't love you and respect you all; we do." It is a normal, everyday occurrence for people to annoy each other. When we're fed up with each other, we need to find a safe place to dump our feelings; we need a friend who will listen so that we can vent our anger in a healthy way; and we need to acknowledge that that is what we are doing. We have to trust that our friends will help us deal with our concerns and move on, so we can all live and work in community.

In the same way, we must sometimes grieve for communities we have lost, and then move on. One of my friends lost her place in a community of black women when she came out to them as a lesbian. She suffered and grieved for her old friends, then accepted the loss. She said, "I'm often the woman who needs the others not to be so much in community that they won't break from the pack. They don't have the courage to stand up against the 'party line' with a different point of view. They can't risk losing their place. Sometimes I can only belong as long as I don't act too gay, or too black." Sadly, our communities are often exclusive, and the price of membership may be being not quite honest about ourselves. I find it surprising when women don't identify with those who don't belong. After all, we've been the outsiders of many circles ourselves.

I noticed some time ago that I feel most discouraged when there is unresolved strife in a women's community. It's not that these communities experience any more tension than other communities I'm involved with; it's that my expectations of them are higher. I recently worked on a project with a group of women who represented a number of feminist organizations around the province. The relationship was a disaster. My expectations of sisterhood were so high that when one woman behaved aggressively toward me, I was too shocked to handle the situation. Further, when my sisters did not support me, I was thrown for a loop. The situation went from bad to worse: I ended up paralyzed with fear, and left the project unfinished. In ten years I had not had such a negative, confidence-destroying experience. I'd worked with government bureaucrats and corporate representatives and ended up with more self-respect than when I worked with this group of feminists. Some friends think I am naïve for expecting more of my feminist sisters, for many women have been hurt in their brushes with the feminist community.

One thing that makes it difficult to work in community with our feminist sisters is that we use the term *feminist* as though it means one kind of woman with one kind of outlook. There are as many kinds of feminisms as there are feminists. We range from conservative to liberal to radical, from communist to capitalist to anarchist. Our own views can change from one position to another in the space of a year, sometimes even a day. Too often we assume that others must have a similar analysis to ours, because we are all in the same community.

Problems are also bound to occur in our feminist communities when we fail to support each other because we can't come together in strength. I once experienced this with a group of peer counsellors. The leader of the group was accused by a group member of being inappropriately sexual with a young woman. In twos and threes we discussed possible actions: perhaps we should write a letter to the group leader demanding he resign, or perhaps we should encourage the young woman to lay charges. In the end, we did nothing. Slowly the group disintegrated, as one by one we left. Years later, a few of us happened to be together and we talked about how passively we'd responded to that crisis. One woman suggested that we all wanted so much to belong to that community, for our own needs, that we were unable to act together in a way that probably would have been confrontational and angry, and that likely would have destroyed the group. I expect this is true. We're often afraid that we will lose something precious to us individually, if we confront problems within our communities.

Another reason we experience tension in our feminist communities is that we get confused about our relationships and roles.

In my recent disastrous project, I had been hired to do a job. Unfortunately, I was never clear about who I was in relation to the group. Was I a staff person hired to do their bidding, or a consultant hired to advise and lead? Was I a friend or a professional associate? We often sat and vented about our common foes in the struggle to end violence against women, and at those times I felt solidly part of the group, but other times my role was unclear. I bounced back and forth between feeling safe with these women's respect and caring, and feeling unsafe when I realized I was having difficulties and could find no support. I was caught between being inside the group, looking out, and being outside the group, looking in.

I believe, however, that the biggest problem in feminist communities is a twofold one: we have difficulty talking openly about the problems we have with each other, and we still haven't found ways to nurture and take care of each other when there's strife. We're still developing, still learning these skills. In the sixties we tried to be collective, to work in non-hierarchical ways. We were pioneers, full of visions of utopia and ill-equipped for the slings and arrows that appeared when we tossed out traditional ways and tried new ones. We needed training and experience that were not available to us then. Many women still bear the scars of foundering in those uncharted waters. Some gave up; others persisted and today have found healthy, more equitable ways to work together.

One of my favourite communities is a women's employment counselling service in Nova Scotia where the staff and the board truly work together to support each other and provide good service. This is the most equal, non-hierarchical setting of all the communities I'm connected to. But, most workplaces, even the most feminist of battered women's shelters, still operate hierarchically, with clients at the bottom of the ladder. The staff report to the director, who reports to the board, and power and control increase as you move "upward." Shouldn't the women we serve be at the top of the hierarchy ladder, if such ladders are even necessary? I want every community I'm a member of to be more equal. This year I'm on the board of the local sexual assault centre, and we're working to have staff attend meetings and have input into decision-making. We need to learn to honour each other rather than protect our positions of control over others, and to help each other be empowered so we can all learn and grow.

I remember, as a young woman, setting out for a walk with my sister, who lived in a village in England. Just as we reached her garden gate, she looked down and said, "Oh dear, I forgot to clean my shoes. Don't want people talking about me, do I?" And she ran back into the house to make herself more presentable. That's one sense of community I don't want. Maybe she was exaggerating how critical her community was; maybe her self-consciousness had more to do with our father, who brought us up to believe that you could tell most things about people from their shoes. But it did tell me how uncomfortable my sister felt just being herself in her community.

That's not to say that I always make comfort my goal. In this new era I am learning to deal with the discomfort of accepting challenges. I need to face my assumptions, and learn to see my own racism, classism, homophobia: the oppressive behaviours that exclude people from our communities. We all need to address inequalities within our communities, because those with less privilege will never feel they truly belong as long as there is disparity. If we cocoon ourselves, we will continue to act out the institutionalized cruelty we are often too close to see. If we open our minds and hearts, we can learn to love with practical, useful compassion. We can stop being strangers to those who are not just like us. We can connect.

My need for community may stem partly from feeling like a stranger in my childhood community in England. After my mother died, my father single-parented my sisters and me. He did a wonderful job, all things considered, but we always felt "different." As soon as I could, I applied for a job in Canada, and here I am, newly rooted, and thirty years is "new" for rooting. At a recent dinner we were talking about Canada's heinous treatment of Italian Canadians during the Second World War and someone remarked that not one person around the table had been born in Canada. We had all come from elsewhere, and we all needed to find our communities among people who shared our work and our politics, among those we lived with, those we could connect with.

Perhaps a sense of loneliness is part of the human condition and the best we can do is find a few people in this world we can truly be with. Perhaps the essence of community is the chance to surface out of the long, dark tunnel of aloneness and connect to others. But all communities are not the same. What is the difference between my community and that of my shoe-conscious sister's, years ago, or the religious community that Di Brandt has left? Don't those communities offer a sense of belonging? A "follow the rules and you'll be accepted" kind of belonging? A barn-raising, summer picnic, sharing kind of belonging?

The important difference for me is that I belong only to communities where I feel among equals, where women are not lesser-than, where we treasure each other as individuals, where we try to be positive and not overly critical, and where the state of our shoes and our souls is a cause for concern, at worst — never for condemnation. I want to know that, if I walk in my community in dirty shoes, my friends will assume it is my choice — or perhaps help me clean them — if they notice at all. I want to know that, with the strength of my community, I can stretch and grow, and even soar. I want to believe that, in community, we can transform ourselves and the world.

# DONNA E. SMYTH

# WOMEN FLYING

## THE ESCHATOLOGY OF NATURE

*Eschatology: the traditional science of the "four last things": death, judgement, heaven, hell.*

— *Oxford English Dictionary*

Wings beat the air, whirrr … past my head. Eyes closed, I am standing at the bird feeder at the edge of the woodlot, where field and forest meet — interzone of ecosystems. Where the action is.

The female red-breasted nuthatch (*Sitta candadensis*), urgent with hunger, calls to me to hurry with the seed. Shadows of wings brush my face, new arrivals … chick-a-dee-dee. Cheeky, cheerful balls of feathers fluffed up against the cold.

"Hello," I say, and "How are you?" "I'm coming," I say, slip-sliding even on the cleats clamped to my boots. Season of ice, of falls and broken bones.

If we had wings.

I shrug the backpack off. Unzip, reach for the seed container. Hulls of sunflower seeds are strewn like petals on the snow-covered ice. The nuthatch moves closer ... Hurry! Hurry! How to translate her call? One of my bird books describes it as "yank-yank," another as "ank-ank-ank."

A clumsy approximation of human language. What I know is that she talks to me, I to her, and we understand each other. Sometimes her mate comes too, but usually he keeps his distance, feeding at the suet hung on the other side of the path.

As I fumble with the container lid, my fingers start to go numb with the cold. How do birds survive it? Sometimes at night, when I hear the wind blowing, I imagine them crouched close to the heart of the spruce and balsam fir, swaying, hunched down to conserve heat, held only by those fine lines of legs, the gripping claws. Above them hangs the Big Dipper, part of Ursa Major, whose slow rotation marks the passage of winter through the night sky. And Polaris, the North Star, mysterious and radiant.

In the mornings I step out the door and look to the north. The bird feeder is hidden beyond the donkey pasture and the field where straggly red spruce are claiming territory. In the summer, both pasture and field are alive with music. Cicadas hummm in the late afternoon and the long twilight, as the earth radiates the heat of day, hummm ... throbbing vibrations. Thousands of them praising the light ... or welcoming the warm darkness? The chorus rises from the ground to greet Venus, the Evening Star, just above the dark line of spruce and pine on the horizon.

In the spring it's the peepers (*Hyla crucifer*), the only tree frog found in Nova Scotia. The first evening we hear them it's usually just one or two shrill voices. Listen! We stand transfixed. Listen, it must be spring! Pe-ep! Pe-ep! Over the next few nights, as the weather grows warmer, more and more peepers join in, until an operatic chorus rises from the maples that stand along the gully on the east line of the farm, and from the beeches along the gully on the west. No leaves at this time of year, only small frogs clinging to branches and stems, singing their hearts' desire to the sliver of the new moon.

Listen, we say, listen! The land is waking up, there is new life here! Persephone is rising from the underworld, feeling her way with her green fingertips. Pussy willows, catkins, alder leaves like cat tongues. Ice crystals of winter collapsing into mud.

Take a deep breath and it will all begin again. We shall plunge headlong into summer, rolling with the sun through the universe. On my hands and knees I sing praises as I thrust seeds into the ground.

But now I am shaking seeds into the tray for the nuthatch and the chickadees. A sleek red squirrel travels headfirst down the spruce trunk, intent on grabbing his share. When I try to shoo him away to give the birds first chance, he stares at me. Stares at me as if to say, Who do you think you are? I live here; you are a mere visitor.

Quite so.

✦ ✦ ✦

I'm trying to write a story about the Great Dyings — mass extinctions, natural holocausts. Scientists call them Extinction Events; it sounds like a catastrophe movie, like the end of the world. The most well-known in popular culture is the mysterious extinction of the giant dinosaurs in the Jurassic period. The Spielberg movie and its successors brush up against the idea of these Great Dyings without much reflection on their meaning. Scientists argue among themselves about their significance. Some incline to a theory of climate change or worldwide fluctuations in sea levels, continental drift, acid rain caused by volcanoes, cosmic radiation. Some believe in death stars — asteroids flashing through the atmosphere, the startled creatures looking up at the light, then impact, explosion. Fires. Dust. Silence.

Robert Bakker, consultant for Spielberg's *Jurassic Park*, argues in *The Dinosaur Heresies*[1] for the theory of disequilibrium of ecosystems, pointing out that "when ecosystems are healthy and well insulated from extinction, no single genus dominates. There will be several nearly equally abundant genera in each ecological category — several large plant-eaters, several big meat-eaters, and so on." But if a foreign species is introduced, this state, which ecologists call equability, is disturbed, especially when that species takes over and dominates the ecosystem. Then, according to Bakker, the ecosystem enters a period of decay, signifying extinction for many of the original species.

We are beginning to understand that even subtle shifts produce devastating consequences. It is estimated that ninety-nine point nine percent of all species that have lived on earth are now extinct. The survivors adapt, new webs are woven, some forms of life go on.

The question haunting me at the end of the twentieth century, is are we in the midst of another Great Dying?

The story I'm trying to write has a bird character, a great black-backed gull (*Larus marinus*) named Linnaeus. Linnaeus and his gull tribe want an answer to a simple question: Where are the fish? Their major natural source of food has declined to the point where it will no longer support their population. The human population of Atlantic Canada is suffering a similar decline due to the collapse of the major cod fisheries. Scientists, politicians and fishers argue about the causes and point fingers of blame: It's the seals, it's the foreign draggers. The government is training fisher men and women to use computers so they will have skills for other jobs — non-existent jobs. Their money is running out and their children are leaving as soon as they can; this next generation will become the new workforce, fluid, flexible, disposable. And now we begin to hear about the decline of the West Coast salmon fisheries.

It's the end of abundance in the oceans, and the oceans are the life-fluid of the planet.

In the midst of all this, it's easy to understand why nobody worries too much about the gulls. They are intelligent and adapt quickly. They turn to other food sources: garbage dumps (in official language, landfills). For many years they have hung in clouds over the Sackville landfill site, just off Highway 101. For years this site received all the garbage from Halifax and the surrounding area. Driving along the highway, I used to watch the gull clouds shift and regroup in mysterious patterns. Sometimes I saw a solitary gull winging through the air, white-silver gleam against the blue. Sometimes, by the side of the road, a heap of bloody feathers ruffled by the wind. Roadkill. The gracefulness of flight collapsed into a carcass in the ditch. The crows will take care of it. Ross Baker, a local naturalist, used to call them "nature's undertakers"— the crows, that is.

Who would mourn the death of a gull? I would. In writing about Linnaeus, I have come to have a terrible affinity for gulls. I worry about them. Especially as the Sackville dump closed at the end of 1996. After fighting for years about where to put the refuse the authorities closed down this site and began to truck the refuse to Cumberland County, a two-hour drive away. What's more, they're talking of building a separate compost facility, some-where, sometime. How are the gulls to know where their food supply has gone?

Stories surface in the media about gulls raiding garbage bags, snatching sandwiches out of the hands of little children in schoolyards. Behaving, in fact, as though they were starving.

In my story, Linnaeus is the wise elder of the gull tribe. He is the storyteller and the time traveller. At a great conference of all the seabirds, they turn to Linnaeus and ask him to seek answers to two questions: Where are the fish? Is the disappearance of the fish a sign of another Great Dying?

✧   ✧   ✧

I talk with my students about nature writing texts. Words, phrases, sifting through the narratives, the images: the End of Nature, the Death of Nature. Elegiac laments placed side by side with celebration. Hopkins, the priest-poet at the end of the nineteenth century: "And for all this, nature is never spent; There lives the dearest freshness deep down things." [2] The sombre challenge of Rachel Carson in 1962: "The obligation to endure means the right to know." [3] This woman who loved birds could not bear the thought of a spring without them. As she was struggling to complete *Silent Spring*, her breast cancer had already metastasized. When the book was published, the chemical industries tried first to discredit her research. When that didn't work, they tried to discredit her. They said she was "hysterical," "alarmist" and so on.

These epithets have often been applied to environmental activists over the last forty years. They are associated with stereotypical negative feminine characteristics — hysteria, the womb rising to engorge the throat; the hysterical female object of the scientific male gaze. Nature as female, female as nature, both signifiers of that which can be manipulated and controlled, or made extinct. Those who are perceived to be closer to nature are equally dispensable: the poor, indigenous people, workers. High technology and transnational capitalism extend invisible webs of control, creeping into the hearts of our homes, our lives. A new ruling class is shifting into place and no place is sacred. There are no boundaries and, apparently, no limits.

Biogenetics and technology have transgressed species integrity, engineering nature in their own image. Some celebrate this transcendence of nature, declaring a liberation from the material world, from the flesh. Donna Haraway, in *Simians, Cyborgs, and Women*,[4] offers the cyborg on the Internet as a signifier of the future. But some of us believe this kind of future holds within itself its own dark virus of destruction. Some of us have taken to living in strange, remote places. We're hunkered down on the land, on small farms, rethinking our connections to nature.

Take turkeys, for example. We used to raise a few turkeys for meat — white turkeys, known as Beltsville Small White, bred to put on weight fast, a large part of it on the breast. This is really the only kind of bird available to backyard growers and, in fact, to most commercial producers. It's a simulation turkey that struggles to become the real bird, the wild turkey (*Meleagris gallopavo*) native to North America. Ghosts of their former selves, these birds grow so fast they sometimes outstrip their vascular system and literally implode. (It's known as "aortal flip.") They can't mate naturally because the males are too heavy with all that breast meat. They are extremely nervous and rather stupid — they don't know enough to come in out of the rain. They would never survive in the wild.

Yet there are traces of their ancestry in the way they strut, in the gleam of their white feathers in the twilight, in the ancient turkey language they still speak to each other. They have a presence and a strange kind of dignity. These traits we have not yet managed to eliminate. But with the increasing sophistication of genetic engineering, who knows what we will call "turkey" in the future? Who cares? In the rich nations, only a few of us have seen a live turkey, let alone a wild one. How can we value that which we do not know?

If this were only a turkey story, perhaps it wouldn't carry much weight. But it's a small sequence in the narrative of modern meat: turkey, chicken, cow, pig, sheep, goat. Artificial insemination, surrogacy, *in vitro* fertilization, freezing embryos, cloning — all the tricks of reproductive technology have been tested and used on domestic animals, as have antibiotics and growth hormones. Move a gene from one species into another, and see what you get. Someone's playing God in the barnyard and the laboratory, to say nothing of the fertility clinics.

That's why this is more than just the modern meat story. Someone's mining cells from indigenous people in exotic places, getting patents on someone else's DNA, patents on seeds and life forms. This is the story of the commodification of nature in its most fundamental units.

✧ ✧ ✧

The end of goat kidding season this year was a sad one. The last doe to kid was Comet, a small black and white Alpine — lively, intelligent, with a look about her that reminds me of her mother, Aino, the grandmother of the herd. Aino was named after my own Finnish grandmother, Aino Mackie-Maniko.

After about fifteen years of keeping goats, I've become a fairly proficient midwife in the barn. But I still dread the necessity of intervention, shoving a hand, an arm into the vulva and heaving birth canal, struggling to see through touch — is this a head, a rear end? Where are the legs?

As Comet goes into labour, Johnny, the two-year-old buck, gets upset. He's jealous that I'm in the pen with her. I ignore him and leave Comet for a few minutes to fetch kidding equipment from the house: rags for cleaning and drying the kids, a basin of disinfectant to wash up in, scissors for cutting umbilical cords, iodine for dipping the navel so it won't become infected.

As I return to the barn, Johnny chooses to challenge me. He's the size of a small pony. Ordinarily quite good-tempered for a buck, he can be a formidable figure when he rears on his hind legs in the goat-dance posture that is the prelude to rushing and butting. Without thinking I grab a snow shovel and hit him on the head. He pauses, stunned. I haven't hit him all that hard, but this is the first time he's been struck by a human. I slip around him and lock myself in the barn. He can still come in through the small goat-door, but I'm hoping he won't jump the wooden wall of the pen where I'm crouched beside Comet.

Johnny comes flying through the door in such an aroused state that he flings himself on top of the nearest doe, who falls under his sudden weight. In goat life the position for penetration and sexual play is also the dominance position. Does do it to other does, just as bucks do it to does. The goat herd is not an egalitarian community.

I watch anxiously as Johnny charges around the loafing pen, scattering the other does and their kids. The doe he jumped gets to her feet warily. Johnny flings himself at the pen wall, rearing up on his hind legs, his front ones braced on the wall so he can thrust his fierce head and long beard into the space where Comet is straining. He stares at me and I stare back. I tell him I've placed a pitchfork just outside the pen — if he comes over the wall, I'll use it.

Standoff.

Then I let out my breath. I can see the hair on the nape of his neck relaxing (when a buck is aroused, the long hair on the nape and along the spine stands up). Johnny is cooling down. Me too.

Already I'm feeling guilty I hit him. We got him when he was just a week old; he rode home in my lap in the car and we bottle-fed him until he was old enough to be weaned. Bonds run deep between us. But now something has changed. He knows it, I know it.

After about five hours, Comet goes into deep contractions. Something black and wet appears, disappears, in the vulva's opening. The familiar rhythm of giving birth. There should be a nose pressed down on front hoofs, or a hoof. Instead it's a breech presentation. I wash up quickly and go inside to help the kid out of the birth canal, pulling as Comet pushes, maintaining her rhythm. As Comet screams, I manage to extract the kid in a rush of mucus and blood. I quickly pull away the transparent sheath from its mouth and nose, but I already sense from its posture and lack of movement that the kid is dead. I place it outside the pen so Comet won't be upset. She's looking around for it but she's also preoccupied with the next one coming. It arrives in a hurry. I see the kid suspended in a clear globe of living tissue. The globe bursts and I catch the kid in mid-fall. On my knees I tear away the sheath. Something is wrong here. The tongue is between the teeth, it's choking. Fluid in the lungs? And the neck is at a funny angle. But at least it's alive. Comet and I work on it. She licks and licks while I use paper towels, then rags. In a cold barn, the kid must dry off quickly or it will be chilled.

After about ten minutes, while I'm still working on the feeble kid, Comet's deep contractions start again. Goats are multiple kidders, and triplets are not uncommon but always tricky. Comet strains hard but nothing shows. I decide to go inside, feeling for this last kid, who is quite small. As I draw it out, Comet screams and I groan. Another dead one.

Johnny is standing on the other side of the wall, very quiet. So are the other goats. The goat psyche is a powerful collective. They know.

Human help arrives and we work on the remaining kid, willing it to live so Comet will have something to mother. In the first forty-eight hours, the rush of hormones is tremendous. Even goats who are not particularly maternal by nature are caught up in this hormonal surge, which produces a sort of mutual bliss between mother and kid. Comet, who is one of the more maternal does, is caught in this life flow. She needs that kid.

After an hour, we admit defeat. Drown the dying kid in a bucket of warm water. Merciful death.

Then we turn to face the grieving mother, who stares at us: Where are my kids?

Anyone who has lived and worked with animals knows they share a range of feelings with us. The sounds of goat grieving are not translatable into human language, but then, neither are the sounds of genuine human grief. All we know is that those of us who remain are under the obligation to endure.

I gently massage Comet's udder and speak to her. She presses against me, licks me as if I'm her kid. Mysterious energy flows between us. Some of the ancient stories tell of a time when animals could become humans, humans become animals. Humans are animals, of course, but the myths suggest we can slip the bonds of our species to share other realities.

After a few days, Comet begins to regain her equilibrium. The tension in the barn relaxes. Goats are stoic philosophers; they go with the flow.

This is the story of a small rural tragedy. For many farmers who keep commercial dairy herds, goat or cow, it's not even tragedy; it's everyday reality. In Britain, commercial goat farmers drown kids at birth as a matter of routine. The milk is for human consumption.

Sometimes I think about writing a new Book of Revelation in which the other species of earth call us to a final accounting. We shall have to wade through rivers of slaughterhouse blood, climb mountains of guts, yellow fat steaming, sacrifices made to carnivorous gods. We shall have to listen to the cries of pain and longing, look into the dark-eyed pools of suffering. Great flocks of birds will darken the sky, risen from the ashes of extinction. Bindweed will hold us and hoofs will pound hearts until we recognize our relations, our selves.

goat-song *(for Comet)*

*sun-swallowed dark,*
*light weak and watery,*
*if I didn't know better*
*I'd think this was the end,*
*there is nothing more*
*than nothing, this endless*
*round of dusty grass*
*is nothing like the lusty*
*green of spring, this pale*
*sun loitering is not himself,*
*ice creeps into water*
*buckets and hearts congeal,*
*each night the stars move*
*closer, deadly beauty in*
*the cold depths of space*

*breathing is difficult,*
*they press upon me so,*
*one, two, three turning*
*in the salty sea, my skin*
*taut as a drum, stretched,*
*pain-knobbled knees*
*swollen, my bones unknit*
*to feed a multitude,*
*when I walk I sway*
*like a ship, I press*
*my head against hard*
*surfaces, concentrate*

*the night before I feel*
*the darkness cracking,*
*between us the air*
*vibrates and we start*
*to tell the stories,*
*the genealogy of the race,*

*the gleaming mountains*
*of Tibet, the ancient earth*
*unfolding to our amazement,*
*we were blue then and white,*
*colours of sky and snow,*
*we flew through the thin*

*air, spinning almost out*
*of control, landing*
*with precision; we knew*
*the caves of birth and death,*
*our bellies transparent*
*membranes veined and globed,*
*the map of constellations*
*etched in lines of blood*
*to feed new generations,*
*each spring the pain,*
*cries and the calling*
*forth while the bucks*
*waited on the horizon,*
*holding sun, stars, moon*
*between their great horns*

*we have this sacred*
*memory within us,*
*like the tips of green*
*buds about to unfurl,*
*it tastes as sweet as bark,*
*balsam fir, popple strips*
*dripping with sap, it warms*
*us in the cold-barn nights,*
*the long captivity and slaughter,*
*cries of kids gushing blood*
*from slit throats, burnt*
*flesh offering; they steal*
*our milk for themselves*
*while they herd us over*

*deserts of their own making,*
*cursing the trembling*
*one who is sent forth*
*to bear it all, carrying*
*sins upon her back,*
*she who is one of us,*
*goat-mothers who suckle*
*the fallen, falling world*
*let it be, let it go,*
*this is the night before*
*the grace of morning*
*recalls us from the dark,*
*this is the night*
*when the kids start*
*their long journey home,*
*may my heart not misgive*
*me, may the milk flow*
*freely into eager mouths,*
*each spring I bring forth*
*the world perfectly made,*
*I lick it dry and nudge*
*it to stand on all four*
*shaky legs, my fierce*
*tongue is like my love,*
*it knows no bounds,*
*it runs through me*
*like a dark river, I no*
*longer know if I am*
*giving birth or being born*

From scientists and the media, we hear that we're in the midst of global changes and environmental crises — and then we hear that we're not. The holes in the ozone layer are growing larger; maybe this has something to do with us, maybe not. There is a global climatic warming trend — or maybe not. We in the rich nations must begin to limit our omnivorous appetites for pro-duction-consumption. Or maybe not. Scientific knowledge is appropriated for the "free market," and legitimate scientific debate is exploited so that it is difficult for lay people to understand whether or not there is a crisis. The result is an obscuration of experience and a denial of accountability. Earth Summits come and go, with political protocols and agendas promising some amelioration of human-wrought destruction. Meanwhile, the fish have gone or are going; the forests are being clear-cut, the oceans polluted, the lakes and rivers and streams acidified and/or polluted, groundwater aquifers exhausted; cities are becoming sinks of pollution and hundreds of species are extinct or endangered due to human activity of one kind or another. Humans themselves are becoming sick or dying from many environmental causes.

Some days my own species sickens me.

Yet I know there has been a shift in consciousness in many people who are working hard to make the changes we know are necessary, for our own survival and that of other species. And I know that these changes must come from a place where wild hope and love flourish like weeds.

This is not another version of the nostalgic pastoral myth. It is a lucid vision of the contingency of life as we know it on this planet. The more we know about how embedded in nature we are, the more miraculous our existence seems. What we have called "natural resources" are really life-support systems that have evolved over billions of years: earth, air, water, other species. For the brief space of our emergence as the dominant species, we are part of an unfolding. We have choices to make, many things to learn. If we make the wrong choices and don't learn the right things, then we too may disappear. We may be part of the last Great Dying.

*she conjures her grandmother, the Finnish witch*

*grandmother,*
isu,
*I've studied hard*

*and learned to raise the dead,*
*each day I trudge*
*across fields of snow,*
*offerings on my back*

*They come disguised*
*as birds: nuthatch,*
*chickadee, blue jay,*
*crow, whir of wings*
*around my head,*
*ank-ank-ank,*
*chick-a-dee-dee-dee,*
*caw-caw-DONG!*
*black forms tumble*
*out of the blue sky,*
*they don't fool me,*
*I can feel them*
*thronging along arms,*
*shoulders, plucking*
*the toque off my head,*
*after eyes, liver, heart,*
*lights, the vital parts*
*that we call offal,*
*after blood to calm*
*their queasy souls*

*grandmother,*
isu,
*the goats have taught*
*me how to dance,*
*at first I was timid,*
*sat in the midst*
*of flying hooves,*
*eyes closed, hands*
*clutching earth,*
*refusing to rear*
*up on my hind legs,*

*twist the body,*
*prance, leap into air*
*with nothing to hold*
*me but ecstasy,*
*in the spring the kids*
*swept like a river*
*along frozen ground,*
*swerved and jumped*
*over the moon's pale*
*shadow, left me*
*dazzled and free*
*to slough off gravity*

*grandmother,*
isu,
*I reach for your hand,*
*I need to yank you*
*out of your grave,*
*we must fly to Finland*
*where it all began,*
*North, northing,*
*past the North Star,*
*seek lucidity among*
*the Lapps who feed*
*reindeer magic mushrooms*
*so potent the very piss*
*will make a poor woman*
*swoon and she lies*
*a shaman in the snow,*
*around her the reindeer*
*snuffle up the bit,*

*red and white scraps,*
*they know this ritual:*
*first they dance, bow*
*and pirouette, toss*
*of head, antlers gleam*

*in the sun's cold eye,*
*they begin to leap*
*higher and higher,*
*over the shaman's body*
*till she rises and flaps*
*her arms, jumps a small*
*hummock, leaps into the*
*wild dance of the flying*
*reindeer, higher and higher*
*they go, swirling so fast*
*they are a blur of light,*
*woman and reindeer,*
*they pass out of sight*
*into the next galaxy,*
*leaving traces behind,*
*music of the spheres*
*rings in the inner ear.*

## Endnotes

1. Robert T. Bakker, *The Dinosaur Heresies: New Theories Unlocking the Mystery of the Dinosaurs and Their Extinction* (New York: Morrow, 1986).

2. Gerard Manley Hopkins, in W.H. Gardner, *Gerard Manley Hopkins: A Selection of His Poems and Prose* (London: Penquin, 1953), p. 27.

3. Rachel Carson, *Silent Spring* (Boston: Houghton Mifflin, 1962).

4. Donna J. Haraway, *Simians, Cyborgs, and Women: The Reinvention of Nature* (New York: Routledge, 1991).

# CAROL ROSE

# OUT OF EXILE

## A SPIRITUAL QUEST

Trying to write about my spiritual journey is difficult, not because I don't remember the details, but because life experiences often expand beyond our ability to talk about them. I'm afraid that, like most people, I've grown comfortable in an "old telling": trapped in a particular version of my story, unable to make contact with the missing pieces. I hope to recreate my journey in such a way that the fragments come together in new patterns, new formations that allow the depth of the story to shine through. I suppose I'm hoping to tap into the "soul level" of the journey, the level that transcends the personal and becomes more than just an individual tale.

I don't know whether I can pinpoint the beginnings of my spiritual quest. I don't know because I can't remember a time when I wasn't involved with Spirit, when I didn't believe in a divine power. I also don't know whether my current spiritual journey is new, or whether it's just a continuation of an older story, one that began long ago, in another time, another place. Actually, I don't know very much about the "whys" of my journey, but I do know that I've been searching for a long time. I also know that being a woman and being a Jew are part of that journey; I was born that way, socialized that way, and both aspects continue to be a vital part of my self-definition.

Ever since I was a child, I've prayed to a deity that I felt connected to, a personal God. This wasn't something I was taught, nor was it modelled in the conventional way, by pious parents or grandparents. Rather, my connection was intuitive. I believed that there was a purpose to everything, including my being a Jewess. That's not to say that I was always happy about it. I often wished that I could be "ordinary," that this personal deity would continue taking care of the world, leaving me and my people alone.

I grew up in New York, in the great silence of those who survived the Holocaust. My family didn't discuss the war, didn't discuss the difficulties they had faced as immigrants, didn't discuss why God had allowed this horror to happen. They didn't even discuss whether there was room for a God in their *Weltanschauung* (world view). I really didn't know what my parents believed. I only knew that I was their "golden child," their promise for a future in this new land of freedom.

My mother's message to me was about living a "balanced" life — not too Jewish, nor too assimilated. One had to know one's history, one's culture, one's ancestral language and one's religion. Coupled with that, one also had to be modern, educated and tolerant. That was her credo — especially tolerance, respect for all people. It was what she had brought with her from Germany, along with my grandmother's candlesticks. It was her inheritance … and mine.

My father was more emotional, more passionate. I remember him crying during a Rosh Hashanah service. When I asked him why, he said, "I'm just talking to God — it's called prayer." That was the first time I realized that he and I shared a sense of intimacy with the Divine. I can also remember him singing loudly, to the chagrin of my rather conservative mother, on Hanukkah. Now I recognize how these two memories have become laminated onto my own prayer life. Whether in silent devotion or in joyous song, Jewish prayer is the language of my heart.

My parents valued education so, in addition to my general studies, I was sent to a synagogue religious school (somewhat unusual for girls in my neighbourhood). There I studied Torah — the five books of Moses, the commentaries, the prophets and other sacred writings. In Hebrew school I developed a deep love for this ancient tradition that dared to struggle with the big questions, questions about the meaning of life.

Those questions continue to intrigue me, and I'm eternally grateful to my parents and my teachers for encouraging me to ask them. In fact, the ability to question is what has kept my dialogue with Judaism alive, even after I realized that it was a system that taught its history, interpreted its laws, and prayed to a God fashioned (mainly) in the image of masculine experience. Fortunately, it was also a system that argued with itself, that engaged in intertextual and intratextual discourse. And it had elasticity; it was capable of stretching across centuries, even into the future. (There are all sorts of discussions about what will happen when the Messiah comes, for example.) So I believed, and continue to believe, that one just had to learn how to ask, to unlock answers that were already hidden there. I felt that one had to love this tradition enough to wrestle with it, to challenge it, to force it to yield new and creative responses.

But I certainly didn't know that in Hebrew school! I had to go through life's usual hoops: elementary school, junior high, confirmation (in my circles, only very privileged girls had a bat mitzvah) and then high school. Along the way, I joined a synagogue youth group and I began to travel and meet folks from other communities. Despite the fact that no one in my family went to synagogue on a regular basis, I regularly attended late Friday-evening services. Those services were filled with sights and sounds that gave me a sense of Sabbath peace. Every time the

cantor sang the Sabbath melodies, every time I read the special
Sabbath psalms, every time the rabbi discussed the weekly Torah
portion, I was transported to another level of self. I always stayed
until the very end of the evening, hoping to hear more Torah,
hoping to hold onto that Shabbat feeling, sensing that I was part
of something very ancient, very holy. While my family accepted
my Sabbath pattern, they wondered about it. Perhaps I was a
genetic throwback, they joked. My maternal grandmother
(whom I was supposed to resemble, and had who died in Ausch-
witz) had been a pious woman, a Sabbath observer. Perhaps, they
speculated, I had inherited her soul. And who knows? Perhaps I
had.

My mother became quite ill during my adolescence, and I
nursed her at home until she finally had to be hospitalized. Then
I managed to arrange my schedule so that I could go to school in
the mornings and visit her every afternoon and evening. Those
mornings were very precious. At least at school I was still a lively,
inquisitive, fun-loving kid, albeit a kid with tons of responsibility.

That same year, several Israeli students entered my high
school and I befriended them. They were full of Zionist vision
and fervour. I listened to them, imagining what it would be like
to live and work on a kibbutz. I learned the words to Hebrew
songs and the steps to Israeli folk dances. I visited the Israeli cafés
that were beginning to appear on New York's Upper West Side.
I began thinking about *aliyah*, about making a pilgrimage to the
Holy Land. As far back as I can remember, I dreamed about
Jerusalem.

My life was a balancing act — school, homework, hospital
visits and home responsibilities. At night I'd relax at one of the
cafés. On weekends I'd go down to the Village, where life was full
of newness and people were willing to share their talents and
ideas. Conversations were lively and animated, moving from art
to politics, from Zen Buddhism to Hare Krishna, from meditation to love. Somehow, even in that "beat" environment, I was
always the Jew. That was true when I was with my Israeli friends,
as well. In fact, they really weren't interested in discussing

spirituality or religion. Zionism was their passion, and I learned from them a great deal about the love of land and the love of people.

During my final year of high school, my mother died. Though I wanted to move into an apartment of my own, I continued to live at home in order to maintain a sense of family for my younger brother. I had more time to myself after my mother's death, and I used it to read works by contemporary Jewish philosophers. I was particularly drawn to the writing of Martin Buber, and I especially loved his retelling of Chassidic tales about saintly rabbis and holy beggars who, through their simple faith and joyous outlook, discovered pathways to healing, transformation and enlightenment. In fact, I longed to meet Jews who lived like those Chassidim, with joy and simplicity, with holiness and intentionality. But even then I realized that, because I was a woman, I'd have difficulty gaining access to that world.

One Saturday night, a Chassidic-looking man — bearded, with a black hat and dark suit — came into my favourite café. I couldn't take my eyes off him. People from his world didn't usually frequent cafés, so I was certain we were destined to meet. Some of my friends seemed to know him; they even knew his name. I gasped when they told me who he was because several weeks before, at the home of my great-aunt, I had met his parents. They were distant relatives, an elderly rabbi and his wife, who had come to make a condolence visit. They seemed kind, though she was a little intimidating. She asked me if I knew her son, and said that if I had any questions about Judaism I should talk to him. She insisted that I come back to my aunt's house the following Sunday to meet him. I never kept that appointment — my father went in my place — but the son didn't show up either. Instead, he left me a recording of his original songs. I fell in love with his music and, though I didn't understand a word of what he was saying, his songs touched my soul. I sang them to myself, often.

Now he was standing in front of me. "Hi, I'm Shlomo Carlebach," he said. "What's your name?" I introduced myself and he said, "Oh, you're my little cousin, the one I was supposed to meet a few weeks ago." We laughed and joked about how things come to pass despite our efforts to the contrary. I asked him to sing for me, and I joined in, not realizing how unusual it was for an Orthodox man to sing with a woman. He complimented my singing and told me that soon he was going to Israel. Quite spontaneously, I asked him to take me with him. In true rabbinic style he responded with a question: "What if I said I was going to Spain?" Without even thinking I answered, "I suppose I would ask you to take me with you anyway." That was the beginning of a relationship that lasted thirty-five years, until his untimely death in 1994. From the night of our meeting, my life would be forever linked to his; he was my teacher, my friend, my eternal soul companion.

Shlomo introduced me to the world of Chassidic thought. For almost three years he studied with me every night, in person or by phone, calling from wherever he was, sharing his insights and those of the teachers he loved. Sometimes I travelled with him. This allowed me to see, first-hand, that he was a living bridge between the world that had been — the world of European Jewry — and the spiritual world that was yet to be. Despite the male orientation of Chassidic thought, Shlomo always made me feel that my interpretations of Torah were significant, and that women's teachings were, in fact, vital, a missing link in the ancient chain of Jewish knowledge.

Shlomo also brought me to the Lubavitchers, a Chassidic community in Brooklyn, and arranged for me to meet their spiritual leader, "the Rebbe," Rabbi Menachem Mendel Schneerson. For a while I was in close contact with the Rebbe. I even considered him a guide in my own spiritual development. However, the Rebbe was not the community. The Chassidic world is based on rules about behaviour, and role demarcations are clearly defined. It strives for total conformity among its members, and I could easily have lost my sense of self in that world. I was suspect: a modern woman who was (and always would be) part of the outside world. Because I was a woman, I was excluded from any real intellectual or spiritual participation. Nevertheless, for many

years the Rebbe was extremely warm to me. Once, during a
private audience, he told me a parable about a horse. "She was so
beautiful and free that everyone wanted to own her," he said.
"One day someone captured that horse. They saddled her, bri-
dled her and turned her into a milk horse. No longer was she wild
and free; no longer did she possess her own beauty. Remember
that story," he concluded, and I did. It was a gift, a liberating
nugget that I always held on to.

One of the most significant trips I took with Shlomo was to
meet Rabbi Zalman Schachter, the Hillel director at the University of Manitoba. One of the giants of contemporary Jewish life,
Zalman is the founder of the Jewish Renewal Movement, a fully
egalitarian organization that encourages the study of Jewish
mystical teachings from the perspective of New Age consciousness. I looked forward to meeting this man Shlomo had told me
so much about, this man he called his closest friend. He came to
pick us up at the airport, dressed in an old RCMP beaver coat.
He looked like a bear, and he hugged like one too! He was very
jovial, very warm, very welcoming. After spending time in
Chassidic communities where men barely tolerated my existence, I was surprised at how affectionate he was to me. Zalman
was a professor of Jewish mysticism who also understood the
language and culture of the sixties. He was a "groovy" rabbi, and
his students loved him. After only a few hours, so did I! Though
he was clearly delighted to see Shlomo, he included me in every
conversation, making sure that I understood the Yiddish or
Hebrew words that flowed between them, translating kabbalis-
tic concepts into metaphors I could grasp, communicating difficult ideas in imaginative and poetic ways.

I lived with Zalman and his family for a week. For me, those
were seven days of spiritual formation. From the moment I got
up to the time I went to bed, Shlomo and Zalman were busy
instructing me. They taught me as one teaches a little child,
lovingly washing my hands as they helped me recite the morning benedictions, feeding me different foods so I could learn
the appropriate blessings, singing songs and telling stories to

illustrate a point. During the day, they conducted classes and seminars for a Jewish students' retreat, the main reason for our trip to Winnipeg. Every prayer session was filled with joy and with a longing for union with the Divine. At night, Zalman would take me down to his famous basement, filled with colourful lava lamps, incense burners, mandalas, Tibetan bells, Indian music and pictures of great Chassidic teachers. On the eastern wall there was a large meditation chart, a focusing device that listed various Hebrew letter combinations to spell the names of God. He taught me to meditate on these, and with him I learned breathing techniques, concentration skills and chanting. To this day, he is a dear friend and wise mentor.

I was a good student, and I had great teachers. Shlomo was my rebbe of faith, striving to prove that everything existed in the Torah if we only knew how to look for it. Zalman was my rebbe of doubt, challenging me to look everywhere, even in the teachings of other traditions.

To say that I was transformed by my experience in Winnipeg is an understatement; I came home unable to fit into my old Jewish lifestyle, unable to fit in anywhere. Although I had grown to love the ecstatic prayer of the Chassidim, as a woman I was unable to join in. I could watch the men sing and dance, but I wasn't allowed to participate. I no longer felt satisfied with the services at my own synagogue either. The inner experiences I had shared with Shlomo and Zalman, I discovered, didn't really belong to the world they had initiated me into. I was a woman and I had a definite place, and unfortunately that place had nothing to do with public worship or learning, let alone with what was, for me, the essence of Chassidic life — the celebration of the Divine in the midst of every act, in the midst of physical reality. I didn't understand this at the time, and it would take me years to realize that this was what I was looking for.

In the meantime, I tried to understand what it meant to live as a Jewish woman. I enrolled in evening classes at an Orthodox women's *yeshivah* (educational institute), but I lasted there only a few weeks. Then I tried to learn as much as I could from observing the women themselves. I visited the Chassidic community every Sabbath and I watched how things were done. I spent the holidays at the home of Shlomo's sister, or with friends in other religious Jewish communities. I asked tons of questions, mostly "how to" questions, since I quickly learned that these were valued while "why" questions were frowned upon. I absorbed a great deal of information about Jewish customs and ritual, learning the choreography of prayer and the rubrics of Jewish law. Even as my soul was dying, I tried hard to fit in.

On weekdays I returned to my life in the city, still longing for opportunities to practise Jewish mystical exercises. I began reading the life stories of Eastern and Western mystics. Often I felt that I had more in common with seekers in other faith communities than I did with religious Jewish women and men. I felt a particular kinship with those involved in Eastern mystical practices; they seemed alive and happy in their bodies, even as they searched for ways to connect their souls to the Source of Life. I compared my own ecstatic experiences to those of friends who were experimenting with mescaline and LSD. The claims of all inner traditions (including the sacred "medicine" paths) seemed true to me; after all, all roads led to The One. Of course it was best if one had a living teacher to help map the way.

While extremely liberal in their understanding and interpretation of Jewish law, Shlomo and Zalman were guided by strict observance of its principles. They were Sabbath observers and they kept the dietary laws. Although they conducted mixed services for students on campus, they themselves prayed in Orthodox synagogues, where men and women were seated separately. However, they did understand my desire for *yichud*, for union with the Divine, and they were dedicated to helping me find the inner meaning of Jewish spiritual practice.

I found other teachers who "lived between the pages" — initially in Chassidic stories or in the teachings of the old masters, and later in the writings of Dr. Abraham Joshua Heschel. I sensed that what these teachers knew came from deep personal encounters with the Divine. I suspected that there were also women who knew these things. After all, biblical women were prophets and seers. However, whenever I raised questions about the spiritual life of women, people changed the subject or, at best, told me about "eccentric" women. It was even suggested that I'd be less interested in mystical experiences if I settled down, got married and led a "normal" life. No matter how hard I searched, Jewish inner experiences just weren't available to me. It seemed that unlike other traditions, Judaism didn't encourage women mystics.

I continued studying, attending classes wherever I was welcome. I even began to look outside of Orthodox institutions, although the prejudices I had developed against non-Orthodox Torah study were hard to shake; for years I had considered the Orthodox approach to be the only authentic one. During one of my classes I met Neal Rose, a rabbinical student at the Jewish Theological Seminary, who had also studied at Lubavitch. He seemed to understand my desire for a spiritual life that was wedded to physical reality, and he shared my perspective. "People like us will always have to walk between two worlds," he said. Sometimes Neal helped keep me from falling through the cracks; sometimes I supported him. Eventually we married, and together we continued walking the path between the worlds.

Along the way we met other like-minded, like-spirited folks, and in time we created our own way. Every Wednesday evening, Neal and I attended a course in Tanya (a Chassidic text) led by a Lubavitcher Chassid who was willing to teach women and men together. On Thursday nights, Shlomo would teach from the works of Rabbi Nachman of Bratzlav, an insightful mystical storyteller. Our home in New York became a Sabbath retreat for many, and we grew as our guests challenged our assumptions and convictions. Then came a wonderful opportunity. Zalman, who was the head of the Department of Near Eastern and Judaic Studies at the University of Manitoba, invited Neal to apply for a position, and shortly after Neal's ordination we moved to Winnipeg with our two young sons.

After three years in Winnipeg, we took a sabbatical and moved to Israel, settling in the city of my dreams, Jerusalem. We lived there for two years, and our third son was born there. Those were magical days — messianic, in fact. There was a resurgence of interest in Jewish spirituality, a resurgence of Jewish pride and a renewed love for the land of Israel. Former hippies, drop outs from the 60s and disillusioned executives all started to arrive, coming in search of meaning, and to rediscover their Jewish roots. New _yeshivot_ opened their doors. However, just as traditional Jewish values impacted on the new arrivals, so they too had an influence — especially the women, who were unwilling to put up with restrictions and attitudes that kept them from full participation in the religious life they had come in search of.

Those Jerusalem years were very broadening. I met Jews from all over the world, and I began to appreciate their quest, so much like my own. These people had lived through the sexual revolution, and had fought for and in many cases won equality in their workplaces, and in their educational settings. Now they were seeking entry into a spiritual community where opportunities for women and men were not entirely equal. Since Neal and I had returned to the spiritual practice of Judaism, rather than being born into it, we became role models; we had a worldly sensibility and a secular education, yet we seemed comfortable living an the intensely Jewish lifestyle we had chosen. As a couple, we represented the merging of the new and the old.

However, in spite of our progressive outlook, I felt that I had some serious soul-searching to do. For years I had divided my feminist self from my Jewish practice. Now I had to face that bifurcation, and it terrified me. How could I lead an authentic Jewish life and still be true to myself as a feminist? I had chosen to be guided by Jewish law (Halacha), but did I have the patience to wait for the Halachic process to respond to the needs of women, as I believed it would someday? Did I want my sons to grow up believing that the spiritual needs of women were less important than their own? That the spiritual contributions of women were less significant than those of men? Could I live with myself if I didn't challenge the customs and laws being taught to my children? Could I stand up to the tradition that I loved and hold it accountable? Fortunately, I didn't have to solve all these issues alone. There were other women struggling with them, women who were beginning to write about their frustrations, and about the ways we could work towards change.

In the midst of all my searching, the time came for us to return to Winnipeg. Leaving Israel was difficult; I would miss the diversity of Jewish life, the ease with which one could observe the Sabbath and the festivals, and the sense of being connected to the land. In Israel I had felt, for the first time, the agricultural link to the holidays, and I loved the earthiness of it all. Israel had given me a sense of God Immanent; of the Divine Presence experienced in the earth as well as in the heavens.

In Winnipeg I returned to teaching and going to university, and I connected deeply with the interfaith community. Neal and I became popular interpreters of Judaism, speaking to organizations in our own and other faith communities. We began alternative high holiday services for Rosh Hashanah and Yom Kippur, in which the use of contemporary poetry and music seemed to create a sense of holiness and community. Zalman had been active in dialogue, especially with Catholic clergy, and we happily continued that work. Soon after our return to Winnipeg, our fourth son was born.

At this stage I became interested in the writings of feminist theologians, and curious about the emerging women's spirituality movement. Together with Elana Schachter, I started Winnipeg's first Rosh Chodesh (New Moon) group, which combined the best of a consciousness-raising group, a study group and a place to explore ritual. The members were professional women, students, artists, writers and mothers; we were feminist women interested in spiritual exploration. We created healing rituals, rituals of birth, divorce, death and loss, and rituals of transformation. We wrote welcoming ceremonies for baby girls, composed original songs and told original stories. Like many Rosh Chodesh groups, we developed our own woman-centred Passover Seder: a parallel celebration of liberation.

The Rosh Chodesh groups turned out to be radically transformative! In them we learned to take charge of our spiritual lives,
to choose those components that helped us feel more deeply
connected to the holy. Originally we had wanted to gain confidence in our ritual and interpretive abilities, but for many of us
Rosh Chodesh celebrations became our most significant religious
experience, and several of us grew to enjoy them more than we
enjoyed synagogue services. As our understanding of our own
spiritual preferences deepened, some of us became impatient
with normative religious practice. Experimenting with language
and imagery, we developed connections to what the kabbalists
called Shekinah, the feminine facet of God ... and we loved Her.
She spoke to us of banishment, of exile and of power. She called
out to us and we identified with Her, recognizing Her condition
as our own. Sadly, some of us were unable to share these experiences in our synagogue communities or with our families, and
outside of our Rosh Chodesh groups we had no place to honour
Her presence. Our spiritual lives were split between women-only
celebrations and our synagogue lives, and we experienced a sense
of being cut off from the deepest part of ourselves. (I believe this
has become a problem for women in other faith communities, as
well.)

Some of us realized that we'd never again be satisfied with the
practices in our houses of worship, even those that were egalitarian. We'd continue going to Temple or synagogue to celebrate the
Sabbath and the festivals, and to observe life-cycle events with
family and friends, but we needed to supplement our religious
lives with our own ceremonies and teachings in order to feel
whole. Others were determined to become active participants in
synagogue life, bringing new rituals, especially healing rituals
and welcoming ceremonies, into the heart of traditional services.
As the Jewish feminist movement grew, those of us who stayed
within the establishment succeeded in challenging it. In Liberal
synagogues, women were given greater ritual and political power.
Liberal seminaries began admitting women to both rabbinical
and cantorial programmes. I was pleased with all of these

changes, happy that women could learn and finally assume positions of leadership. But personally, I was still searching.

Our family took another sabbatical, once again settling in Jerusalem. I became a part-time student at PARDES, a *yeshivah* where women and men could study the same texts and could teach and learn together. I also began a course of private study with Madame Colette Aboulker-Muscat, a psychologist and wise woman who teaches a form of imagery work used for healing and personal transformation. I first met Colette when she was seventy, and I thought she was one of the most beautiful women I had ever seen. Her ancestors were physicians, healers and teachers of Sephardic kabbalah, and she is heir to a deep esoteric knowledge passed down for generations in her renowned Algerian family.

In my work with Colette, I've finally found the practice I've been searching for, a practice that draws on the teachings of biblical, liturgical and Jewish mystical writings. Colette encourages an awareness of the "Presence of the Presence" in all things, and a life of spiritual cleanliness, honesty and generosity. It directs us to recognize that we are all created in the image of the Divine; that we are, ourselves, creative and quite likely divine! Her exercises are designed to bring us into a state of health, wholeness and holiness. We are challenged to live in the moment, to act rather than react to life; to do our part for all creation, and to do our best. This is personal work, quiet work, that strives to break habitual patterns of behaviour and thought. Using Colette's approach, there are times when I've experienced heightened states of awareness and times when I've felt great joy and ecstasy. Mostly I have learned (to quote Colette) to be "in life," to live my life fully and gratefully. I have called her my teacher for the last twenty years, returning to study with her every summer. At the same time I continue to be part of the larger Jewish community, to pray in egalitarian synagogues, to study and learn from our tradition. Because of my work with Colette, I sense, much more deeply now, what lies behind those teachings.

When our only daughter was born, I hoped that I'd have answers for her; that I'd know exactly what to teach her. I remember asking Shlomo for a blessing: "Let me have clarity for her." "Clarity? You want clarity?" he asked. "Clarity isn't all it's cracked up to be. A little mystery would be better, don't you think?" And mystery is all I have to offer my daughter — and my sons.

In the year or so preceding our daughter's birth, I began dreaming about biblical women. Sarah, Rebekah, Leah and Rachel were my new dream-time companions and, along with other matriarchal figures, they came to teach me about the power of myth, about what happens when women become the tellers and interpreters of sacred story. As my dreams evolved, I learned to trust the wisdom that came from them. I understood that we women need to learn to trust our dreams again, to open ourselves to the flow of imagination, especially when we are trying to understand the texts we call holy. As a result of my dreams, and other images I had at Colette's, I created (with illustrator Lu-Ann Lynde) a set of cards called Walking The Mother Path, which contain visual and poetic story fragments (*midrash*). When I was developing the cards, I sensed that they were a beginning, a channel into a new oral tradition based on women's insights. Possibly they are a continuation of an older tradition that, like the Shekinah, has been in exile. I use these cards in workshops, as tools for making contact with women's wisdom — the very wisdom I have been searching for for so many years.[1]

I've been given a loving family, wonderful companions and enlightened teachers on my journey. I've made blunders and progress, and have learned as I've taught. I've lived to see the changes that women's consciousness has brought to my tradition, and to our age. I think of the biblical sentence, "I am that I am becoming" as my personal affirmation, and I try to focus on it every day. Recently, Di Brandt challenged me to look at "my poet" as a spiritual guide, and of course it is the poet in me that gives voice to those enormous moments of transcendence and love. It is my poet that struggles with oppression and pain, and it

is my poet who strives to find language for what we call the
ineffable.

Several years ago, Jewish folklorist Dov Noy, then nearly
eighty years old, reportedly said, "I'm glad that I've lived this long
because today women and men are able to hear the stories of our
people told from the perspective of women, and that's never been
done before." I'm glad too, and I feel privileged to be part of the
change that is reforming our heritage. I'm delighted not only to
hear those tales but to tell them, and in doing so to bring balance
to a spiritual path that has, for too long, kept the Shekinah in exile.


## ENDNOTE

1. For more about the development of the cards, see: Joan Turner (ed.),
*Living the Changes* (Winnipeg: University of Manitoba Press, 1990). For a
description of how they are being used, see: Shohama Wiener (ed.), *The
Fifty-Eighth Century: A Jewish Renewal Sourcebook* (New Jersey: Jason Aron-
son, 1996).

# SHELLEY DAVIS FINSON

## SEEING WITH NEW EYES

### MOMENTS OF SPIRITUAL AWAKENING

*F*or the past twenty years, I have been interested in the experiences of women who are critical of how Christian tradition has affected their lives. I know that my own religious questions and reflections about the meaning of what is holy or ultimate have arisen at times of brokenness or connection. Hearing others, and recalling my own story, I recognize that as we intentionally relive moments of changed consciousness, we realize that we have not always been where we are now, that we see things today that we did not see before.

As a feminist I have integrated into my spirituality the central element of feminist consciousness, including the cornerstone of feminist theory — namely, the understanding that the personal is political. To know women's personal lives is to know the politics of their situation. Similarly, to know something of women's personal lives is to know their spirituality. That which I name as Spirit comes to me through experience and symbols totally inseparable from human community and history. My spirituality is expressed in everything I do, from how I spend money to with whom I align myself politically and to whom I give thanks.

The spirituality of Christian women has been truncated by the fact that it has had to find itself expressed in a society that is patriarchal — that is, male-centred, male-dominated and male-valued. As a Christian feminist theologian, I see my task as recognizing and exposing the nature and effect of patriarchy on the lives of women, and pointing to the places where women's spirituality can flourish and has flourished.

When I speak of women's spiritual journey, I do so less in terms of "stages of faith" development than in terms of moments of changed consciousness, which I like to describe as "seeing with new eyes." Changed consciousness brings about new understanding of what it is to be in relationship with the self, as well as with others. Research on women published by the Stone Center, at Wellesley College in Boston, has established that the significance of "being in relationship" goes beyond women simply valuing relationships; it is also about how women grow and change in relation to each other.[1] Judith Jordan writes that "the deepest sense of one's being is continuously formed in connection with others and is inextricably tied to relational movement."[2] Spirituality too involves growth in our relationships — human relationships and our relationship with the Divine.

Reflecting on my life story, I increasingly recognize the magnitude of my debt to mentors, colleagues and friends who have made visible a path for me to follow. The biblical image of the "cloud of witnesses" provides a vision of those who have inspired me, who stand as a tower of strength and encouragement, who beckon me forward and sustain me.

My "seeing with new eyes" concept also leads me to recognize quite diverse forms of living out the faith. For some women, the Divine is God, the God of the people of the Hebrew and Christian texts, for example. Others speak of the Divine within themselves as energy, power or a personal sense of wholeness and integration. For still others, their spiritual guide is the Mother Goddess, who was banished and destroyed by the patriarchal Father God centuries ago.

Finally, I am someone with a built-in sense of the unfairness of life. Accordingly, my spiritual life has involved the necessity of coming to a consciousness that lets in the world, especially the suffering of women and other disenfranchised persons. It has also meant trying to live an accountable life that keeps before me more than just the daily maintenance of my own being.

I was born into a British working-class family three years before the beginning of the Second World War, in 1936. The war saw my father conscripted, my mother abandoning her two children to seek her fortune with an Allied soldier and my brother and me evacuated to South Wales. I have few memories of my early life until I returned to England to live with my great-aunt, Thirza, at the age of nine. (My brother, meanwhile, returned from the evacuation to live with our grandmother.) Thirza Ann, born at the close of the Victorian era, was my grandfather's sister. She had managed to avoid going into domestic service by securing work as a seamstress, something she used as a means to financial independence during her married life. She liked to remind her family that she had been born within the sound of Bow Bells in London, and was hence a Cockney. I remember her as a shamelessly uppity and irreligious woman, and as extraordinarily self-reliant. She stayed away from responding to feelings, and her main remedy for ills of the spirit was to put the kettle on for the next cup of tea.

Thirza's primary relationship with the church was playing cards at whist drives and attending the occasional church fête. It does not seem strange to me that she drew comfort from the spirit of both her deceased mother and her young son, who had died at age nine. She was my first encounter with a voice against injustice in the world family. I am convinced that the presence of her indomitable spirit has accompanied me since those early days.

My own relationship to the church included zeal for little religious pictures awarded for attending Sunday school, and singing hymns to give me comfort against the darkness of night. To me, God was a father figure in the sky who was keeping an account of my misdemeanours in His Book and whose barrelled beer, Thirza assured me, was being delivered during the rumbling of thunderstorms.

At age thirteen, I joined my father and his new bride in Jamaica. Here I learned the lessons of what it means to be different. My only previous encounter with people of colour had come when Thirza called me to witness a black soldier passing our front door on his way to the local military establishment. In Jamaica, I became a member of my stepmother's prominent West Indian family. I attended school with Chinese, Indian, Pakistani and Jamaican children; I was the only white child. As well, I spoke with a rather odd accent. Because my schooling had been interrupted by the war, it was minimal. Therefore, I was tutored by the teacher, Miss Bell, a large, very black woman who sat me next to her at the front of the room, facing all the other students. Up until this point, my primary academic aim had been to achieve the lowest place in the class; my best friend and I had schemed to compete for that privilege. However, Miss Bell was a dedicated teacher and saw potential in me. Wanting her praise, I took up learning with great enthusiasm and became her star pupil. I remember being conscious of the fact that school was one place where I felt I had a hold on my own destiny. Here I learned that, with work, I could achieve positive ends.

I attended the local parish church and was confirmed, but my Sunday mornings were conflicted times. At the Half-Way Tree Parish Church the drama of class and colour barriers presented itself. I was aware of the discrepancy between the pomp and circumstance inside the church, and the incredible need of those on the outside. Thirza had thoroughly tutored me on British class structures and the differences between "them" and "us." Their tea would include fancy sandwiches; ours was lovely bread and jam. The "toffs" didn't have to work for their money; we did, working for them in their houses or their offices. The "mucky-mucks" had people to take care of them; we should look out for ourselves, because no one else would. But now I was one of "them"! And so I struggled, as an adolescent, to sort out where and how I was to fit into this strange culture. I recall being confused by my father's disapproval of the various "unacceptable" friends I tended to make. This too became part of my struggle. With whom was I supposed to talk, play and share confidences?

The sense of isolation I felt was aggravated by what I later recognized as sexual abuse. This was undoubtedly an excruciating and confusing period for me. My very soul had been attacked. I withdrew from my plucky adolescent persona to a state of solitary disconnection. The full impact and meaning of my experiences was only unveiled years later, during a time of healing in my mid-thirties.

Fortunately for me, two extremely important connections gave me an identity and provided support for my self-esteem and my survival as a young teen. The first was with Miss Bell, who seemed to take pride in the fact that she was able to teach this "misfit"; I was thrilled by her special attention. The other was my involvement in the Girl Guide movement, which provided me with activities in which I could succeed and be proud. In Guides I had contact with folk who did not seem preoccupied with race and class culture, which was a great relief. Furthermore, the Guides were led by a certain lieutenant who captured all of my adolescent adoration.

Returning to my Aunt Thirza in England at age sixteen, I entered the workplace as the "girl" in a printing company. This seemed to be a natural step for a teenager with no particular career goals or direction, but the duties of running errands, making tea and collecting the mail soon lost their glamour, and I became determined to find a life that offered more. On the day I turned seventeen and a half, I mailed in my application to become a member of Her Majesty's Royal Air Force. For a second time I became immersed in the experience of new learning: the identity of the uniform and the possibility of travel.

I flourished in the company of other young women who were also trying to sort out who they were. I soon realized that, although I had had tentative experiences with heterosexual relationships, mostly my heart was stopped by these women. However, the heavy homophobic environment within the military in the mid-1950s was enough to curb any ardour I might have felt.

After less than two years, I left the air force to keep house for my brother, who had contracted tuberculosis. Once again I tried my hand at the working world, believing I had moved up when I entered a typing pool. However, within another year I resumed my search for something that would give my life more meaning; being a housekeeper at home and a robot at work wasn't enough. I was restless to find a connection that provided some purpose.

I set my sights on Canada. In 1956 I left my Aunt Thirza for the final time, although she would continue as a constant in my life, by way of letters and visits, until she died years later, at age ninety-two. At her funeral, where I was cast in a pastoral role because by then I had become a minister, I was painfully aware that few knew what Thirza had been for me. I was grieving the loss of a mother, rather than an aunt.

For years I wondered why I chose Canada as a destination. Was it the influence of the Canadian teacher who came to my elementary school with astounding stories of hot springs and Mounties? Was it the fact of knowing many Jamaican adolescents who went to Canada to finish their schooling? Or was it because the Canadian embassy was just down the street from where I worked in London? Not until 1974, almost twenty years after arriving in Canada, did I track down my birth mother's new family in Vancouver. I had repressed the fact that the Allied soldier she had left home and family for was a Canadian.

I immediately felt at home in Canada. Now I was Shelley, not Sheila. I had come by courtesy of the Canadian government, and a job was waiting for me in Toronto. This time I had been given a really big promotion; I alone ran the office of a small manufacturing company. Everything was new and once again I was perceived as different, someone with a strange accent. But this time, being different was exciting and not particularly unique. At the YWCA where I lived, dozens of newcomers were finding temporary shelter while passing through Toronto on their way to a new life. I found community and friendship among other young working women. In the fifties, "waiting and dating" in hopes of meeting Mr. Right took up a great deal of women's interest and time, and I was no different. I recall with some sadness those experiences of relating to men and trying to sort out my feelings and needs, aware of the social pressure to find someone and "go steady." I also remember the intense feelings of attraction I had for certain women. However, at that time I had neither the insight nor the language to describe my feelings.

Once again, two connections stand out as significant. The first was with a young prostitute, Peggy, who turned up at my door at the "Y" one night. Her belief that I could make a difference in her life, just by my interest in her, seemed to touch something deep within me. I began mentoring Peggy and she continued seeking me out for many years. The second was with a young adults group at the Queen Street United Church — a church with a bowling alley! Friends had invited me to bowl with them, and the bowling group was led by a young minister and his wife who regularly engaged us in discussion. In introducing the "God factor" to me, they were dealing with someone with no experience with religious talk. I found these discussions very exciting, as I discovered the world of ideas and meaning in the connection between myself, what I understood to be God, and a communal relationship. This was an experience of "being found." It was akin to Thirza's complete willingness to receive me into her home when I felt like an outsider in other places, and my sense of being recognized as someone with potential by Miss Bell.

Feeling some sense of responsibility to the young adults group, I soon joined the church. What followed was a period of massive turmoil. Quite suddenly I quit my job, left a man who had expected to marry me, packed up my belongings and headed to a Christian retreat centre. I needed to think and to talk. My primary preoccupation was the fact that my life had no direction or meaning; I had no purpose other than keeping up relationships that were stressful. Although my decision to leave everything behind appeared irrational to others, I can only explain it as a moment of conversion. At the end of two months, I became convinced that I had a call to work for the church. In time, I was mentored by two women in ministry who provided me with a vocational image, a deaconess in the United Church.

Though I now identified myself as "religious" and was absolutely sure that I had a "call," I was determined not to look like, sound like or act like any of the stereotypical "religious" folk I had encountered. I considered it a badge of honour when someone remarked to me, "You certainly are not like any religious person I've known." Quite intentionally, I kept to the boundary of the traditional religious community. The social separation I had felt as a youngster between "them" and "us" once more came into play as I identified myself with the marginal, as opposed to those who were "established." Describing myself as working for the church, not in the church, I maintained a relationship as a critic of the church, challenging the structures to be more responsive to the needs of the marginalized, particularly youth.

When I was reluctant to put my trust in an institution that so consistently failed to hear its own message, I felt secure in the work I was doing, and in my belief that the church exists where the Spirit is present. Spiritually, I identified myself with workers for civil rights, the anti-Vietnam voices and the youth movement leaders. Like so many of the folk on the political left, I joined marches and sang songs related to each of those movements. Finally my life had meaning, purpose and direction.

In retrospect, as I put this time into a spiritual context, I realize that my boundary living reflected my understanding of the early Jesus movement as a marginalized, counter-cultural community, before it lost its way in the institutionalization of its religious practices. I knew that the Spirit was working in the world through the lives of freedom fighters, resisters and young folk struggling for new life. I believed we were going to change the world!

Still, I felt somewhat ambiguous about my vocational identity. Mary Daly captures something of the critical tension that is
part of living on the margin, something of the difficulty that I
believe was part of what I was feeling.

> ... *creative living on the boundary should not be confused with
> having one's cake and eating it too — a subtle perversion of the
> real thing which may resemble it superficially. Real boundary
> living is a refusal of tokenism and absorption, and therefore it is
> genuinely dangerous.* [3]

I was not initially conscious of the real problems implicit in
being marginalized, however. While I studied theology in prepa-
ration for full-time ministry, I had no sense of anything problem-
atic with the way theology was being taught. I was aware of how
the theological school marginalized women students, as well as of
the general stereotyping of women in the church, but these were
accepted as normal, as were other forms of discrimination and
oppression. Consequently, I felt no opposition to my theological
education. While I was conscious that folks around me were
sometimes upset by my persona and my way of being in the world,
I took the places of incongruity to mean that others felt there was
something wrong with my perspective. Besides, it was not new for
me to feel odd. At the same time, my call became clearer: I wanted
to reach those who were identified as "displaced youth." So I
worked for several years in outreach projects with teens who had
few links to any system, certainly none to the church.

After some years of working, and as the women's movement
was beginning to be more visible, I began to meet with a group of
women church workers from different denominations. Gradually, we realized that there was something radically wrong with
the Christian theology that had been transmitted to us. As we
heard each others' stories, we began to recognize that the dis-
criminating factors that affected the lives of women in other
institutions were also present in the church. Like women in the
secular community, we were paid less for work of equal value;

fewer women were in decision-making positions; and sexual harassment was present in most of our lives. Several members of the group felt called to ordained ministry but came from denominations that vehemently opposed women's ordination. This was not a problem for me. (The United Church of Canada has ordained women since 1936.) We began to learn about the theological arguments for and against the ordination of women, and we joined our sisters at numerous meetings and on picket lines. So it was that, as a group, we learned that the personal is political: that our individual experiences were more than that, they were a social phenomenon, a political issue.

The group of church workers grew and flourished. We called ourselves the Friends of Hagar. We began to see the pervasiveness of sexism in the theology and patriarchal practices of the institutional church, and to ask ourselves, "What can we do?" Like women around the globe, we organized ourselves to work for change. No longer content to be called "sons of God" or "men" or "brothers," we turned to reconstruct the religious tradition by rewording scripture, reshaping liturgies and recasting prayers and hymns. This reconstruction included changing language to include women — for example, changing "mankind" to "humankind." We also introduced new metaphors for God, such as Friend or Mother or Lover, introducing a feminine face to this concept. Further, we were learning feminist interpretations of the old stories. From feminist biblical scholars we learned that Genesis does not point to the sin of woman leading the helpless man astray. Rather, it illustrates the sinfulness of patriarchy and how the relationship between women and men is distorted by power and abuse. As well, feminist examinations of church histories revealed that there were many women active in the early life of the church, so using the writer Paul as an argument for women's silence was unfounded in tradition as well as in scriptural interpretation. By challenging the sexism in the traditional theology of mainline Christianity, we were taking the initial step of feminist liberation theology. We were seeing the Christian faith tradition and its alternatives with new eyes.

Out of the Friends of Hagar, a number of women established a project called the Movement for Christian Feminism. For several years I functioned as the co-ordinator of this ecumenical venture, which was funded by numerous churches. The project was designed to reach out to Christian women who were struggling with the issues raised by the women's movement. At this time there were few women faculty in theological schools, and the numbers of female students going into ministry were just beginning to rise. National church offices were starting to form task groups to examine the changing roles of women and men in the church and society. Women were coming to feminist consciousness and beginning to challenge the lack of women's presence in the decision-making bodies of the church. Women's salaries and conditions of employment were scrutinized, and women's spirituality became something to explore.

This awakening process was a profoundly spiritual time of defining ourselves as women of faith, and not just people who belonged to particular denominations. Finally we had tools to develop a conceptual base for understanding the world around us and our place in it. Much of our networking and sharing of resources was accomplished through conferences and workshops, and via a newsletter. Organized events brought women together to tell their stories — stories of the harm done by distorted theology and discriminatory practices. Though the written history of women was at that time scanty, we found enough to show us that women before us and like us had searched for ways to actualize their faith and express their spirituality. We had a sense of continuity with these subversive activities of women in the past, women who refused to be bound by the expectations of their day. Now we knew that we were born to be neither the handmaid of our brother, nor his seductive temptress. The importance of non-inclusive language became clear to us as we wrestled with such biblical stories as the woman's search for her lost coin. We had been told about the shepherd (God) looking for the lost sheep. We had been told about the father (God) welcoming back the prodigal son. But about the woman with the lost coin as God — never!

In addition to meeting and working with like-minded women, I read every feminist theology book available. These books not only changed my way of thinking, they opened my eyes. However, seeing the world with new eyes was not without pain, as I became aware of the pervasiveness of patriarchy and the complicity of Christian theology within it. All the same, my work in the Movement for Christian Feminism project made this an extraordinary time in my life. It was a period of standing with other women and at the same time standing on the shoulders of those who had gone before. Often I would turn to the wisdom of women like Aunt Thirza, who demonstrated the possibility of resistance. At the same time, I knew myself to be stirred by something I call the Spirit, and I came to understand my choice to identify with the vision of a just world associated with the Jesus story.

All this activity did not go unnoticed. Like many of the women I was working with, I encountered the incredible anger and hostility that are directed towards those who try to live into the vision of justice. Feminists working in other spheres of the community (and in other eras) have commonly been caricatured as foolish or self-serving. The same phenomenon happened within the church. This reaction is usually triggered in conservative thinkers when we identify women as participants in the founding events of Christianity, and as significant subjects within the biblical story itself. For men and women who identify with the dominant patriarchal traditions of interpretation, this transformative theological activity is a threatening phenomenon. These traditionalists protest that "radical feminists" are misappropriating the Bible, rewriting scripture and reinventing themselves and God. Often, however, the prospect of "new" truths being invented is only a secondary cause of the critics' anxiety. The primary threat is the scandal perceived in biblical work that lifts up a new/old possibility: that the eternal verities of faith can be claimed by women, and reconstructed on behalf of women and other marginalized groups.

The years following my time with the Friends of Hagar were marked by an ongoing process of faith redevelopment along a road that would bring me home to myself spiritually. Inspired first by my early years in ministry working with youth on the street, and then by the Movement for Christian Feminism, I followed a path that eventually led me to teaching in a theological school. By now I had acquired post-graduate degrees in religious education and social work and was beginning a doctoral of ministry programme. Feminist liberation theology had come of age, and feminist courses were being taught in theological schools, where a growing fifty percent of the students were women. Now in my forties, I seemed compelled to move into yet another stage of knowing more about myself, this time as a lesbian.

As a Christian lesbian feminist I lived a double life. I spent most of my time "passing" or "colluding" in order to survive within heterosexual society, and I knew the necessity of these actions. As Thirza would so aptly say, "What the ear doesn't hear, the heart doesn't grieve about." The expression of my lesbian identity was constrained by the rampant homophobia and the cloak of silence that surrounded homosexuality within mainstream society, including the church. There seemed to be little or no appreciation of or compassion for the pain and suffering of gays and lesbians living in a heterosexist community.

This was a time when younger lesbians were jumping out of the closet and demanding that older lesbians follow suit. I desperately wanted to be "out," to experience the freedom and joy of living with integrity, not having to hide or pretend. I also wanted to be out for the Christian lesbians who were already out, for I was painfully aware that these women were alone with the hatred and rejection that swept through the church. However, despite my desire to live openly as a lesbian, my thoughts were dominated by my awareness of the price others had paid for being out, and the prejudice I would certainly face if I followed them. I believed I could not risk coming out because it would affect my ability to continue the ministry to which I felt called. For years I had been the focus of misogynous energy from Christian folk; facing the hatred that accompanies homophobia seemed far more than I was able to carry. Of course, I realize now that much of the negativity I experienced over the years was likely rooted in homophobia; to many in the church, being a feminist meant hating men, and was associated with being lesbian.

At the same time that I was closeted within the church, I was out in certain women's communities. My straight feminist friends often provided cover for those of us who were developing a lesbian network within the larger community of Christian feminists. This was a gift, for without their support it would have been much harder for lesbians to find each other and our own sense of lesbian community. Only in these community groups did I have the freedom to speak as a lesbian. For the first time, I heard my own lesbian voice, speaking from my own experiences. For the first time, I could speak about lesbians inclusively, not as if their lives were not my own.

Just before my fiftieth birthday, and after almost thirty years in Toronto, I yet again broke with the familiar, taking a teaching job in Halifax. I was on my own again. In this new setting I was not yet designated as "that Christian feminist woman," nor did I want to be typecast as such. Teaching was exciting; it gave me renewed opportunities to integrate a passion for justice by raising students' consciousness about power and privilege, oppression and liberation. However, in Halifax the church context of my teaching was already affected by the "issue" — that is, the debate over the ordination/commissioning of lesbians and gays. As I settled into my new life, the polarizing dynamics of this debate swirled around me. After enduring two excruciatingly painful occasions in the courts of the church, when people were arguing about whether or not homosexuality was a "God-given" way of being, I withdrew beyond the boundaries of the debate. Despite my years in ministry, despite the depth of my faith, these people would question my existence and my vocation. Reasoning that I would have to remain underground, I opted to go on living a life that was split.

Again, I searched for and found a lesbian community where I could be myself. There was more life for me in the lesbian world than in the church, and it was in the lesbian community that my spirituality was nurtured. Reflecting on this time, I remember the despair of not being able to bridge my two worlds. And yet I knew from my experience that who I was and what I was about had something to do with learning to integrate all the dimensions of my life. I no longer wanted to live a divided life, being "out" in one place and not another, telling some people and not others. Through work with an able feminist therapist, I was able to explore some of the infractions against me as a child and adolescent, and to revisit some of the decisions I had made as an adult seeking lesbian relationships. The therapist called forth my spirit and enabled me to recognize afresh that my energy of resistance, my profound convictions about human value, my dogged tenacity and hopeful vision, were, in fact, all qualities of my spiritual life. At that time, I finally decided that I needed to claim my lesbian voice within the church. It only remained for me to live into this decision.

During the year following my sixtieth birthday, I spent a great deal of time pondering this coming of age. Fortuitously, I was asked to write a reflection on a loss experience. I finally settled on what I identified as a sense of loss, and wrote of the loss of my youth:

*I have lost a sense of myself as I knew and I liked myself. I often say I am unashamedly vain! I loved the way I have been able to live in the world ... I have known myself as attractive, strong and energetic ... I am not talking here of physical beauty but rather about an essential way of being. Now I can feel my body, my older body changing ... My flabby arms are there for all the world to see ... I have far less energy.*

It had taken me a year to accept the aging process. An encounter with breast cancer, five years previously, had told me that I was not invincible. I continued to reflect on the meaning of my loss:

*I know my loss is nothing of any real consequence when measured
against the significance of Life itself. Life is enormous. Life involves
others. It involves the pain of the world. My loss is my personal
pain. The connection is that as I know pain myself, I am in some
way connected to the world's pain and to God who abides in this
world, particularly with those in pain …*

Aging raised questions about my self-identify and my way of
being in the world. What ultimately seemed to make sense to me
was to recall the presence of a stirring that has animated my soul
since my mid-twenties, when I was touched by the Spirit at the
time of my conversion. That stirring has led me to work at things
that I think have importance, and that in some ways contribute to
the coming Shalom, peace with justice. I finished the reflection
on loss by commenting on the gains of aging:

*My vanity prevails as I am conscious of presenting myself to the
world as an "older" woman who does not look her age! I enjoy the
fact that I now most often win the top prize for my age category
in road races, since I am the only one out there over sixty. I mostly
feel comfortable with who I am, flabby arms and all. I really like
not having so much angst about my personal life as it leaves more
energy to be able to engage life more fully. And I appreciate the
wisdom that seems to attend the aging process.*

Functioning as an "out lesbian" is simultaneously a frightening and an immensely exhilarating time. On the one hand, I fear
my lack of courage to keep going. On the other, I am full of
excitement about the possibilities this new self-naming will open
up for me. It is essential to me that I live the rest of my life known
as a lesbian. I have been informing most of my family and
friends. At our fall faculty meeting, I announced to my colleagues that, as a lesbian, I would be doing research into the lives
of other lesbian women. There have been no earth-shattering
responses. I suspect that this declaration has been far more of an
issue for me than for anyone else. I am told that everyone knew

I was lesbian, although I firmly believed that no one knew unless I told them.

Recently, I have been preparing for a sabbatical year. The research project I have settled on is to capture the stories of women who were in pastoral ministry during the "issue" debate on the ordination of homosexuals. What were their spiritual resources? Who were their supporters? Why did they stay or why did they leave? Preparing for work that will be written in my lesbian voice has generated strange and unexpected emotional responses in me. As I proceed, I have come to an understanding of my own experience as a lesbian in the church. The questions I want to ask other lesbian women are my own questions. Have I had a particular spiritual life that nurtured and provided me with the strength and enthusiasm to remain connected to the church and its Jesus story? Why have I stayed? What stopped me from leaving?

Through the years, I have discovered that it is difficult to walk away from the church, despite the pain and stress. Staying in the church as a lesbian feminist makes no sense at all, except when I recognize the potential that this particular structure might have in creating a different world. I have refused to leave the church because I have recognized the need for the liberation of women, both inside and outside the church, from a theology that is oppressive. What stopped me from leaving was the fact that I could not imagine where else I would go and be able to do the things I wished to do. It has been the right decision for me. I have been given the extraordinary gift of experiences that have added meaning to my life. There have been riches beyond my wildest dreams — deep friendships, knowledge, insight and opportunities, to name only a few.

In spite of the church's own injustice, it has a history of resistance to injustice, and I claim the "cloud of witnesses" to injustice as my ancestors, my family of faith. Specifically, my role models have been women who insisted that the core message of the Bible was one of justice. Women like Elizabeth Cady Stanton, whose 1898 writings are an example of the deconstruction of distorted ideas and teachings.[4] Stanton's work stands as a record of resistance to the biblically grounded attacks by clergy on women in the suffrage movement. Also serving as an inspiration to me is Nellie McClung, who used her marvellous way with words on many occasions in the courts of the church, demonstrating how persuasive debate can further a cause. And of course I can't forget Aunt Thirza, who always spoke, even when not spoken to.

I soon will be travelling on a road I have never see before. In three years, I retire as a teacher and face the possibility of looking for something else to do with my energy and time. I will no longer be in active ministry. What does an ordained, lesbian, feminist academic woman do in her retirement? That has yet to be discerned.

Despite my journey's countless turns, I have rarely travelled alone for very long; there have been numerous companions along the way. And despite my fearfulness about the future, I have rarely been without hope or a vision; there always seems to be possibility ahead. Thirza's spirit is never far from me, nudging me to speak out and bring injustice to the attention of the powers that be. The eyes of Peggy still meet mine in the women in the sex trade, the homeless and lost. Over and over again, I have heard Miss Bell encouraging me in the voices that have inspired and sustained me as I tried to do things far beyond my own expectations.

My life has been one of questioning and searching, with a deep desire to be free to live openly and honestly. As I continue to seek an integrated and embodied spirituality, I have dared to use my lesbian voice, first to myself and then more publicly. I have moved to yet another "moment of changed consciousness." As an older lesbian woman, I am again involved in the task of inventing myself. I am convinced that my spirituality will be reawakened and deepened as I contend with a society that prefers to believe that, and to behave as though, homosexuals ought not exist. My spirit is eager to meet the new challenge, and I will continue to draw on the support of my companions.

## ENDNOTES

1. The Stone Center was established to provide therapy for women and to carry out psychological research on women.

2. Judith Jordan, "A Relational Perspective for Understanding Women's Development," in *Women's Growth in Diversity*, Judith V. Jordan (ed.), (New York: Guilford, 1997), p. 15.

3. Mary Daly, *Beyond God the Father: Towards a Philosophy of Women's Liberation* (Boston: Beacon Press, 1973), p. 55.

4. Elizabeth Cady Stanton, *The Women's Bible* (Seattle: Coalition Task Force on Women and Religion, 1974).

# CHERYL MALMO

# *JOURNEY TO THE GODDESS*

### DISCOVERING A FEMINIST SPIRITUALITY

*G*rowing up in a prairie village that boasted many different Christian churches, but not "ours," I experienced numerous forms of Christianity. The positive message invariably was "Jesus loves the little children of the world." However, the elitism disturbed me — each church believed that its faith was the right one. It seemed to me that judging people by their religion was hypocritical — didn't Jesus love all the little children? — so early on I became a cynic.

Our own church was my mother's, Anglican, twenty-five kilometres away, which we attended on religious holidays when I was older. Here I appreciated the organ music, tall brass candlesticks and brocaded cloths decorating the altar and podiums, colours changing with each season. I liked the formality, the ritual, that for communion we drank wine. However, the words of the prayers and hymns, the language of the Bible readings and the sermons felt stilted and alienating. Having faith seemed to require being a blind and unquestioning follower, something I was not. So while I participated by kneeling, I always kept my head up and eyes open, consciously challenging the speakers' words and assumptions.

When I left home in 1963 to attend university, religion briefly took on a new dimension as I met members of the politically and socially conscious Student Christian Movement (SCM). Eager to travel to Toronto in the summer, I took advantage of the opportunity to work in an SCM mental health work camp, with students from across the country. More important to me than our political protests were our attempts to educate ourselves on mental health issues. My interest in psychology persisted. I returned to Ontario the following year to work at Warrendale, a summer camp for disturbed children. There I met and fell in love with Mitch, our recreation director, a Jewish man. The following year we had a non-denominational wedding on the university campus in Edmonton, with a minimum number of references to God, readings from Kahlil Gibran and vows we had written ourselves. For two years we lived in Ontario, near my in-laws. Always interested in learning about other cultures, I anticipated I would now be able to experience Jewish rituals firsthand. Sadly, I attended only one Seder and one Bar Mitzvah during this time.

Pursuing our common interest in psychology, Mitch and I moved back to Edmonton in 1969 to begin graduate school together. There, another student, Lorette, introduced me to feminism, lending me Betty Friedan's *The Feminine Mystique*, and inviting me to join her consciousness-raising group. At last I had found a home for my critical thinking. While I was still in the midst of my studies, my son, David, was born in 1971. I allowed him to be circumcised to satisfy my husband's Jewish tradition, something I now perceive as barbaric, but my consciousness-raising group hadn't yet dealt with that issue. We were still focused on examining our socialization and experiences of devaluation and discrimination. I had no interest in having my son baptized;

I did not believe that he was born in sin and had no interest in his receiving a blessing from any patriarchal institution. Mitch left four months later. I divorced him, not because of differences in spiritual belief or background, but because of our very different attitudes towards sexual intimacy and commitment — I believed they were integral to our marriage; he did not.

The late 1970s brought more changes: commitments to doctoral studies and to a new long-term relationship with Ray, a sensitive artist with a gentle spirit. For the first time I was with a man who offered me everything that was important to me — healthy sexuality, commitment, and respect for my strengths and interests. When I expressed fear that he would leave me when our baby was four months old, he would humour me: "You'll see; I'll be here." In 1978 I gave birth to Ryan, my second son. Ray stayed.

I believed that I could do a better job than could any religious institution to instill in my sons a morality that challenged prejudice of all kinds. People had many different ideas about religion, and no particular religion was the right one, I explained to my sons. I also taught them that women were as valuable as men; that everyone deserved to be loved, respected and treated kindly; that speaking out against injustice was important; that sex was for fun as well as for making babies; and that women could love women and men could love men, just as men and women could love each other. I knew I had been successful on the latter point when David, aged six, asked at a cousin's wedding, "Are those men marrying each other?" Likewise, I knew I had succeeded when Ryan, aged nine, returned from a Saturday-night sleep-over that included a Sunday morning church service. I asked, "So, how was church?" He replied, "Disgusting! They're racist!" "What makes you say that?" I inquired. "The pastor talked about Jews not believing in Jesus," he explained. I said little but silently cheered, pleased that Ryan's consciousness enabled him to be critical of the elitism he had sensed.

In the mid-1980s, my work as a psychotherapist took an unexpected turn. After two years in therapy dealing with the

ramifications of child sexual abuse, one of my clients began
remembering incidents of abuse by family members in a satanic
cult. Her growing awareness that she had been abused spiritually
as well as physically, psychologically, emotionally and sexually,
forced me to face the reality of evil, and to examine my understanding of spirit. Together we explored the depths of her trauma
and engaged in activities to facilitate her healing. As was routine
in my work with survivors of childhood trauma, I had already
assisted her, using hypnosis, to imagine a safe place and a spirit
guide. Her spirit guide was a guardian angel, and we both began
to collect angels, for ourselves and for each other, for protection
and for healing.

Around this time I read Marion Zimmer Bradley's *The Mists
of Avalon*. The intuitive powers of women in this book intrigued
me, as did their opposition to the repressive Christian church,
which was committed to extinguishing them. I persuaded Ray to
read the book and he too found it compelling. When I received
notice of a meeting of the European Congress of Hypnosis in
Oxford, England, in 1987, I knew that I must attend, and that Ray
must come too. We could visit Glastonbury, the setting for
Bradley's book, the place where the Celtic priestesses encountered and struggled against the invading Roman Christians. We
could enter Bradley's fantasy and climb the Tor, the high hill that
was home to the priestesses of Avalon. We could experience the
magic of the ancient spirituality of Bradley's fiction that had so
enthralled us.

## THE FIRST JOURNEY

We began our quest in England by visiting numerous spiritual
places — the beautiful old churches and chapels of Oxford, as
well as the ancient stone circles of Stonehenge and Avebury,
located in the surrounding countryside. While I could easily
relate to the churches through my own Anglican background, I
was even more intrigued by the stone circles, powerful and

mysterious symbols of a spirituality I did not comprehend. Similarly, I marvelled at the giant white horse embedded into a hill, not yet aware she was the symbol of the Goddess Ryan. However, the highlight was Glastonbury, not the wonderful ruins of the town's cathedral where it was claimed Arthur and Guinevere were buried, but the Tor, the high hill, home to Morgan, sister to Arthur and priestess of the ancient pagan religion at Avalon. We found a bed and breakfast with a view of the Tor and, too excited to wait until the next day, approached it at dusk. Once we began the hike, we couldn't stop, even as it got dark. Pretending we were visitors to that ancient time and place, we climbed by starlight along a well-worn path to the top of the Tor, crowned now by the steeple of St. Michael's Chapel. I remember this hike as the most magical I have ever experienced.

Later, as we drove to the ruins of Tintern Abbey in Wales, we heard a BBC radio programme that further fed our excitement. Experts explained that, like most other Christian churches in Great Britian, Tintern Abbey was built on a "power spot" originally located by the Celts. To test this, some people had spent nights among the ruins, recording eerie sounds that were broadcast as part of the programme. This information was confirmation for Bradley's portrayal of Christianity as usurping the power of the ancient pagan religion. It also validated our experience of powerful energy within the stone circles, on the Whitehorse Hills, and on the Tor.

Back home, I continued my practice of feminist psychotherapy. I had not yet connected the ancient spirituality of Glastonbury with the emerging feminist spirituality, not yet understanding how the Goddess was central to nature-based pagan beliefs and practices. I also had not yet differentiated religion from spirituality. I was a social scientist, and religion seemed a waste of time — valuable time needed for facilitating psychological change and taking political action. I remember watching Mair, a member of our feminist community who worked in the women's programme at the university where I regularly taught workshops, crocheting medicine bags during meetings. What had this to do with feminism, I wondered. I also remember a celebration of the women's programme that took place outside in winter. A dozen or so of us had settled into a steaming hot tub. When Mair pointed to the moon and hollered, "There's the Goddess!" I couldn't relate. I had no intention of bowing down to any higher being, even if She was female.

In 1989 the National Film Board of Canada released Donna Read's film *Goddess Remembered*, and a group of women in my neighbourhood met to view and discuss it. The film documented a spirituality in which women's power to give birth and nurture life had been central to early cultures. We learned that the idea of Goddess was qualitatively different from God; whereas God was considered a superior being to be worshipped from afar, from the bottom of a hierarchy, the Goddess was respected as the life force within us all. The film was both an eye-opener and inspirational. This kind of spirituality, so different from the institutionalized religions we had all grown up with, existed not just in Bradley's fictions but in reality. I remember saying to my friends as we parted, "So, we got ripped off by the patriarchy in the spiritual realm, too." In the spring that followed our viewing of Read's film, we met for our first Solstice Ritual.

## THE SECOND JOURNEY

In 1990 the European Congress of Hypnosis was meeting in Konstanz, Germany, and Ray and I planned to travel together beforehand, this time taking Ryan. Bradley's latest novel, *The Firebrand*, about the priestess Kassandra (sister to Paris, who was Helen of Troy's lover), inspired me to visit Greece. Ryan, who would be twelve when we made this journey, had developed an interest in Greek mythology, and was as keen as I was to see this part of the world. We agreed that our next spiritual pilgrimage would be to Greece. My friend Kathy suggested that I read *The Chalice and the Blade*, by Riane Eisler, which presented archeological evidence of a Goddess-based culture in

Greece. We would travel to Crete, the last Goddess-centred civilization to survive the influx of aggressive and warring sky-god worshipping northerners. There we could visit the archeological ruins of the Palace of Minos at Knossos where, according to Eisler, there existed "for the last time in recorded history, a spirit of harmony between women and men as joyful and equal participants in life." [1]

Travelling by bus, train and ship, with long hours in the heat, much waiting, and considerable discomfort, we felt like true pilgrims. Our journey took us through Italy, where two sites provided glimpses of what was yet to come. The first was the Garden of the Temple of the Vestal Virgins in Rome, a peaceful and beautiful feminine space in the midst of the overwhelmingly masculine forum, and near the monstrous Coliseum, scene of so much violence and death. In the Garden of the Temple, statues of women surrounded cement pools of water filled with water lilies, and rose bushes climbed against ancient brick walls. I still smile remembering three young women mimicking the postures of the statues, posing excitedly for photos. How wonderful it was for young women to have priestess statues to identify with! My second heartfelt memory of Italy is of a statue of a woman in the Tivoli Gardens outside Rome. Called the Fountain of Nature, her arms were held out to her sides with palms up, water spraying from her many breasts. She was breath-taking! At the time I had no idea of her identity as the Goddess Artemis, but knew I must have a picture of her with me in front, mimicking her stance as best I could, as the young women had done several days before.

I also had some thrilling encounters with the Goddess in Greece before arriving at Knossos. The Caryatids at the Acropolis in Athens deeply moved me. These statues of women, supporting the upper part of a temple on their heads, radiated such power and beauty that I couldn't keep my eyes off them. A few days later, walking through the narrow streets of Navplion in the cool of the evening, I found in a small shop a reproduction in white marble of the Cycladic Goddess, from the third millennium BC.

She stands thirty centimetres high; her arms are folded and her face is blank. I learned later from my readings that this blank face suggests a state of trance or meditation, and that a reverence for altered states of consciousness is related to the stability and non-warring aspect of the ancient culture of the Cyclades Islands, as is the case in other Goddess-centred cultures.

Two other incidents in Navplion warmed my feminist heart. Early in our travels I had finished rereading *The Firebrand*, and Ryan and Ray had both started it. Whenever we returned to our hotel room, father and son argued about whose turn it was to have the book. I was secretly thrilled. One night Ryan commented, while reading about the Trojan war, "Mom, Paris sure is a jerk, isn't he?" What more could a woman want?

Travelling on an overnight ship to Crete, we arrived in Herakleion at dawn and soon found a local bus to take us to the archeological site at Knossos, half an hour away. Upon arrival we hired a guide, a graduate student in archeology who was as enthusiastic about the site as I was. While waiting for her to collect a group for her tour, Ryan helped me gather a handful of small white pebbles from just outside the gates, under a sign warning us to take no stone or object from inside.

Finally entering this site we had travelled so far to see, I was at once overwhelmed. I knew that the women who had lived here between 2,800 and 1,100 BC had been valued as women. Reflecting on what it must have been like to live in a place where female power was truly honoured, I realized that only in such a society could women feel completely safe. And for a fleeting moment, I felt just that, safe! A tidal wave of feeling washed over me. I burst into tears. This was a sacred place! Looking out across the parched brown earth, down the long roadway that led to the city gates, across the stone ruins of the temple, palaces and storage houses, to the sycamore trees and the olive groves beyond, I relished every view. Breathing in the hot, dry dusty air outside or the cool air inside the thick-walled and deeply recessed, naturally air-conditioned buildings, I hung on every story our guide told. I was profoundly and deeply moved. The morning spent at Knossos was an experience unlike any I had ever had before. Whereas I had engaged with the Tor as a delightful fantasy, I now engaged with Knossos as a wonderful reality. For the first time I experienced a meeting of the spiritual and the scientific. Now I understood in my body as well as in my mind, that like the personal, the spiritual is also political.

Back in Herakleion, I purchased from a street vendor a small bronze statue of the Minoan Snake Priestess, raised arms entwined with snakes and breasts proudly bared above her flounced skirt. She is a treasure from that pilgrimage, and a tribute to Cassandra, whose understanding of snakes informed her predictions of earthquakes at the oracle. Back in our hotel room, Ray announced that he had a surprise for me, and handed me a film canister filled with dusty brown earth. He had scooped it up from the queen's chambers — not a stone or an object, just earth. I wept again as I realized how lucky I was to have a partner who understood, respected and supported my spiritual quests.

We spent the afternoon in the cool of the Archeological Museum, which houses the artifacts unearthed from Knossos. Here were statues of the magnificent Minoan Snake Goddess, in ceremonial dress, posed for a ritual, and of acrobats, female and male, leaping over bulls. Here were frescoes of dancing Minoan women and of beautiful creatures — dolphins, partridges, blue birds and mythical griffins. Here were crystals on ropes of silver or gold, just like the crystals now being worn by women at home. Here were the giant butterfly-shaped double axes, used ceremoniously in Goddess rituals. Here, also, were the kitchen butcher knives that, according to Riane Eisler, Victorian male archeologists had incorrectly assumed to be weapons, because they could not imagine a culture that did not engage in war. Here was scientific proof of a Goddess-centred society where people lived peacefully for 3,000 years, connected to nature, the cycles of the real world, enjoying the abundance of life and respecting the reality of natural death. When we finally arrived home, it gave me enormous pleasure to share a little bit of sacred earth from Knossos with my friends.

## The Third Journey

When the next European Congress of Hypnosis was announced for Vienna, 1993, it was time to plan the next Goddess pilgrimage. I consulted Eisler's book. Turkey, known as the Land of the Mother Goddess, was the obvious choice because of Çatal Hüyük, the archeological site of the oldest known Goddess civilization in Eastern Europe. This time Kathy, a colleague with an interest in hypnosis as well as the Goddess — the same friend who had introduced me to *The Chalice and the Blade* — would be my travelling companion.

The first thing we did when we landed in Vienna was to visit the Natural History Museum, which houses the ancient Goddess of Willendorf, an image of female fertility from 30,000 BC, along with numerous other stone and clay Goddess figures. Called Venus von Willendorf in Austria, the Goddess is a clay figure only ten centimetres high, a magnificent shape with heavy breasts and buttocks, a pregnant belly and visible pubic triangle and labia. Her legs end in tapered points so that she can easily be inserted into a niche in a cave wall. Her braided hair encircles a blank face, interpreted as a face in trance like that of the Cycladic Goddess, or the face of everywoman. I can relate to both interpretations, the hypnotherapist in me seeing her in trance, the feminist viewing her as everywoman.

Kathy and I were disappointed that the gift shop at the museum sold no replicas of the Goddess of Willendorf; not even a postcard was for sale. However, later, on the way to a boat tour on the Danube, I found a postcard stand filled with cards of this ancient Goddess. Although it may seem insignificant, finding these postcards was tremendously important: postcard images of the Goddess can be shared; shared images facilitate shared knowledge; and knowledge is power. This find not only validated the reality of women's ancient spirituality: Goddess postcards were political.

The boat trip on the Danube was wonderful, taking us past vineyards and mountains, church steeples and castles. The most exciting moment came with the announcement: "On your right you can see the village of Willendorf, where the Venus von Willendorf was found." I was thrilled! How sychronistic it felt to be cruising past the home of the Goddess!

When the European delegates at the conference heard that Kathy and I planned to seek out the Mother Goddess in Turkey, they were alarmed; it was not safe for women to travel alone there, they said. We shrugged off their concern until we learned of tourists being taken hostage in Eastern Turkey, and of bus bombings in Istanbul, our first destination. I had a tearful long-distance conversation with Ray the night before we were to depart. Should we go? Shouldn't we? He gave me just the push I needed. Of course we should go, he said; we had planned the trip for so long; it meant so much to us; we had come so far. We would be fine. So off we went to the airport, with goodbyes and good lucks and the news that Kurdish rebels had taken more hostages in Turkey. As we boarded our plane and the Austrian airline flight attendant gave us the traditional blessing, "Gruss Gott" (God be with you), we changed it to "Gruss Göttin." We were certain now that the Goddess was with us, and that we were meant to take this trip.

Our first day in Istanbul, we headed out from our rather seedy hotel to see what adventures awaited. Noticing a small sign, "English Books," we entered a courtyard and were immediately drawn to some beautiful kilim carpets on display. Kathy excitedly pointed out some Goddess symbols in the carpets, attracting the attention of the shop's owner. When she started explaining to him about the Goddess images, Reçep politely informed us that he knew all about these images — he taught the history and meaning of these ancient symbols at the university, and hired people in the countryside to weave reproductions of original designs. We were enchanted. I bought three carpets on the spot, and the kilim with the Goddess figure rests on the floor beside me now as I type.

We flew on to Ankara, home of the Museum of Anatolian Civilizations, which houses the most famous statue of the Mother

Goddess of Çatal Hüyük, believed to be the most highly developed neolithic centre of the Near East. Hers was the image we had travelled so far to see. As we approached the museum, a beautiful modern building at the top of a hill, we felt we were approaching a shrine. Once inside, however, our hearts sank. We were told that the neolithic exhibit was temporarily closed, and many pieces had been shipped to an exhibit in Istanbul. However, some Goddess figures were still on display in the foyer, so perhaps we had not come in vain. Sure enough, there she was — the Mother Goddess from Çatal Hüyük, estimated to be 8,000 or 9,000 years old, sitting amidst her contemporaries. She was fabulous: round, bulging, powerful, strong. Made of clay, she sat twenty centimetres high on a throne, giving birth, her arms supported by two leopards. Was this the first birthing chair, I wondered.

Unlike the museum gift shop in Vienna, this shop was overflowing with clay, stone and bronze reproductions of Goddesses, as well as heaps of postcards, jewellery and books illustrating the Goddesses we had seen and others we had not. We purchased our Goddess treasures, delighted with the thought of bringing these images into the lives of our friends and clients. As we strolled back down the hill through narrow streets to our hotel, we noticed a shop displaying mannequins in long white wedding gowns trimmed with red velvet ribbons. What a contrast to the images we carried safely in our bags, and in our hearts!

We next travelled to Cappadocia, a vast geographic area of volcanic sandhills, appearing otherworldly, where people lived in cave dwellings until as recently as 1955. Here, during a day-long tour of the cave dwellings and countryside, we continued to come across symbols of the Goddess. While Kathy climbed high into the caves, I sat happily on the dusty ground, heart pounding and knees weak from peering straight down the side of a cliff a few minutes earlier. Bored with my fantasy of how I would get Kathy home in a body bag should she fall, I turned my attention to my surroundings. Some images carved above the cave doorways caught my eye. To my astonishment, there was the sacred triangle, just as

Riane Eisler had described it: a symbol of the Goddess in the shape of a woman's pubic area. The same day we visited a pottery studio, where we saw two huge clay statues of a Goddess from Haçilar, both seated with one hand resting on a breast. Resigning myself to the fact that these statues were too big to carry home, I contented myself with a photo of me squatting beside them, mimicking their pose.

Our next stop, Çatal Hüyük, was our major destination in Turkey. We knew from Eisler that the egalitarian civilization that developed here around 7,000 BC had survived for 1,500 years without warfare. One of the most impressive discoveries at this site was a birthing shrine — a room with a red-painted floor where women gave birth in a ceremonial context, accompanied by midwives, priestesses and music. Death was similarly celebrated, again confirming the notion of the Mother Goddess presiding over both life and death.

Our guidebook warned us that the closest city, Konya, was very conservative; local women typically dressed in dark robes and veils, and we should take care not to offend the devout Muslims with our Western dress and behaviour. As we disembarked from the bus, two young men — boys, really — approached us, determined to help us with whatever we needed. Ahmat and Ahmet insisted they could show us a cheaper and better hotel than the one we had planned to find. Since they also insisted on carrying our bags, which had grown considerably heavier, we agreed.

On the walk to the hotel, we told our young escorts the purpose of our trip. They knew all about Çatal Hüyük, had a friend Abduhl who was a cab driver, and would arrange for him to pick us up in half an hour. Not only that, but they would come along to protect us from bad Turkish men and snakes. I teased, "You want to be our bodyguards? You're not very big. Are you sure you're strong enough to protect us?" In response, Ahmet pulled from his wallet a Kung Fu identification card while Ahmat insisted we needed bodyguards in the country because "bad things happened to a British woman who went alone." "Fine, you can be our bodyguards," I told them, watching Kathy's eyes grow wide with surprise.

Abduhl proved to be a terrific tour guide as we bounced over dusty gravel roads, past sugar-beet fields, stork nests atop power poles, harvested wheat fields and a band of gypsies sitting outside their tents. Ahmat and Ahmet admitted that they were university students, and that they routinely picked up tourists at the bus station so they could practise speaking English. When we arrived in the little village near the Çatal Hüyük site, we stopped to draw some water from an ancient well consisting of a very long pole on a balance beam. Some curious villagers came out to shyly view us, and we, equally curious, watched them in silence. Finally, at the gate to the archeological site we were met by Mamet, the guard, who spoke little English but graciously invited us for tea. We asked if we could tour the site first and have tea later and he agreed, so off we went for what was to be the highlight of our trip, in the company of four strange but friendly Turkish men.

Although there were plans to resume excavation of the site — Mamet told us the archeologists had left just before we arrived — it had been neglected for almost thirty years because of lack of funds, and earth had filled in most of the excavations. Nevertheless, we could see outlines of walls and buildings, and bones and horns showed through the earth. Mamet had instructed us to take no object from the site, but allowed us to take samples of earth from the temple area, enough to fill two film canisters. Kathy exclaimed that she could feel energy in the temple site, but I knew that my moment of connection had not yet come.

When we reached the highest point of the site, a dry, barren hill from which we could see the surrounding countryside in every direction, I knew I had found the place I had come to experience — a power place. We asked to spend some time there alone, and the four men withdrew to Mamet's small office. There on the hilltop in the intense sun, with the sound of buzzing flies and with two butterflies, one yellow and one black, dancing around us, we sat quietly on some rocks, trying to absorb the significance of Çatal Hüyük, memorizing in our bodies our sense of being there. Feeling the need for a ritual of some kind, we held hands and I said a few words about the power of the Goddess entering our bodies through the heat of the stones and earth, and filling us for our work. With the butterflies still dancing, we cried together, moved by the sacred female energy that people had acknowledged here so long ago.

Back at the guardhouse, Mamet sprinkled ritual lemon cologne on our hands, face and hair to refresh us, and served us apple tea in the shade of the vine-covered patio. Keen to learn how to speak English, he brought out his correspondence lessons and read from a list of phrases he had been studying: "Do not go. Do not touch. It is forbidden. Keep out. Not now. Later." We all told stories, and Kathy showed photos of her grandchildren, and I of my children. As I told the group that today was my sixteenth anniversary and that I was thinking of my husband, I began to cry. Mamet responded by jumping up and picking a flower for me. Then all the men picked flowers for us — blue morning glories and red dahlias, which we pinned in our hair. Finally, Mamet broke his own rule, and presented each of us with a tiny shard of obsidian from the site. We left the site, thrilled with everything that had happened. Our sense of elation must have been contagious, for this time when we stopped in the village, women approached us to share delicious, juicy slices of sweet melon.

Back in Konya, Ahmat and Ahmet became our guides to the city. Our last stop before dinner was the Selimiye Camii mosque, where worshippers were celebrating the birthday of Mohammed. Shoes off, draped in veils, Kathy and I entered and gazed around the huge open space, empty except for dozens of beautifully coloured carpets on the floor. A few men prayed on their knees. In a back corner, a ragged grey cloth screened off a small section of the room. Ahmet explained, in a hushed voice, "For the women." "Then that's where I want to go," I whispered.

Kathy and I slipped into the tiny space, to find it crowded with about twenty women. Some were kneeling and praying on the carpet, others standing at the back, waiting for their turn. When one woman motioned me to take an empty spot, I moved to fill it, kneeling hip to hip on the carpet with the others. Listening to their murmurs, feeling their breath and the warmth of their bodies, I felt intimately connected to the women in that crowded little corner of the mosque. For once, bowing my head and closing my eyes seemed the right thing to do — it helped me focus on what I was feeling and thinking, and besides, there was no leader to watch, listen to or judge. Kneeling there, I was very conscious of how privileged I was to be able to travel halfway around the world to experience Çatal Hüyük and this unexpected spiritual moment. I was also aware that, in spite of their bodies being so heavily robed and veiled, their lives so constricted, and their praying confined to this small, dingy corner, the spirits of these women were strong and would never be extinguished. I reflected that this was the situation of women everywhere: restricted and oppressed in some way or other, but with spirits still very much alive. As I thanked the Goddess for this opportunity to learn, I realized with some astonishment that I had prayed spontaneously twice that day.

After dinner, Kathy and I walked back to our hotel, still accompanied by our bodyguards. Before they left us the two young men insisted we close our eyes. Trusting that nothing bad could happen at the end of such a wonderful, magic day, we complied. We felt them pinning something to our tee-shirts, and when we opened our eyes we saw that we were both wearing tiny embroidered butterflies, Kathy's black and mine yellow. I can still hear Kathy squealing, "Oh, oh, oh!" and feel the pounding in my chest as we stared at each other in disbelief. We had not told these boys of our encounter with the butterflies on the hilltop.

We planned our next destination to provide a change of pace; rather than tour museums and archeological sites, we would visit the natural hot springs of Pamukkale. Although our intent was simply to swim, rest and read, our encounters with the Goddess continued. In a small bookshop we found a wonderful little book, *Anatolia Land of Mother Goddess*[2] by Resit Ergener, a professor at the University of the Bosphorus in Istanbul. Not only did this book give information about the Mother Goddess from Çatal Hüyük, it explained how the Goddess is still present in all religions and cultures. It described how blood, a symbol of women's fertility and power, is used in religious stories around the world. For example, the Koran tells that God created man from a clot of blood. Rituals using blood were also present in every culture, according to Erenger. In medieval Europe women sowed seeds from bags stained with menstrual blood or poured menstrual blood directly onto the soil; in Anatolia, they covered clay statues of the Goddess with menstrual blood and buried them in the fields during planting.

As religions became patriarchal, however, rituals began to change, requiring sacrifice and bloodletting by males. It is no coincidence that an image of Judaism is of Abraham prepared to sacrifice his son to prove his love to a male God, and that the image of Christianity is of Christ sacrificed on the cross to save those who believe in the same male God. I reflected that the Christian mass involves a symbolic drinking of Christ's blood, and that in Orthodox Judaism women are considered unclean after giving birth. I recalled signs on temple doors in Southeast Asia forbidding menstruating women entry, and remembered that a Thai woman who once lived in our home for several months would not pick vegetables in the garden while she was menstruating, for fear of killing the plants. Patriarchy had usurped women's power, and reversed the meaning of women's blood. Ergener's stories went on and on, through culture after culture: human sacrifice, animal sacrifice, body piercing, washing in blood, drinking blood, bloodletting, priest castrations, male-child circumcisions, blood wiped on foreheads and brides dressed in red. An image from Ankara returned — the red-velvet ribbons trimming white bridal gowns. Then I made my own connection — the red roses traditionally carried by brides back in the fifties, a last remnant of the Mother Goddess for Christian women (at least for Protestant women who lack a special connection to the Virgin Mary enjoyed by their Catholic sisters).

Walking along the main street in Pamukkale one evening, we noticed a bus tour to Aphrodisias and its temple of Aphrodite. Unable to resist another archeological site, we signed up for a tour the next day. The site at Aphrodisias was large and wonderfully preserved. Most beautiful was the temple, modelled on female genitalia: while the outer foyer symbolized the outer labia and the inner foyer the inner labia, both preceded the entrance to the inner sanctum, the most sacred place in the temple, the womb. After touring the grounds in the heat, we were thankful to enter the coolness of the museum. Much to our surprise, in the gift shop, seated on a shelf among her Turkish sisters, was the Goddess of Willendorf — not valued enough in her native Austria to be available there, but valued here in the Turkish countryside.

Dalyan, an idyllic town on the Mediterranean, offered another time-out from our pilgrimage. After a few days of boating, swimming and snorkelling, and another unexpected visit to yet one more archeological site, we decided to spend a day in the shade of tall trees at an outdoor café, reading and writing in our journals. Suddenly the sound of horns and drums blasted into our peaceful reverie. "What's going on?" we inquired. "A parade for a circumcision celebration; you know, snip, snip," a man explained, scissoring his index and middle fingers. We hurried into the street, following the sounds of the band.

At the head of the parade was a father leading his little boy, aged nine or ten, on a donkey. The boy wore a bright red satin cape and hat trimmed with white fur and sequins. He looked terrified, and our hearts broke for him. Behind him was a truck carrying a four-piece band, followed by two cars filled with men, honking and cheering. What really caught our attention, however, was that draped over the neck of the donkey, and over the hoods of all the vehicles, were bright red sheets —another example of the patriarchy's usurping the power of women's blood for their rituals.

The following day, we travelled to Selçuk, near the ancient city of Ephesus, believed to have been founded by the Amazons. Strolling through this site, we were awed by the size of the excavation and its immense structures. Amazing details stared out at us from among the ruins — the Amazon warriors carved into the portico of one building, and the Goddess Adidas on a broken stone, resting at the side of the road. The outside of the beautiful Celsus Library features four huge statues of women symbolizing wisdom (Sophia), knowledge (Episteme), intelligence (Ennoia) and virtue (Arete). Experts believe that the vaulted niche in the centre of the library, which reaches up two storeys, once held a statue of Athena, Goddess of wisdom and learning. These Goddesses, however, are all derivations of the Great Mother Goddess, whose power was broken and divided in the classical period of Greece.

The oldest and most famous site at Ephesus is the Temple of Artemis, which was once the second-largest temple in the world, and was considered one of the seven wonders of the ancient world. It was at this temple that small carvings were found of priests dressed in women's clothing. Ergener explains that priests today wear long robes because the transfer of divine authority from women to men was first achieved by dressing priests in the sacred robes of priestesses. Here at the temple site, dressed in our long skirts, we ceremoniously ate peaches in memory of Artemis, convinced She would have relished in the sweet juice running down our chins and around our wrists.

At the archeological museum in Selçuk, we saw what are probably the two most exquisite statues of Artemis in the world. The Great Artemis, made of reddish marble, is about four metres tall and wears a three-layered headdress, the upper section of which is an Ionian temple. The Beautiful Artemis, made of finer white marble, has no headdress. Now armless, the two statues once held lions. At either side of their heads, and on their upper chests and skirts, are flowers and animals — rams, goats, stags, bulls, sphinxes, griffins and bees. On their lower chests are rows of bulbous protrusions, symbols of fertility — breasts or eggs, depending on the interpretation. Myth has it that this Mother Goddess, believed to be present at the birth of all living things, escaped destruction by the Christians who destroyed her temple because she was assisting at the birth of Alexander the Great. Archeologists believe the statues survived because Artemis was beloved by the people and they hid her images from the marauding Christians. The statues moved us to tears. The smaller one, especially, has exquisite detail, and the soul of Artemis radiates from it — so affirming of the beauty, strength and power of women.

Replicas of both Artemis statues, as well as the other Anatolian Goddesses, filled the adjoining gift shop, and we added to our growing collection. As we left the museum in a state of bliss, Kathy talked of the abundance the Artemis statues represented to her, the abundance she had grown up with on a prairie farm, and the abundance that the world could provide to every human being if the values of the Goddess were honoured. Suddenly, the traffic noise, the air pollution and the overwhelming presence of men and absence of women in Turkish public life, shocked us back to reality — a world under patriarchy.

## MUSINGS ON MY JOURNEYS

My journeys have added a richness to my life that I could not before have imagined —a connection to some part of me not acknowledged by patriarchal religion, and to something greater than me that is hard to define. I am aware now that I began this journey long before I consciously planned trips to Britain, Greece or Turkey. Since my young student days I have collected images of women, infusing my home with their spirits. After discovering feminism, I joked that I needed images of women around me to balance the testosterone-driven energy of the males I lived with. I was already on an inner journey, but I didn't know it.

I now believe that evidence of the Goddess, of respect for the powerful creative and nurturing aspect of women, and for our connection to nature and her cycles, is everywhere in all cultures, if we just look back far enough in time. Archeological sites, museums and antiquities shops hold the evidence, and it is in these places that I continue my quest, wherever I travel. In Paris for my fiftieth birthday, I fell in love at the Louvre with a beautiful statue of Ishtar, Great Mother Goddess of the Babylonians, from 1,000 BC. Once known as the Lady of Vision, she is the all-encompassing Goddess of fertility, birth, death and resurrection, and symbolizes an individual's inner journey to self-discovery and spiritual growth. In l'Orangerie in Paris, I was deeply moved by a life-size marble statue of Eve, naked, holding an apple, the serpent winding at her feet. Poor Eve! She was devalued in her status as the Great Mother, alienated from the snake, restricted from the tree of knowledge, banished from the garden, and portrayed by patriarchy as the downfall of mankind.

On my trip to the most recent Hypnosis Congress in Budapest in 1996, I found in a folklore and icon shop an Egyptian painting on wood. Serendipity was at work again —at the time of this discovery I was reading Pauline Gedge's latest novel about ancient Egypt. The painting kept haunting me — I even dreamed about it — so after several days I returned to the shop and bought it. My knowledge about Egyptian culture was restricted to what I had learned from Gedge, so I had no idea who was depicted in this painting until I got it home and found an exact copy in Hallie Austen's book, *The Heart of the Goddess*.[3] It was Isis leading Queen Nefertari, copied from an Egyptian tomb from 1,300 BC. Isis — known as Au Set to the ancient Egyptians, She from Whom All Becoming Came Forth — was considered the Great Goddess of Egypt, mother to the deities, the sun and the world. As always, first I had the personal experience by following my intuition, then at home I researched and discovered the context; first right brain, then left. Egypt is high on my list of places to visit in the future.

I have learned during winter vacations in Mexico that the Goddess really is everywhere. A small museum in Puerto Vallarta houses about a dozen Goddess statues from the preclassic period of the Olmecs and the classic period of the Toltecs. Interestingly, the guide book to this museum describes the preclassic period as "The Mother Culture," just as Turkish Anatolia is referred to as "The Land of the Mother Goddess." A small museum in Cozumel displays Goddess images from the early Mayan culture. Goddess images are still very present in Mexican culture. A huge sculpture of Ixchel, the Mayan Goddess of the moon, healing and childbirth, sits in a square in the middle of town on Isla Mujeres (Island of Women). A small archeological site on the south end of the island marks a temple where pilgrims came to pray to Her. Images of Ixchel giving birth are carved into the limestone buildings at various archeological sites, including Tulum and Chichén Itzá. The Aztec, too, acknowledged women's power to give birth. When the Aztec Goddess Tlazolteotl is depicted squatting in the final stage of labour, she is sometimes presented as a healthy young woman, and sometimes as a severely emaciated old woman, reminding us that her power is linked to life and death. I was thrilled to learn that the Aztecs honoured as warriors women who died in childbirth, recognizing that when a woman gives birth, she faces her own death.

Most recently, in the expansive and beautiful archeological museum in Quito, Ecuador, I was thrilled to find hundreds of Goddess statues from the Inca culture, and from the Valdivia, the Bahia and the many cultures that came before the Incas. The experience of walking through this wonderful museum, surrounded by Goddesses from many ages, felt more sacred than the trips we made to the numerous churches in the old city. A more up-to-date version of the Goddess is found in many virgin images, common in the religious artwork and culture of both Ecuador and Mexico. In Mexico today, people still pray to the Virgin of Guadalupe, who in the sixteenth century was considered a symbol of freedom from European invaders. Representing unconditional mother love, she is virgin in the original sense — whole unto herself.

I have also discovered images of the Goddess close to home. Native Albertans make a pilgrimage every year to nearby Lac St. Anne, named for the mother of Mary, to bathe in her sacred waters. Statues of Kuan-yin, China's Goddess of Mercy, abound in any Chinese store that carries porcelain. As the story goes,

Kuan-yin was a kind and gentle princess who defied her father by refusing to marry and instead became a nun in a temple, tending to the needs of the ill. After her father had her killed, she tended to those in the underworld. When the people demanded that her father resurrect her, he did so and she became a healer in both worlds. India and Japan have their own versions of this Goddess, I've learned. Travelling exhibits from other cultures invariably portray their own beginnings with Goddess imagery and explanations of their pagan beliefs and practices. A recent exhibit from Egypt introduced me to the Scorpion Goddess, Selket, who guards the four sides of Tutankhamen's tomb.

I also have statues of other Goddesses from Indonesia, India and Africa whose names and origins I do not know, gifts from friends and purchases from import shops. I am especially fond of an artifact from northern Syria, third millennium BC, a Goddess with a bird face on a woman's body, connecting her intimately to the natural world. She reminds me that the neolithic roots of the Goddess teaches about living with respect for and in harmony with nature, with the reality of all our cycles including birth and death. She and my many Goddess images validate my femaleness, inoculating me against the devaluing of women that persists in our culture, and filling a void left by a dominating and hierarchical patriarchal religion.

Just as my journeys have enriched my personal life, so too have they enriched my work as a psychotherapist. In the 1970s, while travelling in Thailand, I volunteered to teach communication skills to young counsellors eager to learn the practice of western psychology. They told me stories of Buddhist priests who gave talismans to people to help them with their problems. How superstitious this practice seemed to me then! Now, recognizing my clients' needs for spiritual support, I sometimes give them tiny worry dolls from Guatemala to symbolize traumatized parts of themselves that need to be cared for. At other times I might have them choose a coloured stone that carries a positive message they need to remember. When I sense that a client needs to feel a connection to and a valuing of her female spirit, I give her one of the little white pebbles from Knossos. Finally, my clients choose a beautiful crocheted medicine bag, specially made for me by Mair, to hold their treasure.

Also in my work, I use Goddess energy when I introduce my clients to the idea of a spirit guide, a being or energy that may take any form, that is intelligent and powerful and offers unconditional love and support. Of course, the guides imagined are not necessarily of a Goddess. The power of nature and the energy of the life force come to us through whatever messengers we find meaningful. My clients' spirit guides have taken many forms: people, animals, other aspects of nature, their own higher selves. Whatever form the guide takes, the qualities invariably include those of the Mother Goddess: wisdom, power, love and support.

I believe that my journey to the Goddess will continue throughout my life, that I will continue to develop spiritually just as I continue to develop intellectually and emotionally. I have already discovered that the spirit of the Goddess is in all of us, women and men alike, in our desire to nurture and support life through actions that contribute to the protection of all living things and to the creation of a peaceful and loving world. This realization is a gift I will treasure forever. Secure in my knowledge that the Goddess was the basis for cultures living in peace, cooperation and harmony with nature and each other in the past, I have found a reason to be hopeful for the future.

## ENDNOTES

1. Riane Eisler, *The Chalice and the Blade* (San Fransisco: Harper & Row, 1987), p. 31.

2. Resit Ergener, *Anatolia: Land of Mother Goddess* (Hitit Publications [undated]).

3. Hallie Iglehart Austen, *The Heart of the Goddess: Art, Myth and Meditations of the World's Sacred Feminine* (Berkeley, CA: Wingbow Press, 1990).

# NAIDA D. HYDE

## RAVEN ON MY HEAD

### FOLLOWING
### MY VISION TO
### SOUL CONNECTION

*Once you live any piece of your vision it opens you to a constant onslaught. Of necessities, of horrors, but of wonders too, of possibilities ... like meteor showers all the time, bombardment, constant connections.*[1]

*— Audre Lorde*

*M*y tale is a tapestry woven of personal psychological healing and shamanic healing. It is the story of connection with my soul and connection with the spirits and teachers in nature. And like the process of healing, this tale of my journey to soul connection is not linear; there is no starting place and there is no end in sight. It moves backward and forward, a wave — gaining energy, losing energy, increasing momentum, resting, disappearing and then magically reappearing with magnificent intensity when least expected.

In June of 1990, I set off to attend a workshop on alternative healing methods at Esalen, Big Sur, on the California coast, a centre I had always considered to be a bit suspect if not downright "flaky." The first session began in the evening and I had more than a little trepidation as I entered the room. I sat down in the circle feeling shy and anxious, aware that I was probably the only Canadian in the group. In the soft dusk light I suddenly saw a huge standing grizzly bear; she had positioned herself so that I could see her from where I sat. As I sat looking at her, I knew that she was there for me. I had met animal spirit guides before, as part of guided imagery work, but this was the first time an animal guide had appeared to me unbidden.

A couple of days later, the workshop leader told us that we were going to do a shamanic journey to the fast beating of two drums. We were told to find a hole in the earth and go down through it to nonordinary reality to find our "power animals," and to journey with them. Immediately I could see my entry point. I knew that I would enter the earth through the roots of a solitary old fir tree in the garden of our Vancouver home. The drumming started and the shamanic journey began.

My animal guides accompanied me as I walked through Monet-like flower gardens, vibrant colours everywhere. I found myself flying a long distance on Eagle's back, over mountains. The Himalayas, I thought. After some time, we landed in a grassy place with soft, rounded green mountain ridges at our backs and in front of us. From off to my right but out of sight there came the sound of a rushing mountain creek. Eagle, Bear, Seal and I sat in a circle. They told me that I needed to come to this place and start a healing centre for women. Eagle gave me the acuity of her awareness; Bear gave me the abundance of her love; and Seal gave me her deep and quiet wisdom.

During this shamanic journey, I was fully conscious of my surroundings. I had a sense of how much time had passed, and it seemed not unlike guided imagery I had done before. But when we returned from journeying and it came time to report my experience to the rest of the group, I began to tremble and cry. I could feel the vibrations of the drum go through me. I found it difficult to speak. I could not get control over my shaking and crying. I was suffused with a feeling I had never experienced before. I called it joy, but now I know it was ecstasy. As well, I know now that shamanism is called "the crying way," signifying both the tears of grief and pain that wash our wounds, and the tears of ecstasy that mark our connection with the spirits and our healing. As I described my journey to the group, I knew that the place I had been to was not the Himalayas but the Selkirk Mountains in the Kootenays, a beautiful area in southeastern British Columbia that I had visited only once.

For many years I had worked as a psychotherapist with women trauma survivors, and I had taught other mental health professionals how to do trauma work. Over time I had realized that psychotherapy must acknowledge and heal trauma to the spirit, and that traditional psychotherapy is not enough to transform trauma into healing. My experience is that healing and transformation cannot fully take place without in some way accessing energy that is external to both client and therapist and to the psychotherapy relationship. None of us has within herself the enormous energy required to fuel transformation of the deep wounding that so many of us as women have experienced. However, I am not presenting a prescription to follow. Instead, I am describing what I know "fits" for me, and inviting each of you to seek healing energy in a way that fits for you, and to take action on your own behalf using that energy.

When I came home from California, my partner, Helga Jacobson, and I drove to Nelson, a mountainside town on Kootenay Lake in the Selkirk Mountains. The experience in my shamanic journey had been the first of its kind in my life, and I was impelled to go and check out what I had seen and heard. I felt a single-mindedness, focus and energy unlike any I had previously experienced. I even went to the bank and did the paperwork for a mortgage. But when we arrived in Nelson after a long day's drive,

I got cold feet and just wanted to drive around and look at the area. Helga said I would be disappointed to go back to Vancouver without doing what we had come here to do. Everyone needs at least one enlightened witness to mirror her truth, and Helga was mine at that moment. My anxiety galvanized into energy and I was ready to act. And so we found a real estate agent.

I could hardly walk into a real estate office and say, "I have had a vision of some land and I wonder, if you aren't too busy today, if you could take me to it?" Instead, I asked to see some land with a house on it, somewhere out of town. The second property the agent showed us was exactly the place I had been to in my journey. The mountains were behind and in front, the creek flowed through the land out of sight to my right but not out of hearing, and I could see the grassy area where I had sat with my animal guides. I was walking in ordinary reality where I had been in nonordinary reality just the week before. I wandered the land, scarcely able to take in the possibility of living in this beautiful place. I was filled with anxiety. I know that taking action is a vital part of any transformation, but I was in psychic and emotional shock at what I felt was required of me now. Again Helga was my enlightened witness. She walked the land with me and quietly affirmed that the power of the shamanic journey was intended to carry me through into action, and that the time for action was now. Two hours later, we bought the land.

Over the next year and a half, I closed my practice in Vancouver and finished my work with many wonderful women. We left our home of many years and said goodbye to friends and colleagues. I endured this huge loss to go to a place where I knew no one. It was the most difficult thing I have ever done, but it was also the most strengthening and exhilarating adventure of my life. I have had to grieve for many losses and feel incapacitating loneliness. I have also had the unprecedented opportunity to connect with the land and with the earth. I have learned to listen to Raven and to Steller's Jay, and to grow vegetables and flowers. I have had the quiet and leisure to notice my impatience — how I want my difficult feelings to be over with and gone, just as I want the cucumbers to form and grow before the plant is ready, and the tomatoes to ripen before their time. My city-busy energy has slowly dissipated as I have moved inside the inexorable dance of the days and the seasons.

During the first spring on our new land, as I struggled to make space to grow vegetables and flowers, I made a commitment to the earth and to the birds, butterflies and insects who visited with me: I would grow organically, I would help the earth to heal. Early mornings in the garden, ravens talked to me. They flew over me so close I could hear their wings beat the air, their shining black bodies celebrating daybreak. Our land and home became RavenSpirit. At the time I did not know the full meaning of that name, but I knew it was right. Later I was told by my power animals — Raven now among them — that RavenSpirit is actually my own name, honouring my present transformation. And I began to write about my experiences with shamanism and the spirits of nature. One morning as I sat writing, I could feel claws digging into my head. It was Raven, standing on my head, directing my words.

Shamanism makes deep sense to me; my soul connection with the earth now has a name. It makes sense to me that every part of the living earth is sentient, that each has a spirit of its own, a living intelligence. Each rock, tree, dewdrop, plant, bird and animal holds wisdom, knowledge and integrity. Over time I have learned that the spirits want us to heal. They want us to be whole; they want us to be in a healing relationship with each person with whom we come in contact, and they want us to heal the earth. It also makes sense to me that indigenous people worldwide and throughout history have made similar connections with the spirits in nature, for a minimum of forty thousand years, understanding that, as people, we are only one small part of a larger whole.

Learning to use the healing power and wisdom inherent in a shamanic understanding of the universe has been my work for the last seven years at RavenSpirit. For the first few months after moving here, I could stay outside for only brief moments before the power in the land caused me to flee indoors, full of inexplicable anxiety. Over time, I began to take in the abundance of the earth and sky. Growing up, deprivation had been my familiar, and so abundance was new and frightening. Despite what I had considered to be my perfect family, I had grown up in an atmosphere of invisibility and emotional neglect. It is so difficult to give up family loyalty, loyalty to the familiar — and break family silences — but my soul was the price my loyalty had exacted. Now I had begun the painstaking process of taking back my soul, walking the land, feeling the soles of my feet connect with the earth, breathing wilderness air.

Gradually, I slowed my life down so that I could listen to what the spirits of the land were telling me, and receive what they were giving me. Attuning myself to the birds, to the plants, to the trees, to the creek, required me to move to a stillpoint deep inside so that my energy better matched theirs. Only then could I listen to what they had to say and feel their loving energy.

## PSYCHOLOGICAL TRUTH-TELLING AND SHAMANIC DISMEMBERMENT

When I look back on that first shamanic journey and what the message has required of me ever since, I am astonished. What strikes me most is that I was emotionally ready for the power of that journey. What made me ready? What constituted "ready" for me? Joan Halifax writes that to become a shamanic healer "something has to break open inside you; and then that which is discovered within is found to be raw and absolutely naked. It is rare and it is cultivated in the wilderness." She goes on to describe rites of shamanic initiation in indigenous cultures, saying that extended periods of isolation, combined with experiences of shame, grief and fear, "shock at the level of the self, at the core of the psyche, beyond an idea." [2]

I now understood for the first time how I had come to do healing work with women. I understood what had prepared me to listen to the spirits' call. For several years before taking that first shamanic journey at Esalen, I had been doing deep and intensive healing work with women and also doing my own personal healing. I discovered that to have emotional integrity required telling my truth. For too many years I had been sleep-walking through my life, deceiving myself. My lifelong low-level depression and feeling of inner emptiness had been invisible to me; at that time I had had no enlightened witness to mirror my truth to me. I presented such an outgoing, friendly and competent self to the world that I fooled myself into believing that I must be as fine as I appeared to be, and as everyone around me believed me to be.

In 1970, when I had finished graduate school in Boston, my professors had invited me to join their graduate faculty. Soon after receiving my doctoral degree, I had become the acting head of the department of psychology at the hospital where I worked. Any position I wanted was mine over the next few years. My choice of partners was much less successful, but it took me years to work out that I had chosen partners who carried deep trauma similar to that which was as yet unconscious in me. And so I rested in the solitary and grandiose notion that I was clear about my life, and did not need help from anyone. I embodied my family's cardinal rule that I must "go it alone," always. I did not see the inconsistency between this belief and my clarity about women clients: they had been alone in their wounding and so they needed to be accompanied in their healing, and I was their ally to help them heal their lives.

Reading Alice Miller's book *The Drama of the Gifted Child*[3] woke me up. When she described the inner child who lives in solitary confinement in her soul, I knew she was describing me. She was naming the pain I had lived as a child, and I felt the healing power of her recognition. She was my enlightened witness, long before my grandiosity fell apart and I was impelled to re-examine my values and find a psychotherapist.

In my own therapy, I finally had a place to feel and name the immense grief I carried for my cut-down, truncated childhood.

Horror has always been my reaction to bonsai; I know how those trees feel. I was invisible to my mother; she couldn't see the wonderful little girl I was, alive with hope and possibilities. Instead, I became the reservoir and reflection of her secret wounds and deep disconnection, her wordless pain and suffering, suffering that came also to me as it had to her. My father, whom I adored, loved me from a distance too great to touch my loneliness or mirror my intelligence, musicality or creativity. As I delved deeper and deeper into the truth of my life, I contacted the bedrock of my sadness. About two years into my therapy, I mentioned something to my therapist about my maternal grandfather, whose home we shared from my birth and who died when I was ten months old. My therapist said I must have missed him when he died. I had never given my grandfather much thought, beyond seeing baby pictures of myself basking in his gaze as I sat in a washbasin having my bath.

Without warning, as I recalled those baby pictures, my body became immobilized, frozen. I could not speak. I sat petrified, oblivious to time, reverberating to images of my grandfather putting his fingers in my vagina and his penis in my mouth. My world split open in that moment. I became aware of my therapist being unusually silent and removed, so I told him what I was experiencing, thinking that he might not understand what I was feeling since I was the expert on sexual abuse, not he. He remained silent and I felt deeply betrayed. I buried my feelings because I depended on him, but that was the beginning of the end of my therapy. I had held those memories deep inside until I felt safe to bring them out and look at them in the fresh light of healing. I spent the next twenty-four hours in bed in fetal position, wordless silence resonating through me. My whole life made sense to me now, for the very first time. My work with women made sense to me. The radar I had for women's pain and terror came from my own pain, my own terror. Finally, I could begin to live and work in the strength of my integrity.

But the price of integrity is high. Telling the truth brought an end to my life as I had known it. I started insisting on visibility with my parents and my brother. I turned back their shaming looks, sounds, words, all their efforts to shut down my new-found, hard-won words and actions, to silence the true me. I knew that my life depended on my naming abuse and saying no to it, just as I had supported women in doing for years. And so my world split open once more. The day came when I knew that I could no longer survive contact with my "perfect" family. To compromise myself, to live a lie, to live in bad faith with myself was killing me, suffocating my soul energy. My family did not want to know me, the real me I had wrested from a life sentence of solitary confinement in a prison of accommodation, taking care of their needs at the expense of my own.

How little my family wanted to know me shook me to the core. The ease with which they all gave me up in favour of the status quo seared my soul. I was also stunned and hurt by friends and even psychotherapist colleagues who censured me when I told them I was no longer in contact with my family. I could see that these women had painful, limited relationships with their own families, and were frightened by my action, but this was cold comfort at the time. I entered a long period of isolation in which I grieved deeply for the loss of those I loved, and the loss of the illusions that had shored up my life for forty years. This was my shamanic initiation.

My psyche stripped to the bone, I experienced the soul-level annihilation that is the necessary precursor to the new self, the real self, stretching, moving, blossoming. I now know that it is only in the coldest, bleakest darkness that we can gather the enormous energy necessary for our transformation. Each winter I watch the fruit trees in the solitude and quiet of the dark, buried for so many months under feet of snow. Then, as the light lengthens and the birds begin to sing, the trees bud and blossom with the magic of renewal. So it is with our own growth.

In shamanism, there is a healing method called dismember-ment that is a soul-level parallel to the emotional dismembering and re-membering of the self. Being dismembered and stripped to the very essence, the deep core, allows for re-membering in a healed way, leaving behind what was enervating and soul-destroying. In shamanic journeys I have experienced this kind of nonordinary-reality dismemberment and have felt the healing and empowerment that come from it. However, I am keenly aware that my first true dismemberment was in ordinary reality, when my world split open again and again. Beneath the loss and grief my own spirit was coming alive, beginning to stretch into freedom and vitality.

Following this time of emotional and shamanic dismemberment, I was ready for the challenges and demands of life at RavenSpirit. The biggest challenge was building a workshop and sleeping space for the women who would come. At a workshop in the Sonoran desert, a large rock that was my teacher in a journey said, "The name of the centre you will build is Bear Lodge." Startled, I answered, "But where is the money coming from to build it?" "The name and what it signifies are more important than the money. It is to be called Bear Lodge because it signifies the healing power of Bear medicine; Bear moves into the quiet, moves into the solitude of hibernation, to birth her cubs. Similarly, a woman's transformation happens in the quiet and solitude of her own deep inner experience of herself." The shamanic experience with a rock in the desert carried the feeling of ecstasy for which shaminism is known.[4]

I came home from the desert with new energy and focus to build Bear Lodge. However, the next year was a nightmare of construction fiascos. Just because the spirits are directing an enterprise doesn't mean that builders or contractors are any more competent than they would otherwise be. To make matters worse, the project got off to the wrong start when I took control in my old, left-brain, high-achievement way, the way that had previously worked well in my life. I noticed over time that the ravens had disappeared from the land and had ceased to accompany me when I drove through the countryside. My power animals became silent and seemed faded out, not clear and present and strong in their energy, as they had been in my earlier experience. I missed them, and I missed Raven.

I learned only slowly that when the spirits become silent and fade out, in both ordinary and nonordinary reality, that is a message that I am on the wrong track. Power animals are not withholding, vindictive or punitive. They are also not co-dependent, so I have to ask for help — it is not given just because I need it. Learning to ask is a difficult but critical part of healing. Listening to the answer and taking congruent action is even harder. I had made the mistake of charging ahead, ego first, instead of asking for direction and trusting that they would provide it. I finally got on the right track and asked my power animals and teachers for help in finding and building exactly the Bear Lodge that they envisioned. A new building idea suddenly presented itself, and Raven came to me, marking the event. Raven and I were in connection again. No, now I was back in connection with Raven.

And so we have Bear Lodge, two buildings in the big cedars. Bear Lodge contains a beautiful workshop room, a big, inviting kitchen, two bathrooms and sleeping space for twelve. It is a welcoming space for renewal and healing. Because women are always taking care of others' needs, Bear Lodge is a place of abundance where they themselves feel taken care of, physically as well as emotionally and spiritually. Outside, the gardens burst with flowers and herbs and vegetables. The fierce love and protection of Grizzly as I first experienced her is present here. During Bear Lodge's first summer of operation, I came outside one morning during a workshop to discover that Bear had visited in the night and had pulled down four branches of a big cherry tree, leaving one branch lying in each of the four directions. It was an auspicious blessing.

Several times a year, Bear Lodge welcomes women for five-day residential workshops. I teach and facilitate the workshops with Helga, and recently Willow Brocke has joined us. Helga and I combine our professional backgrounds in feminist anthropology and feminist psychology, respectively, with our understanding of shamanism and shamanic healing. Willow brings group and community skills from her feminist social work background, in combination with her gifts and training in ecstatic movement, dance, song and shamanic theatre. The central focus of our workshops is always transformation and healing; these workshops are for women who are pursuing their own healing. Each workshop teaches women the shamanic knowledge and skills to connect with their power animals and teachers, and to access the healing power and wisdom of spirits in nature. During workshops I feel enormous gratitude and joy as I witness women shed their exhaustion, move their focus away from caretaking others and onto caring for themselves, as they learn to connect with the spirits.

Because workshops are the focus of our healing centre, envisioning these workshops is an enterprise we must share with the spirits, if the workshops are to be effective. In the quiet and solitude of winter, Helga and I follow what now, after several years, seems an organic process. In the early winter we rest up from all our work harvesting the land and the orchard and giving the workshops of the year. At some point we feel ready to start talking about ideas that have come to us about our topics for the next year. Last winter the spirits provided us with a particularly clear example of how they help with our envisioning. One day in the dark of winter, Helga announced, seemingly out of nowhere, "Let's do a workshop called 'Coyote and the Curse of Perfectionism.'" I thought that was a great title and said we must write it down. Neither of us did, and we promptly forgot about it.

A month or so later, I was doing a shamanic journey about something that was troubling me, and I was feeling disconnected and unclear about what my power animals and teachers were telling me. And so I did something I rarely do: I asked them for a sign that I had understood correctly. Coyote showed up, front and centre, and said, "'Coyote' will be in the title of one of your workshops." I thought this was very interesting and told Helga. She remembered what I did not — that she had already thought of the title "Coyote and the something of Perfectionism." It took a while for us to remember the whole title, and then, as so often happens when we are in connection with the spirits, the power animal who has come in a journey comes in ordinary reality. The next morning, very early, I was sitting at my computer. As I gazed out the window towards Bear Lodge, Coyote sauntered across the snow, bushy and beautiful — a surprise and a gift. I had seen Coyote only once before on our land, the first summer we were here. At that time, I was so new from the city that I thought it was a very thin dog!

To ready us for giving the workshop, Coyote gave Helga and me many lessons about what a curse perfectionism is, more than we ever wanted or asked for. I have learned what a brittle defence perfectionism is. At its core is the very-early-induced shame of not being good enough, not being enough just as we are. As adults, then, any hint of criticism, judgment or making a mistake, either real or imagined, zooms the perfectionist straight into her core shame and self-hatred. For the perfectionist life is serious and difficult, and self-esteem is always precarious. Coyote, however, is a trickster, and trickster lessons, while never easy, celebrate how lovable each of us is. Tricksters teach us by turning our world upside down, so that we have the opportunity to see from a new perspective and to learn a different way of thinking, and of being in relation to ourselves, our work, our relationships and our life as a whole. Tricksters bring us a form of shamanic healing that is unexpected, disarming and full of expansive laughter that helps us to "lighten up" and enjoy our real selves. In his book *Coyote Medicine*,[5] Lewis Mehl-Madrona writes about "a healing surprise," the gift of healing from a trickster spirit who surprises us into a leap of healing. Coyote, it turns out, is the perfect teacher for a workshop on perfectionism!

## SOUL RETRIEVAL AT RAVENSPIRIT

Ravens fly around me this morning when I go out early with the dogs. They sit high in a cedar, talking to me as I look up at them. Later, Eagle flies very low over me at the beach. I feel their gift of power for this writing, urging me on.

In learning about shamanism, I was galvanized by the concepts of soul loss and soul retrieval. In a shamanic understanding of trauma, when we are wounded, when we are traumatized, either as children or as adults, we lose a part of our soul. Soul parts leave us and go to nonordinary reality, where they are safe from the harm that is going on in this reality. Those soul parts that leave carry with them the life energy that we need to be whole, that we need for our healing. The limitations of psychotherapy that I had experienced over the years with deeply traumatized women now made sense. Women had worked hard to heal but, almost without exception, they seemed to leave psychotherapy feeling less than optimal vitality, connection and joy in their personal bodily integrity. Now I knew why. No matter how healing psychotherapy is, energetically it cannot fill the spaces left by missing soul parts. Soul retrieval became my new work with women.

Soul retrieval is done in concert with a power animal who guides the shamanic healer to bring back a person's lost soul parts. I learned early on that soul retrieval requires ongoing and deep connection with my power animals, not easy with the demands of everyday life. Taking time before a soul retrieval to ensure my connection with Eagle, my soul retrieval power animal, and all my teachers is crucial. To make this connection and ask for help in the healing work, I do a shamanic journey before each person who comes to work with me arrives. In my first year of soul retrieval work, and from time to time since, Eagle used this journey to return parts of my own soul that someone had stolen, or that had left me or that I had given away. Although I was surprised when this happened, spontaneous soul retrieval made good shamanic sense. I felt the power and strength that came from my returned soul parts, and consequently used myself better in my work. Eagle put into action the principle of the wounded healer: I must be healed first, in order to help others heal. I had learned this as a psychotherapist and now was experiencing the same principle in shamanic healing work.

To have honesty and integrity as a healer requires me, as a professional, to take responsibility for healing my wounding.

"Helping" professionals who turn away from knowing their own woundedness hurt many people. Shoring up their own denial, they are blind to how they disappoint the clients who count on them for help. Clients always know, somewhere deep inside, when they have been shortchanged, when their deepest self has been invisible to their therapist.

To integrate soul retrieval into my psychotherapeutic work with women has been deeply rewarding. I have seen the way women respond when their lost soul parts are returned. They cry tears of relief and tears of joy to have their soul parts back within them. They feel their own life energy come back at a visceral level. One woman arrived from southern Ontario for a soul retrieval and asked me if I had ever before worked with a dead woman. She wrote of her experience with soul loss and soul retrieval:

> *I give my soul away because I don't stay able to give my self or live my self whole, loving. Unable to do that, I "go away" which means I give myself away, or just lose soul essence by a sort of slow leakage. I have done that for years. Live untruly. No wonder I have so little energy. But no more. Today I feel I will truly be able to take action, if only because I understand as never before the cost of inaction: soul loss. I long to be the possibility I've seen here: soul-full, soul-abundant, soul-energetic, soul-generous, soul-open to the sacred everywhere, soul-true.*

At the end of our work together, she left me this note in Bear Lodge:

> *I feel as if I am finding lost years, putting them on like good pounds — healthily, happily. It's as if I've landed. Getting grounded is next. That feels attainable here. In the high winds of home I'll need my hefty Stag. Thanks for him, and Owl and Frog, and all my soul threads knit together, pulling together.*

It is now one year later, and this woman has succeeded in leaving the toxic marriage that so enervated her. She is excited about birthing herself into her own life and immersing herself in her passion, writing. For this she now has available both the energy of her returned soul parts and her power animals.

## STEPPING FORWARD INTO TRANSFORMATION

A few years ago, while trekking in Nepal and later in Bhutan, I had to cross roaring gorges of swirling mountain water on configurations of vine and rope and air and wood the guide called bridges. As I looked far below, mesmerized by a tumult of water, everything in me screamed to turn back. What propelled me forward was that there was no way back: our guide was moving forward and I knew I must follow. I stepped out onto fraying vines, cracked and split boards, unimaginable distances between them. Somehow, what looked impossibly flimsy held me. Stepping forward, I conquered my fear. Reaching the other side I touched solid ground, bursting with pride, energized by my new good feeling about myself. Crossing those bridges, walking those challenging mountain paths, transformed me. It was there that I began to understand transformation at an energy level, as I experienced it in my body. On those treks, my body taught me that I don't have to let fear stop me, or exhaustion for that matter. Calling on my own choice and my will made the difference. I learned I could do what seemed impossible to me. Trekking, I had to push through my fear, walk a long way past my exhaustion. Women who stop when they hit the wall of their fear and collapse when exhaustion threatens to overwhelm them sadly miss leaning to fire their will into steely determination and their choice into a life-affirming right. The guides helped me on those treks. Now I help women find and use the strength from their core.

Transformation is change and healing at soul level. To heal at this core level, we must undertake core-level energy changes: change from self-hatred to self-love and self-respect, change from loyalty to our family of origin to loyalty to ourselves, change from life-constricting energy choices to life-enhancing energy choices. We must transform our shame into anger and love. The dark impenetrable cloud of our depression must give way to deeply felt real feelings. We must explode our self-defeating attitudes and beliefs, learned so early that they permeate our nervous systems, our musculature. Our stance in the world must change from passivity to agency. We must replace "I can't get there from here" and "no one will give me what I need" with "I am the author of my own life." and "I can create the love, trust and connections I need for myself." As Gabrielle Roth says, "If you don't do your dance ... who will?"[6]

Each step in a journey of transformation must be grounded in truth. Personal truth-telling in the presence of an enlightened witness fuels our energy change. Telling our own personal truth is life-affirming and energizing. To stop the lies we have had to tell ourselves for our survival, to tell our truth instead, is life-affirming. Each time we have the courage to tell even a small piece of our own truth, we are enhancing our life and freeing up the energy that ripples inside us.

What happens to the woman who resists stepping forward into her own transformation? She may pretend to step forward, perhaps talking about healing or even seeing therapists for short periods, until she finds reasons not to continue. She deceives herself and others with her words. But at the first difficult necessity to act, to expand herself and take responsibility for her life, to take in the abundance of others' caring as well as her own personal success, she is seized by fear. A new landscape of esteem and empowerment is opening up before her, instead of her familiar environment of disregarding her own needs and a sense of emptiness. She rushes away, feeding her fear. And what does she do when she chooses to give more energy to the environment of her wounding than to the landscape of her healing? One woman who grew up as a hated child became a perfectionist in her striving for love. Her perfectionism became a cover for her own self-hatred; she now hates herself for any failure to be perfect. She constantly follows the inner template formed in her childhood, in which she invites negativity in and gives it space and energy. Unfamiliar feelings, such as caring and support, she twists and invalidates. She projects blame outward onto others, refusing responsibility for her own life and choices.

Alice Miller says that each of us must have an enlightened witness in order to face, see and feel the real truth of our childhood. She defines an enlightened witness as one who "works for the truth about childhood."[7] It takes great courage to face the truth about our childhood, and it takes an enlightened witness who has the courage to face our hard truths with us, a witness who will not flinch. Not being alone with the knowledge and pain, as we were back then, is critical to transformation. Otherwise, we maintain the lie of our aloneness. To ask someone for help is a life-and-death struggle for many women. Allowing a therapist or a friend to give help and be a true enlightened witness often contravenes the strictures of family loyalty. Most women do not know how to ask for help, feeling deep shame when they even contemplate the possibility. We develop a loyalty to the belief that we are alone and must remain alone, a loyalty to our original wounding and to the primary relationships in which we were wounded and were left alone with that wounding. Grandiosity then becomes our hallmark, making a virtue out of necessity — "I can do it myself; I can figure out my stuff. I don't need anyone else's help."

Living in bad faith with oneself and others is the inevitable result of the choice not to heal. Living in bad faith means choosing to live in a landscape of lies and partial truths. The woman who lives in bad faith lies to herself and others, and welcomes into her life others who are afraid of the truth. Lies are toxic and their effects fester in her body, causing dis-ease and pain. Telling the truth would ease her dis-ease, but when a woman has turned her face away from her personal truth this healing avenue is no longer open to her, so she must mute her body's dis-ease. Addictions are attempts to silence our bodies: work, cleaning, food, alcohol, reading, caretaking, perfection, chaos — an endless menu is available. But no matter what lies we learn to tell ourselves and each other, our bodies are on our side; they remember our truth and will not be silenced. Our bodies are always our allies in the pursuit of truth. Our cells, our nervous system, our musculature, our bones help us wake up by giving us ever stronger signals which we ignore to our detriment.

A woman academic who had chronic fatigue syndrome for years met Bear as her power animal, asked for help and dissolved in healing tears as she felt the warmth and love of Bear's arms around her, encircling her as she nestled in Bear's fur. Initially she had felt frightened to take in Bear's love. She was surprised at her own reluctance, and then she felt the enormity of her own core self-hatred, never evident to her before, which was holding her back. It was a stark contrast to the love that was coming to her from Bear. An abundance of love was new to her, unfamiliar. Now her healing task is to learn to live her life in a self-loving way. She is exhausted, her life energy sapped by her efforts to drive herself to greater and greater achievement to cover up her self-hatred. Psychotherapy has helped her to change her patterns, but it is not enough. She needed Bear's energy, energy from her power animals, from the spirits. Without the energy that comes from that source, it is impossible to transform self-hatred into self-love, and self-criticism into self-caring. Without the loving kindness that comes from nonordinary reality, we cannot shift what has been inculcated since birth.

During workshops, Helga is given shamanic dreams. In one dream she saw Coyote dancing outside Bear Lodge. As he danced, he sang, "I am a celebrated gift! I am a celebrated gift!" She brought that dream gift into the workshop and each of us sang and danced that simple sentence, experiencing its affirmation, freedom and joy.

It is autumn now. Each morning I am greeted by fresh bear scat in our apple orchard. We tell the bear spirits we are happy to share. The apple trees belong to the land, to Bear, as well as to us. And we are all getting ready for hibernation. As I pick apples and thank the trees for the juice and pies ahead, I feel the earth putting herself to bed for another season. The enormous undertaking of the growing and the harvesting is drawing to a close once again. As I write this, my eyes fall on Robert Bateman's grizzly bear painting, *The Keeper of the Land*, which adorns my office wall. Grizzly is the keeper of the land and we all must be keepers of the land. We must be each others' enlightened witnesses and we must be enlightened witnesses for the earth's suffering and the earth's healing. My life at RavenSpirit teaches me how to be an enlightened witness. Sentimentality is not part of Raven's repertoire. The lessons are hard, but the rewards are as exciting as those shiny black wings beating over my head.

I came to this land, RavenSpirit, called by the spirits to build and develop a healing centre for women. In this enterprise the spirits have made sure that the first woman healed is me. It has been a healing surprise to make this discovery. I have also discovered that my life has become a healing life, for others as well as myself. This is the shamanic way.

## *RavenSpirit*

*Raven*
*is*
*calling me*
*calling me home*
*again.*

*Azure blue winter sky*
*diamond light on crusted snow*
*Midday sun journeys just over the ridge —*
*its January accomplishment.*

*His cry greets me*
*behind the cedars,*
*over the creek,*
*calls me to attention.*
*Magnetic soul connection.*

*I look up,*
*riveted,*
*waiting.*
*Black form*
*moves toward me.*
*I am still*

*Breath unnecessary;*
*Raven, over me.*

*Get your act together, girl!*
*Get your life back!*
*Take your life back!*
*Life is too short for whining, crying over spilled milk, lost souls,*
*soul sickness.*
*Get on with it!*
*Look at me. You are as free as me.*
*You know how to fly*
*and make connection where it counts —*
*with the spirits of the land*
*the water*
*the sky.*
*We will never betray you,*
*never disappoint you.*
*We will always see you,*
*love you*
*no matter how hard our lessons.*

## ENDNOTES

1. Audre Lorde, *Sister Outsider: Essays and Speeches* (Freedom, CA: Crossing Press, 1984), pp. 107-8.

2. Joan Halifax, "Shaman's Journey, Buddhist Path," in Gary Doore (ed.), *Shaman's Path: Healing, Personal Growth and Empowerment* (Boston: Shambala, 1988).

3. Alice Miller, *The Drama of the Gifted Child*, translated by Ruth Ward (New York: Basic Books, 1981).

4. M. Eliade, *Shamanism: Archaic Techniques of Ecstasy*, Bollingen Series LXXVI (Harvard: Princeton University Press, 1964).

5. Lewis Mehl-Madrona, *Coyote Medicine: Lessons from Native American Healing* (New York: Scribner, 1997).

6. Gabrielle Roth, in *The Wave: Ecstatic Dance for Body and Soul* [video] (Bluehorse Films, 1993).

7. Alice Miller, *Breaking Down the Wall of Silence: The Liberating Experience of Facing Painful Truth*, translated by Simon Worrall (New York: Penguin, 1991).

# CONTRIBUTORS' NOTES

**Di Brandt** teaches creative writing and English at the University of Windsor. She has twice been shortlisted for the Governor General's Award for Poetry, and has received numerous other awards for her writing, including the Canadian Authors' Association National Poetry Award. Her books include: *questions i asked my mother* (Turnstone Press, 1987); *Agnes in the sky* (Turnstone Press, 1990); *mother, not mother* (Mercury Press, 1992); *Wild Mother Dancing: Maternal Narrative in Canadian Literature* (University of Manitoba Press, 1993); *Jerusalem, beloved* (Turnstone Press, 1995); and *Dancing Naked: Narrative Strategies for Writing Across Centuries* (Mercury Press, 1996).

**Jeannine Carriere** is a Metis mother of two who is has lived in Alberta for many years. She holds a master's degree in social work and is working on a Ph.D in public health sciences. She has more than twenty years' experience working with Aboriginal communities in the areas of education and social work. She is currently developing Aboriginal child welfare policies for the province of Alberta and teaching as a sessional in the Faculty of Social Work at Grant MacEwan Community College.

**Barbara Cottrell** is a researcher, writer, adult educator and long-time activist on women's issues. She has conducted many workshops and projects on violence against women, and has worked with friends and colleagues to produce reports and guides, including *Workplace Learnings About Woman Abuse: A Guide for Change; Liberty: A Manual for Group Facilitators and Survivors of Woman Abuse; Parent Abuse: The Abuse of Parents by their Teenage Children; and Research Partnerships: A Feminist Approach to Communities and Universities Working Together*. Currently she is writing about community partnerships for a book soon to be published in England. She is a mother, grandmother, daughter, sister and friend to many fine people in Nova Scotia and other parts of the world, many of whom are trying to convince her to sit on fewer committees and write more poetry.

**Barbara Dacks** has worked as a professional writer in Alberta for twenty-three years. In addition to writing and editing for various university and government departments and agencies, she has published freelance articles in *Maclean's, America West, Canadian, Western Living*, WestWorld, and Edmonton magazines. She has also worked as a news reporter for CBC Radio, and as a scriptwriter for CITV and CKUA Radio. She has taught non-fiction writing for Lakeland College, and creative writing for Edmonton Public School Board. Currently, she publishes and edits *Legacy*, an award-winning independent cultural heritage magazine that she founded in 1995.

**Shelley Davis Finson**, MRE, MSW, D.Min, is professor of pastoral theology and co-director of supervised field education at Atlantic School of Theology, Halifax, Nova Scotia. She has been in ministry in the United Church of Canada for thirty-three years. Her publications include *Women and Religion: A Bibliographic Guide to Christian Feminist Liberation Theology* (University of Toronto Press, 1991); *Canadian Research Institute for the Advancement of Women Paper 34: A Historical Review of the Development of Feminist Liberation Theology* (1995) and related articles. In addition to being a foremother in the movement for Christian feminism, she is a runner and enjoys entering road races.

**Sheree Fitch** is the author of nine books for children and a book of poetry for adults, as well as plays, articles and essays. She continues to dance with dragons in Chocolate Lake, Nova Scotia, and makes her living teaching, speaking and storytelling. She is an activist for the cause of literacy and much of her work focuses on issues concerning women and children. She was recently awarded an honorary degree from St. Mary's University in Halifax, Nova Scotia. She is currently at work on a book about writing.

**Carroll Dianne Ganam**, Ph.D, is a psychologist in Edmonton, Alberta. She has thirty years' experience working with families, couples and individuals. She acknowledges that her best teachers are those who have been related to her in some capacity of mothering or being mothered. Their presence in her life has brought her all the best and worst of life's gifts, each one a seed for growth. Women she works with often describe experiencing something similar. Carroll is just beginning to write about this.

**Soledad Gonzalez'** present occupation has the official names of adult educator and counsellor, but she would rather call herself a transmitter of human experiences that have been generously shared. She works with immigrants and refugees who, as she has done, struggle to keep their identity alive in a foreign land. Thirty-six years of roaming have brought her to a niche in Halifax, Nova Scotia. Though Soledad's thoughts frequently take her back to the Chilean landscape and its people, her homeland has now become one of many places on the planet she would dearly love to share with her children and grandchildren. She feels enormously blessed by her son and two daughters, who have been her teachers from the moment they were born.

**Naida D. Hyde**, Ph.D, is a clinical psychologist and feminist psychotherapist. Formerly she was in private practice in Vancouver, British Columbia, was director of the counselling service at Simon Fraser University and taught and published in the area of trauma psychotherapy. She has now developed a women's healing centre in the Selkirk Mountains of British Columbia, where she gives workshops for women focusing on the use of shamanic methods for personal healing. Writing this chapter has spurred her to continue work on a book about her shamanic adventures. To obtain workshop information, please write: RavenSpirit, Site 11, Compartment 29, R R#1, Nelson, B.C., Canada, V1L 5P4, or e-mail: ndhraven@mail.netidea.com

**Martha Keniston Laurence**, Ph.D, is professor of Social Work at Wilfrid Laurier University, where she teaches in the clinical and community development streams in both the master's and doctoral programmes. Her areas of interest in practice, research and writing have, over the years, focused on work with the elderly, quality of care and quality of working life for those providing care to women and the elderly, the experiences of women and feminist psychology. Her passion for learning, her own and others', was recently recognized by her receipt of the 1997 Ontario Confederation of University Faculty Associations Outstanding Teacher Award and the 1998 Laurier Outstanding Teaching Award.

**Eva Pando Radford** was born in Santa Fe, New Mexico, and immigrated to Canada in 1969. She received her first degree from Macalester College in St. Paul, Minnesota and her second from the School of

Library Science at the University of Alberta in Edmonton. She first entered the world of publishing with Hurtig Publishers, and later freelanced as an editor, trying to balance motherhood, work and creative expression as a watercolour painter. Under her leadership, NeWest Press was Alberta Publisher of the Year in 1990. In 1996 she joined the multimedia publishing company Oz New Media as director of the editorial department. Eva lives with husband, Tom Radford, their two children and a menagerie of dogs and cats.

**Carol Rose** is a writer, educator, spiritual counsellor and mother of five. Her first poetry collection was *Behind the Blue Gate* (Beach Holme, 1997). She's been nominated twice for the John Hirsch award for Most Promising Manitoba Writer (1996 and 1997) and is a winner of the Stephen Leacock International Poetry Award (1994) and a co-winner in the Sandburg-Livesay poetry competition (1997). She has appeared in Canadian and American anthologies and journals, and is currently co-editing (with Joan Turner) the anthology *Spider Women: A Tapestry of Creativity and Healing*.

**Donna E. Smyth** lives on an old farm in Hants County, Nova Scotia. She has published two novels, *Quilt*, (Women's Press, 1982) and Subversive Elements, (Women's Press, 1986), and numerous short stories and poems as well as a puppet play for children, *Giant Anna* (Playwrights Canada, 1979), and a young adult novel, *Loyalist Runaway* (Formac, 1995). She teaches English and creative writing at Acadia University, Wolfville, Nova Scotia. Her current projects include a play based on the life of the poet Elizabeth Bishop, and a new genre work based on the life and times of a working-class town in the interior of British Columbia.

**Rosa Spricer** was born in a displaced persons' camp in Germany in 1947 and came to Canada when she was three. She was raised in Montreal, and received her BA at Concordia University and her MEd at McGill University. After working for a time as a high school teacher, counsellor and community outreach worker with delinquent adolescents, she pursued a Ph.D in counselling psychology at the University of Alberta in Edmonton, where she now lives with her husband and teenaged son. She is in private practice, specializing in the areas of eating disorders, abuse and trauma and self-esteem.